QUALITY MANAGEMENT SYSTEMS

This book provides a clear, easy to digest overview of Quality Management Systems (QMS). Critically, it offers the reader an explanation of the International Standards Organization's (ISO) requirement that in future all new and existing Management System Standards (MSS) will need to have the same high-level structure, commonly referred to as Annex SL, with identical core text, as well as common terms and definitions.

In addition to explaining what Annex SL entails, this book provides the reader with a guide to the principles, requirements and interoperability of Quality Management System (QMS) Standards, how to complete internal and external management reviews, third-party audits and evaluations, as well as how to become an ISO certified organisation once your QMS is fully established.

As a simple and straightforward explanation of QMS Standards and their current requirements, this is a perfect guide for practitioners who need a comprehensive overview to put theory into practice, as well as for undergraduate and postgraduate students studying quality management as part of broader operations and management courses.

Ray Tricker is currently working as the Senior Management Consultant for Herne European Consultancy Ltd., which offers organisations access to a range of highly skilled and specialist consultants to help companies enhance their business performance.

QUALITY MANAGEMENT SYSTEMS

A Practical Guide to Standards Implementation

Ray Tricker

Routledge
Taylor & Francis Group

LONDON AND NEW YORK

First published 2020
by Routledge
2 Park Square, Milton Park, Abingdon, Oxon OX14 4RN

and by Routledge
52 Vanderbilt Avenue, New York, NY 10017

Routledge is an imprint of the Taylor & Francis Group, an informa business

British Library Cataloguing-in-Publication Data
A catalogue record for this book is available from the British Library

Library of Congress Cataloging-in-Publication Data
Names: Tricker, Ray, author.
Title: Quality management systems : a practical guide to standards
    implementation / Ray Tricker.
Description: Milton Park, Abingdon, Oxon ; New York : Routledge, 2020. |
    Includes bibliographical references and index.
Identifiers: LCCN 2019029098 (print) | LCCN 2019029099 (ebook) | ISBN
    9780367223519 (hbk) | ISBN 9780367223533 (pbk) | ISBN 9780429274473 (ebk)
Subjects: LCSH: Quality control—Standards.
Classification: LCC TS156.16 .T75 2020 (print) | LCC TS156.16 (ebook) |
    DDC 658.4/013—dc23
LC record available at https://lccn.loc.gov/2019029098
LC ebook record available at https://lccn.loc.gov/2019029099

ISBN: 978-0-367-22351-9 (hbk)
ISBN: 978-0-367-22353-3 (pbk)
ISBN: 978-0-429-27447-3 (ebk)

Typeset in Bembo
by Apex CoVantage, LLC

To Claire – in appreciation of 57 years of happy married life

CONTENTS

PREFACE

A management system is mixture of policies, processes and procedures that an organisation has adopted in order to achieve its stated business objectives. A management standard, on the other hand, is a document that provides requirements, specifications, guidelines or characteristics that can be used consistently to ensure that materials, products, processes and services are fit for their purpose. In today's world, with literally thousands of standards available worldwide – on every conceivable topic – it can become extremely difficult in deciding which will be most applicable to your particular form of business.

Virtually every country with an industrial base has its own national organisation producing its own national set of standards. However, national bodies and national standards cannot dictate customer choice. A product that may legally be marketed need not be of universal appeal or internationally acceptable (for example, the three-pin electrical plug used in the UK is totally useless in most other countries!), and this diversity of standards can obviously lead to a lot of confusion, especially with regard to international trade and tenders. Consequently some form of international agreement has had to be established in order to control the quality of the products and services that an organisation provides, and this became the responsibility of the International Standards Organization (ISO).

The ISO [in conjunction with the International Electrotechnical Commission (IEC)] set up a study group in 1983 to produce a truly international set of quality management standards that **all** countries could use regardless whether they were designers, manufacturers, suppliers or end users. This became the ISO 9001:1987 Quality Management System (QMS) Standard, which, due to its adaptability and non-prescriptive nature, users could employ as a template for a management standard that would suit their own particular type o which have adopted the requirements and recommendations of ISO 9001, but the structure of these QMSs is quite different and in some cases (for example, a company manufacturing medical devices, where patient safety has to be taken into account) have had to implement two completely separate QMSs, one for quality management and the other for medical devices.

Indeed most organisations have more than one management system, and many have expressed their frustration at the extra time and resources (not to mention cost!) that it took to implement and certify their various management systems with differing structures, definitions and requirements. In an effort to ease this problem, in 2011, ISO produced *ISO Guide 83*, which was the first formal effort to create consistency in structure and terminology across **all** ISO Management System Standards.

Annex SL grew out of *ISO Guide 83* (which itself was based on and updated with previous editions of ISO 9001) and is a directive that provides a universal high-level structure, identical core text, with common terms and definitions for all Management System Standards. It has been designed not just to make it easier for organisations that have to comply with more than one Management System Standard but to attempt to make the basic structure of all management systems similar.

Under current legislation, all ISO standards have to be reviewed every five to six years to make sure that they are still current and relevant in their marketplace. The 1987 version of ISO 9001 was the starting point for all Quality Management Systems, and the latest revision of this standard (i.e. ISO 9001:2015) has taken into consideration the new ISO rules regarding the common high-level structure of Annex SL with the aim of not only to integrate itself with these other Management System Standards but also to:

- maintain ISO 9001's relevance as the effective "head" of all quality management;
- provide a consistent foundation for the long-term (i.e. next 10–25 years);
- increase the adoption of quality management throughout all business;
- focus on an increased variety of business users (e.g. service industries, office environments etc.);
- address the increasing complexity of the business environment;
- provide an effective solution for a non–office/virtual office environment;
- focus on achieving value for the organisation and its customers; and in doing so
- enhance an organisation's ability to satisfy customers.

 Although the text and layout of the standard has changed, it should be noted that the actual requirements of ISO 9001:2015 **mainly** remain the same as its predecessor (i.e. ISO 9001:2008) but are much **less** prescriptive.

AUTHOR'S HINT

ISO 9001:2015 now replicates **all** of the requirements and recommendations of Annex SL, and for this reason I have used ISO 9001:2015 as an example of a Management System Standard's typical text or in order to describe a certain aspect of management. This book is most definitely meant **not** as yet another book on ISO 9001:2015 (!) but as a book that is applicable to whatever management system you need to use, whether it concerns environment, safety, quality, health and safety, medical devices, aeronautics, information technology or whatever.

The intention of this book, therefore, is to provide quick access to the requirements for the design and implementation of a productive management system, as well as showing you how to maintain the system via some simple internal quality audit checklists.

For the benefit of master's degree students (and other interested parties), a reduced record of ISO 9000's development is still available in the text (see Chapter 2).

Quality Management Systems: A Practical Guide to Standards Implementation consists of a number of chapters covering topics such as:

- **What is a Quality Management System?** – The basic requirements of a Quality Management System and how a QMS can be structured to any organisation's particular type of business.
- **The history of quality standards** – A brief historical record of how quality management standards began, their interoperability and the basic requirements of ISO 9001:2015 are explained.
- **Who produces quality standards?** – Although the International Standards Organization (ISO) is by far and away the largest one producing industrial standards, this chapter provides details of some of the other standards bodies operating in the world today [e.g. the International Electrotechnical Commission (IEC)] and the International Telegraph Union (ITU)].
- **What is Annex SL all about?** – The chapter explains how Annex SL is structured and how (by using ISO 9001:2015 as a generic template) it can form the basis of all Management System Standards.
- **The seven principles of quality management** – There is a quick overview of the principles behind Annex SL that are used as the basis for all current and future Quality Management Systems.
- **Detailed requirements for management systems** – An overall set of recommended (and sometimes mandatory) requirements for a Quality Management Systems are provided.
- **The interoperability of Management System Standards** – A reminder is offered of the requirements and benefits of quality, Quality Control and Quality Assurance as applicable to vast range of publications.
- **The importance of data protection** – A user-friendly description is provided of the requirements for individual data protection as covered by the General Data Protection Regulation (GDPR), which came into effect on 25 May 2018.
- **Self-assessment** – A section covers the often overlooked topic of self-assessment and methods for completing management reviews, internal or external as well as third-party audits and evaluations.
- **What to do once the Quality Management System (QMS) is established?** – The easiest and most cost-effective method of becoming a management system certified organisation is indicated.
- **Bibliography** – This contains abbreviations and acronyms; reference standards for Quality Management Systems; a glossary of terms used in quality management standards; and – of course! – books by the same author.
- **Full Index**

I have also taken the opportunity to:

- Include a lot of (hopefully self-explanatory!) illustrations on the assumption that 'a picture is worth a thousand words';

- keep explanations as simple as possible so as to appeal to students, newcomers to Quality Assurance, or the beleaguered executive with little time to come to terms with the subject.

For convenience (and in order to reduce the number of equivalent and/or similar terms), the following terms, unless otherwise stated, are considered interchangeable within this book:

Product   hardware, software, service or processed material that is the result of an organisational process that does not include activities performed at the interface between the supplier (provider) and the customer

Organisation   a single person or a group of people who achieve their objectives by using their own functions, responsibilities, authorities and relationships (It can be a company, corporation, enterprise, firm, partnership, charity, association or institution either privately or publicly owned or an operating unit that is part of a larger entity.)

Service   the result of a process that includes at least one activity carried out at the interface between the supplier (provider) and the customer (e.g. the delivery of knowledge)

In the margins of the book, you will find the following symbols that are designed to help you get the most out of this book:

An important point or requirement.

An essential requirement, good idea or suggestion

And within the text:

Note: These are used to provide further amplification or information.

Italic text indicates a direct quotation (or précised quote) from an ISO standard, guidance note, international or national Standard or the like.

ABOUT THE AUTHOR

Ray Tricker (MSc, IEng, FCQI-CQP, FIET, FCMI, FIRSE) is a senior consultant with over 60 years' continuous service in Quality, Safety and Environmental Management, Project Management, Communication Electronics, Railway Command, Control and Signalling systems and the development of molecular nanotechnology.

He served with the Royal Corps of Signals (for a total of 37 years), during which time he held various managerial posts culminating in being appointed Chief Engineer of NATO's Communication Security Agency (ACE COMSEC).

Most of Ray's work since leaving the services has centred on the European railways. He has held a number of posts with the Union International des Chemins de fer (UIC) [e.g. Quality Manager of the European Train Control System (ETCS)] and with the European Union (EU) Commission [e.g. T500 Review Team Leader, European Rail Traffic Management System (ERTMS) Users Group Project Coordinator, HEROE Project Coordinator] and currently (as well as writing books on such diverse subjects as international standards, communication electronics, building, wiring and water regulations for Taylor & Francis, Elsevier and Van Haren). He is busy assisting small businesses from around the world (usually on a no-cost basis) to produce their own auditable Quality and/or Integrated Management Systems to meet the requirements of ISO 9001, ISO 14001 and OHSAS 18001. He is also a UKAS Assessor (for the assessment of certification bodies for the harmonisation of the Trans-European, High Speed Railway Network), and recently he was the Quality, Safety and Environmental Manager for the consultancy overseeing the multibillion-dollar Trinidad Rapid Rail System.

Currently he is still working part-time as the Senior Management Consultant for Herne European Consultancy Ltd (http://thebestqms.com) – a company specialising in offering organisations access to a range of highly skilled and specialist consultants to help these companies enhance their business performance.

One day, he says, he might retire – but there always seem to be more books to write!

About the contributor

Chapter 8 of this book was contributed by Samantha Alford (MSc, MCIPS).

Samantha is an established technical author, instructor, business management specialist and data protection officer. She has over 35 years of continuous experience in compliance, governance and oversight and has worked in in the public, private, voluntary and charity sectors. Samantha served in the Royal Air Force for 17 years and had a wide and varied skillset. Her MSc included a specialisation in performance measurement and management and she is also a certified GDPR practitioner, an IOSH health and safety manager, a quality auditor (internal, external and third party) and an experienced instructor.

Samantha has extensive experience in business management at both strategic and operational levels and her skillset includes planning, policy and business documentation, procedure development, contract management and performance measurement. She is a Director of Professional Procurement and Project Management Ltd (https://www.pppmanagement.co.uk) a project services company specialising in procurement and contract strategy, programme and project delivery, project support services and technical authorship. Her forthcoming book "GDPR-A game of Snakes and Ladders" will be published by Routledge in the winter of 2019/2020.

MORE BOOKS BY THE AUTHOR

As previously mentioned, ISO 9001:2015 is now recognised as the accepted template for all new and future Management System Standards.

Over the years I have written a number of books on ISO 9001, some of which you might find useful when reading this current book. These are listed below:

ISO 9001:2015 in Brief **(4th edition)**	Now in its 4th edition, this book is particularly aimed at students, newcomers to Quality Management Systems and the busy executive with the overall intention of providing them with a user-friendly, very simplified explanation of the history, the requirements and the benefits of the new standard.
	Using this book as background material will also enable organisations (large or small) to quickly set up an ISO 9001:2015–compliant Quality Management System for themselves – at minimal expense.
ISO 9001:2015 for Small Businesses **(6th edition)**	The 6th edition of this top selling quality management book includes down to earth explanations aimed at helping you to understand what the new standard is all about and to determine what you need in order to work in compliance with and/or to achieve certification to ISO 9001:2015.
	It covers all the major changes to this revised ISO standard and how they will affect your work, along with direct, accessible, straightforward guidance that has always been part of this series.
	As a bonus, this book also contains a free, customisable example of a complete, generic Quality Management System that can be adapted to suit any organisation, large or small.
ISO 9001:2015 Audit Procedures **(4th edition)**	Fully revised, updated and expanded, this 4th edition completes the trio by providing access to methods for auditing against the requirements of ISO 9001:2015.
	Although primarily aimed at showing how small businesses auditors can complete management reviews and internal, external and third-party quality audits, this book will prove invaluable to professional auditors.
	Containing an overview of the changes made by the 2015 edition of ISO 9001 and how these will affect audits completed in future, the book also includes an extensive range of audit checklists, explanations and example questionnaires.

How to Convert from ISO 9001– 2008 to ISO 9001–2015 **(1st edition)**	The publication of ISO 9001:2015 in September 2015 signalled the start of a three-year transition period during which those organisations wishing to move to the new version of the standard needed to make changes to their existing Quality Management Systems.
	How to Convert provides step-by-step advice to help you through the transition and to realise the benefits of ISO 9001:2015. It maps out a framework that guides you through the options and alternatives, ensuring that you have the knowledge and information you require to seamlessly make the necessary transition.

 Further assistance

For further details about these books and other ISO 9001 consulting services, please email the author at ray@herne.org.uk. or see https://www.routledge.com/products/search?keywords=ray+tricker

1

WHAT IS A QUALITY MANAGEMENT SYSTEM?

 AUTHOR'S START NOTE

Chapter 1 describes the basic requirements for quality management and how it can be structured to any organisation's particular type of business.

1.1 What is quality?

First of all, what is **meant** by the word –**quality**?!

There are many definitions, but the most commonly accepted meaning of quality is that expressed by the International Organization for Standardization (ISO), namely: '*The totality of features and characteristics of products and services or service that bear on its ability to satisfy stated or implied needs*'. In simpler words, one can say that a product or service has **good** quality when it 'complies with the requirements specified by the client'.

THE DEFINITION OF QUALITY

The totality of features and characteristics of a product or service that bear on its ability to satisfy stated or implied needs

But why is the word 'quality' (although an everyday word), often misused, misquoted and misunderstood? Probably this is because, when most people talk about the quality of an object or service, they are normally talking about its excellence, perfection or value. In reality, of course, they should be talking about how much it meets its designed purpose and satisfies the original requirements.

CASE STUDY

Take, for example, a £80,000 Mercedes and a £19,000 Ford. It would be very unfair to suggest that the Mercedes is a better quality car simply because it costs more! Being realistic, both cars meet their predetermined quality requirements because they have been built to exacting standards and are therefore equally acceptable as 'quality' vehicles. It is simply that the design purpose and original quality requirements (i.e. the level of quality) differ.

In other words, quality is based on consumer satisfaction. So in the case of the Mercedes and the Ford, purchasers of Mercedes will be satisfied only if they get leather seats, a totally interactive navigational system and surround sound, whereas the Ford driver is happy with crushed velour and a CD player. Their required levels of quality differ, but each is satisfied with his or her purchase. The characteristics of each car satisfy customer requirements.

Consumers, however, are not just interested in the level of quality **intended** by the designer, manufacturer or supplier; they are far more interested in the delivery of a product or service that is **consistently** of the same quality. They also want an assurance that what they are buying truly meets the quality standard that was initially offered and/or recommended.

Products and services that are of a consistent quality mean that repeat purchases are more likely – something that any car driver appreciates when considering whether to stay with a preferred make and model,

This consumer requirement has meant that manufacturers and suppliers (especially larger organisations) have now had to pay far more attention to the quality of their products and services than was previously necessary. Organisations have had to set up proper Quality Management Systems in order to control and monitor all stages of the product or service process, and they have had to provide proof to the potential customer that these will have the guaranteed – and, in some cases, certified – quality required by the customer. In other words, the manufacturer or supplier has had to work within a Quality Management System (QMS) to produce their products or deliver their service. (See Figure 1.1)

Unfortunately, with the current trend towards micro-miniaturisation and the use of advanced materials and technology, most modern-day products and services have now become extremely complex assemblies compared to those that were available just a few years ago. This has meant that many more people are involved in the manufacture and/or supply of a relatively simple object, and this has increased the likelihood of a design fault occurring.

Similarly, the responsibility for the quality of a products and services has also been spread over an increasing number of people, which has meant that the manufacturer's and/or supplier's guarantee of quality has, unfortunately, become less precise.

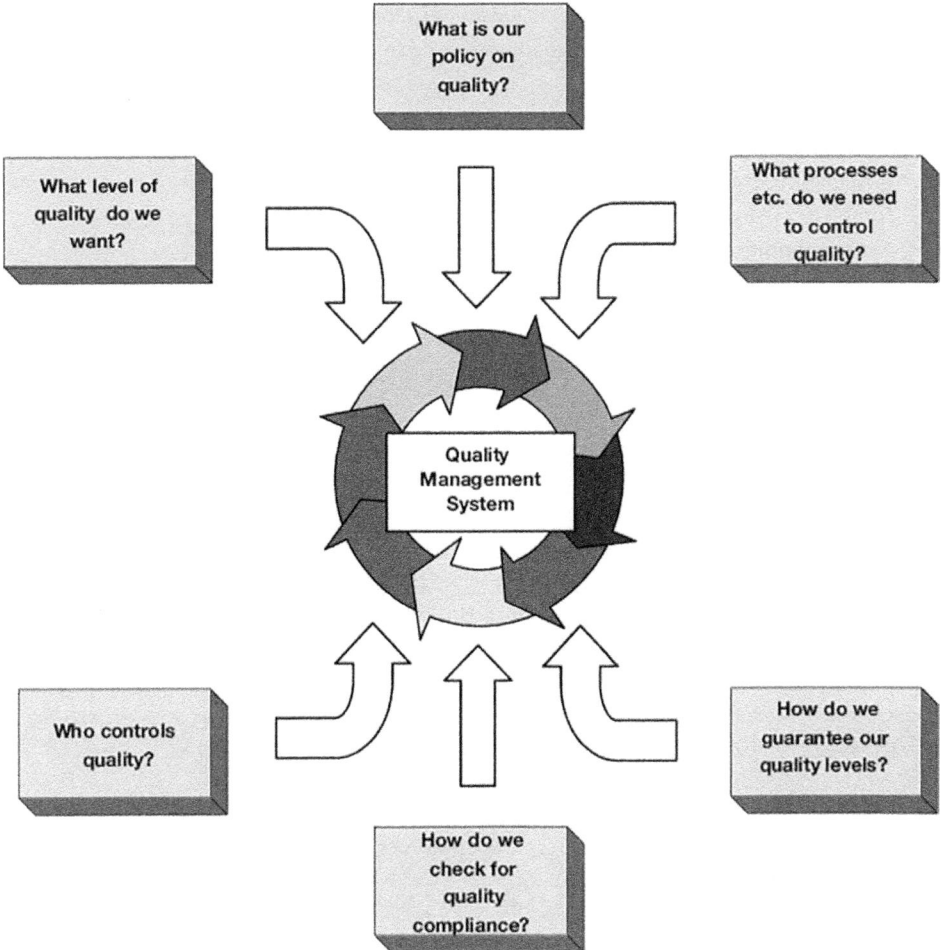

FIGURE 1.1   Some of the questions answered by a Quality Management System

The growing demand for an assurance of quality before a contract is awarded has reinforced the already accepted adage that quality products and services play an important role in securing new markets as well as in retaining existing markets. Without doubt, in these days of competitive world markets, Quality Assurance has never been more relevant, and no longer can suppliers rely on their reputation alone!

Thus the drive towards more quality-controlled products and services now means that today's major purchasers are not just expecting that they are of sufficient quality but are also **demanding** proof that an organisation is constantly capable of continually producing quality products or providing quality services. The provision of this proof normally takes the form of an independent third-party certification, and this is possibly the single most important requirement for a manufacturer, organisation or supplier.

Until the early 1980s, however, no viable third-party certification schemes were available. But with an increased demand for Quality Assurance during all stages of the manufacturing processes came the requirement for manufacturers to work to recognised standards, and this is why the first, truly international, Management System Standard (ISO 9001) was introduced, and it is the basis of this standard, which is now used throughout the world by manufacturers, suppliers and end users.

So in summary, quality **is**:

- a standard that can be accepted by both the supplier and the customer;
- giving complete satisfaction to the customer;
- complying consistently to an agreed level of specification;
- providing products and services at an acceptable cost;
- providing products and services that have auditable proof that they are 'fit for the purpose';
- the totality of features or characteristics of a product or service that bear on its ability to satisfy a given need.

Quality **is not** about:

- complying with a specification (as it is possible that the specification may be wrong!);
- being the best (since achieving this ideal may be very costly and could exceed the price the customer is prepared to pay);
- producing products and services that are fit for the purpose at the point of delivery (as that 'purpose 'may be completely different to the customers' actual needs!). (See Figure 1.2)

FIGURE 1.2   Achieving customer satisfaction

Source: Photograph courtesy of Stingray

AUTHOR'S HINT

One question I am constantly asked is, *'What is the difference between a product and a service?'*

Well, in the words of ISO (the international standard-setting body promoting worldwide proprietary, industrial and commercial standards):

Product is an output that is the result of a process that does not include activities that are performed at the interface between the supplier (provider) and the customer.

Service is the result of a process that includes at least one activity that is carried out at the interface between the supplier (provider) and the customer.

There are three generic product and service categories: hardware, processed materials and software. Many products and services combine several of these categories. For example, a car consists of hardware (e.g. tires), processed materials (e.g. lubricants) and software (e.g. engine control algorithms).

(I hope this helps.)

1.1.1 Benefits and costs of Quality Assurance

Good quality management is capable of helping any size or type of organisation that wants to improve the satisfaction of its customers, increase the effectiveness of its employees and establish a framework for implementing a long-term strategy – all of which can lead to improved profitability and security.

By demonstrating and verifying your compliance with the requirements of a Management System Standard (MSS), you are actively advertising your company's commitment to quality, traceability and continual improvement – which is key to convincing potential clients to utilise your products and services.

It also promotes customer satisfaction and traceability through the implementation of various management system processes.

Other advantages include:

* overall device and/or service improvement;
* increased profits by reducing wastage and errors;
* increased sales;
* a source for finding new clients and a reduction in lost orders;
* effective management (resulting in less time wasted);
* more prospects realised (opening doors restricted to certified suppliers);
* traceability through the implementation of various management system processes;

but essentially:

* greater customer satisfaction;

In practice, some Quality Assurance programs can be very expensive to install and operate, particularly if inadequate Quality Control methods were used previously. If purchasers require consistent quality, they must accept the fact that they will have to pay for it, regardless of the specification or order that the manufacturer has accepted. However, against this expenditure must always be offset the savings in scrapped material, rework and general problems arising from the lack of quality.

From the producers' and/or suppliers' points of view, there is a business requirement to obtain and maintain the desired quality at an optimum cost. The following represent some of the additional expenses that will probably be incurred in a large company:

- salaries for the Quality Assurance Staff;
- training for the Quality Assurance Staff;
- visits by the Quality Assurance Staff to other companies, subcontractors and the eventual consumer, for evaluation and audit of their facilities and products;
- testing equipment that is of a recognised type, standard and quality and that is regularly maintained and calibrated by an accredited calibration centre;
- better storage facilities.

 AUTHOR'S HINT

Obviously, this would not be such a problem with a very small business; nevertheless, account should still be taken of these potential costs – especially if it is the ultimate aim of the small business to eventually gain certification by and registration to a Quality Management Standard.

But why bother with Quality Assurance?!
It is all very expensive to set up and extremely
expensive to run – is it really worth it?!

The short answer, of course, is, '**YES** – it is!'

In order to be part of the enormous European and worldwide market, designers, producers, manufacturers, suppliers **and** sole traders must not merely be aware of the requirements and need for Quality Assurance **must** also be able to prove that they are capable of constantly producing quality products and services that are as good as, if not better than any others available.

Hopefully, organisations will take pride in producing an item of equipment or the design of a system or a piece of software that operates correctly and that will fully satisfy the purchaser – as opposed to something that goes wrong as soon as it is 'switched on'. There will not be many reorders for that particular model!

Insisting on an assurance of quality has got to save money in the long run. It ensures that the deliverable's design features are more dependable and efficient, and built-in quality at every stage obviously reduces wastage and increases customer satisfaction.

So, in a nutshell, see Figure 1.3.

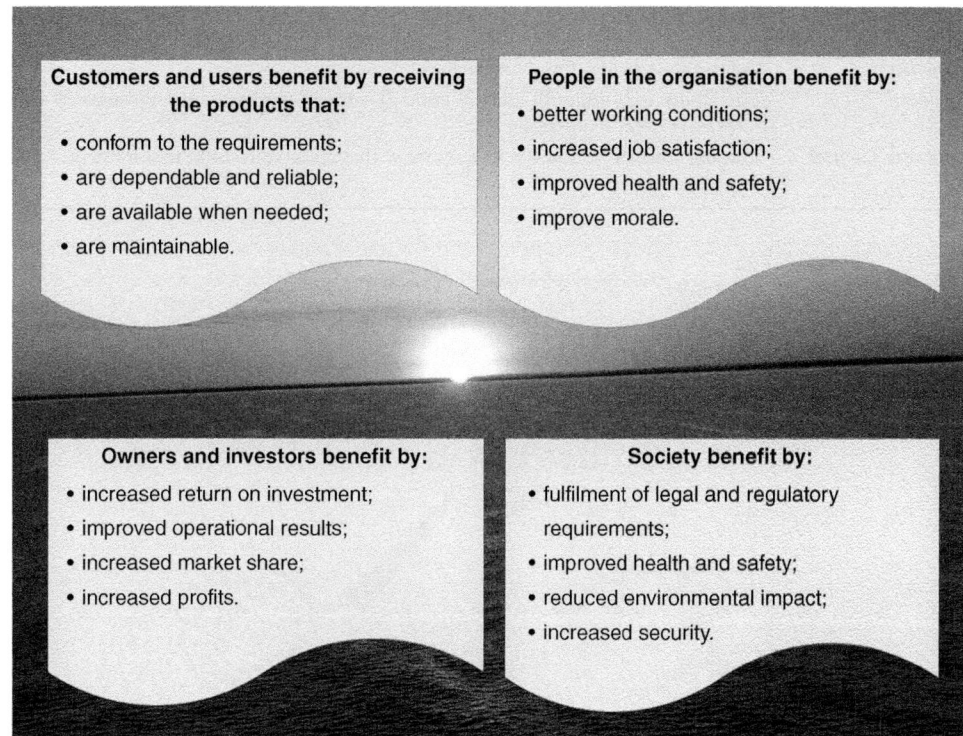

Customers and users benefit by receiving the products that:

- conform to the requirements;
- are dependable and reliable;
- are available when needed;
- are maintainable.

People in the organisation benefit by:

- better working conditions;
- increased job satisfaction;
- improved health and safety;
- improve morale.

Owners and investors benefit by:

- increased return on investment;
- improved operational results;
- increased market share;
- increased profits.

Society benefit by:

- fulfilment of legal and regulatory requirements;
- improved health and safety;
- reduced environmental impact;
- increased security.

FIGURE 1.3 Why bother with Quality Assurance?

1.2 What is the difference between Quality Control and Quality Assurance?

We have already defined what *quality* is all about, but what exactly is meant by Quality Assurance (QA) and Quality Control (QC)?

There seems to be quite a lot of confusion about the meaning of these two topics, and quite frequently people talk about QA when what they actually mean is QC. Although the terms 'Quality Assurance' and 'Quality Control' are both aimed at ensuring the quality of the end product, they are in fact two completely separate processes.

When you think about it, however, the acronym gives the distinction away as the 'C' in QC is all about **controlling** quality via inspections, checks and tests. The 'A' in QA, on the other hand, is about **assuring** quality and involves working out what is required to guarantee quality will be achieved and about setting out processes, standards, procedures and/or policies to do that. (See Figure 1.4)

1.2.1 Quality Control

Quality Control is defined as, *'Part of quality management focused on fulfilling quality requirements'* (ISO). (See Table 1.1)

Quality Control (QC) is the amount of supervision that a deliverable (product or services) is subjected to, so as to be sure that the workmanship associated with that product meets the

TABLE 1.1 Definition of Quality Control

Quality	Verifies the quality of the output
Control	The ability to distinguish what is 'good' (i.e. meets requirements) and what is 'bad' (doesn't meet requirements)
Quality Control	The operational techniques and activities that are used to fulfil requirements for quality

FIGURE 1.4 Difference between Quality Control and Quality Assurance

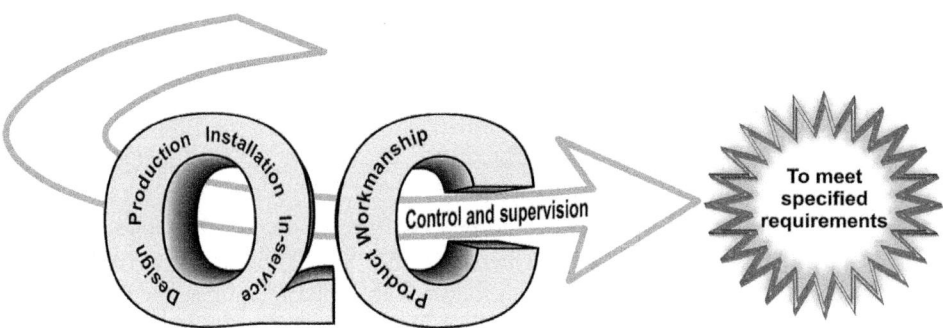

FIGURE 1.5 Quality Control

quality level required by the design. In other words, it is the control exercised by the organisation to certify that **all** aspects of their activities during the design, production, installation **and** in-service stages are up to the desired standards. (See Figure 1.5)

QC is primarily aimed at the **prevention** of errors. Yet, despite all efforts, it remains inevitable that errors can occur. Therefore, the control system should have checks to detect them:

- What error was made?
- Where was it made?

- When was it made?
- Who made it?
- Why was it made?

Only when all these questions are answered can proper action be taken to correct the error and prevent the same mistake from being repeated.

QC is exercised at all levels, and, as all personnel are responsible for the particular task they are doing, they are **all** Quality Controllers to some degree or other.

1.2.2 Quality Assurance

Quality Assurance is defined as, *'The assembly of all planned and systematic actions necessary to provide adequate confidence that a product, process, or service will satisfy given quality requirements'* (ISO). (See Table 1.2)

Quality Assurance (QA) is also a declaration given to inspire confidence that a product or service has achieved the highest standards and that its production, installation, modification and/or repair has been completed in an efficient and timely manner. (See Figure 1.6)

The purpose of QA is to:

- provide assurance to a customer that the standard of workmanship within a contractor's (or subcontractor's) premises is of the highest level and that all products and services leaving that particular organisation are above a certain fixed minimum level of specification;
- ensure that production and/or service standards are uniform among an organisation's departments or offices and that they remain constant despite changes in personnel.

TABLE 1.2 Definition of Quality Assurance

Quality	Fitness for intended use
Assurance	A declaration given to inspire confidence in an organisation's capability
Quality Assurance	A declaration given to inspire confidence that a particular organisation is capable of consistently satisfying need, as well as being a managerial process designed to increase confidence

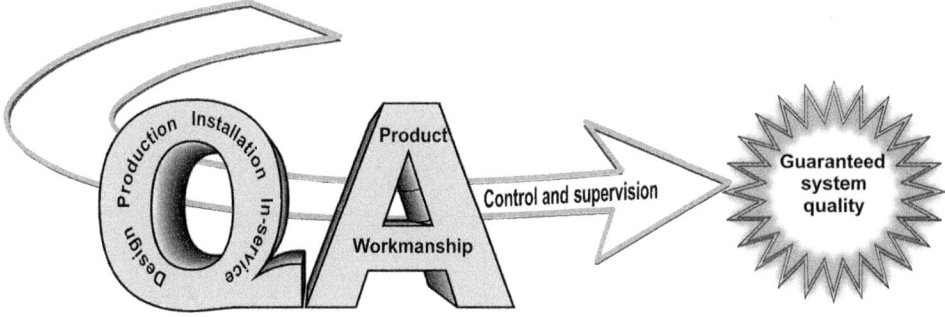

FIGURE 1.6 Quality Assurance

In a nutshell, QA is concerned with:

- an agreed level of quality;
- a commitment within an organisation to the fundamental principle of consistently supplying the right quality product;
- a commitment from a customer to the fundamental principle of accepting only the right quality product;
- a commitment at all levels (of contractor and/or customer) to the basic principles of QA and QC.

 AUTHOR'S HINT

The result of these actions should ideally be checked by someone independently of the work.

 In the case of special projects, customers may require special Quality Assurance measures or a Quality Plan.

1.3 Quality Assurance during a product's life cycle

 AUTHOR'S HINT

Although I have written this section of the book primarily from the point of view of the design, production, acceptance and in-service stages of a product, it is equally applicable whether you are producing an actual device or a document or have influence on any other form of deliverable such as IT products and services.

The life of a manufactured device is made up of four stages (see Figure 1.7). Each of these stages has specific requirements that need to be correctly managed and that need to be regulated by Quality Control.

As Quality Assurance affects the device throughout its life cycle, it is important to realise that Quality Assurance procedures are absolutely essential for the design, manufacture and acceptance stages, as well as in-service utilisation.

1.3.1 Design stage

> *Quality must be designed into products and services before manufacture or assembly.* (ISO)

Throughout the design stage of products and services, the quality of that design **must** be regularly checked. Quality procedures have also to be planned, written and implemented so as to predict and evaluate the fundamental and intrinsic reliability of the proposed design. (See Figure 1.8)

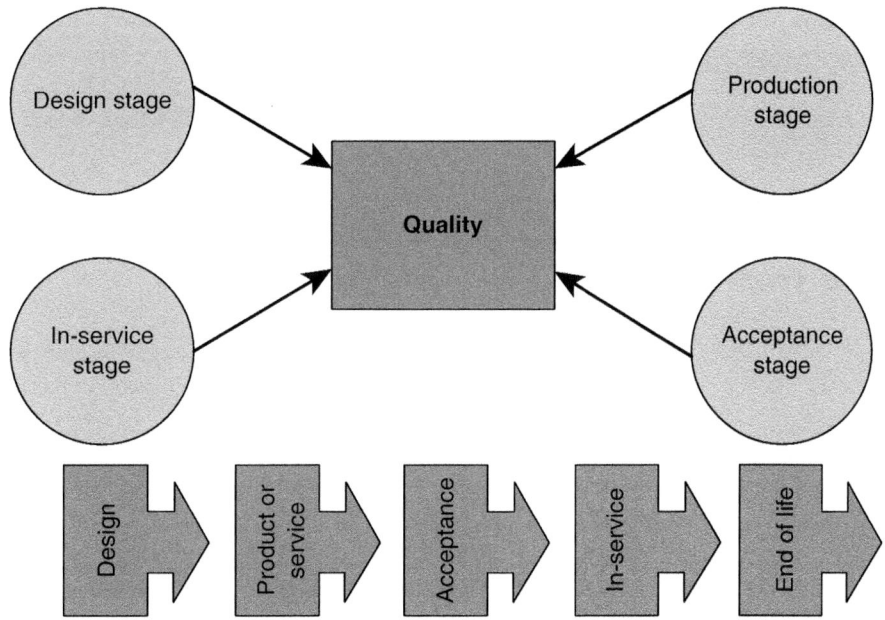

FIGURE 1.7   Quality Assurance during a product's life cycle

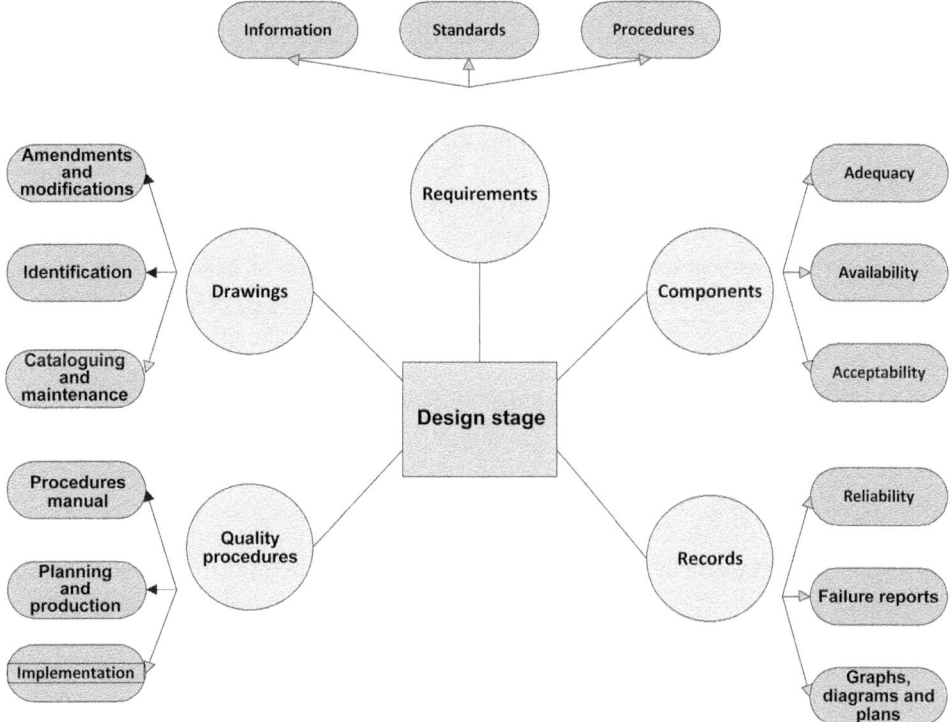

FIGURE 1.8   Quality during the design stage

It doesn't matter whether the responsibility for the design of these products and services rests purely with the supplier or the purchaser or is a joint function. It is essential that the designer is fully aware of the exact requirements of the project and has a sound background knowledge of the relevant standards, information and procedures that will have to be adopted during the design stages.

CASE STUDY

With the introduction of Annex SL and the publication of ISO 9001:2015, much more emphasis has now been placed on an organisation's achieving its (and its customers') quality objectives.

This additional requirement is extremely important to the design office because their actions not only influence the maintenance of quality during the manufacture or supply of the device but will also play a major part in setting the quality level of the eventual device.

For example, if there is no Quality Control in the drawing office, there is little chance of there ever being any on the shop floor, and engineers trying to manufacture or design something to a set of drawings that have countless mistakes have little chance of their ever becoming an acceptable item. In a similar manner, even the production of a simple document or report requires a design stage to show what it is supposed to cover and in what detail – and so on.

Design problems, although not specifically stipulated in a particular Management System Standard, should nevertheless be addressed, and the design office (or team) should ideally produce some sort of *Procedures Manual* that lists and describes the routine procedures required to turn a concept into a set of functional drawings.

These procedures will cover such activities as the numbering of drawings, authorisation to issue amendments and modifications, how to control changes to drawings, the method of withdrawing obsolete drawings and the identification, cataloguing and maintenance of drawings.

In addition to these procedures, the design office will also have to provide a complete listing of all the relevant components, their availability, acceptability and adequacy **and** have to be aware of all the advances in both materials and equipment currently available on today's market that are relevant to the device.

It is imperative that the design team maintains a close relationship with the remainder of the organisation throughout these initial stages so as to be aware of the exact requirements, the problems, and the choice of components etc., to assist in the analysis of failures and to swiftly produce solutions and forestall costly work stoppages. One of the main problems to overcome is the ease with which the design office can make an arbitrary selection but then find that the size and tolerance are completely inappropriate (for example) to the manufacture or assembly process.

In order for the statistical significance of a particular failure to be assessed and for a correct retroactive action to be taken, it is essential that the design team has access to all the relevant documented information such as failure reports and other data as soon as they are available within the design office or shop floor.

The storage, maintenance and analysis of reliability data will require the design team to follow the progress of the products and services throughout their productive life cycle and its many maintenance cycles and to take due note of customers' comments.

The compilation and retention of design office reliability data are essential to the reliability of the actual device being produced and the manufacturing facility itself.

Nowadays, of course, most design offices – particularly in larger organisations – are computerised and use processors to store their records on internal or external hard drives or even cloud-based systems, so that these records can be continually updated and amended. This information (data) can then be used with standard software such as Computer-Aided Design (CAD) programs and computer-aided design facilities to produce lists, graphs and drawings. The possibilities are almost endless, but there are associated problems, such as security against virus attack and computer crashes.

1.3.2 Production stage

Manufacturing operations must be carried out under controlled conditions. (ISO)

During all of the production and manufacturing processes (and throughout early in-service life), the device (assembly or item) being produced must be subjected to a variety of Quality Control procedures and checks in order to evaluate the degree of quality. (See Figure 1.9)

One of the first things that must be done is to predict the reliability of the device's design. This involves obtaining sufficient statistical data so as to be able to estimate the actual reliability of the design before products or services are manufactured.

All the appropriate engineering data has to be carefully examined, particularly the reliability ratings of recommended parts, components, software and the like. The designer then extrapolates and interpolates this data and uses probability methods to examine the reliability of a proposed design.

Design deficiencies, such as assembly errors, operator learning, motivational or fatigue factors, latent defects and improper part selection, are frequently uncovered during this process.

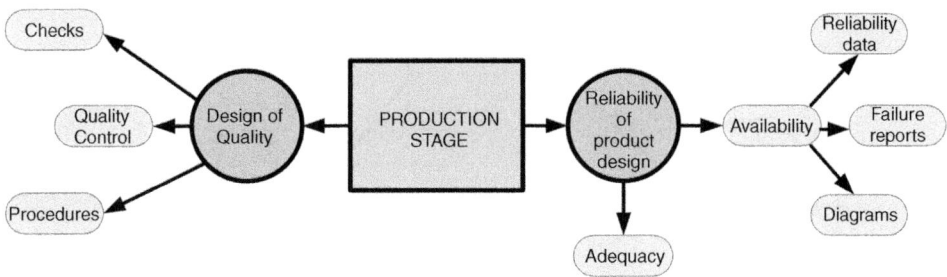

FIGURE 1.9 Quality during the production stage

1.3.3 Acceptance stage

> *The quality of products and services must be proved before being accepted.* (ISO)

As stated in ISO 9001:2015: '*The outputs of design and development shall be provided in a form that enables verification against the design and development input and shall be approved prior to release*' (ISO).

During the acceptance stage, the device produced will need to be subjected to a series of tests designed to confirm that the workmanship fully meets the levels of quality required or stipulated by the user and that the device performs its required function correctly. Tests will range from environmental tests of individual components to field testing complete systems. (See Figure 1.10)

Three mathematical expressions are commonly used to measure reliability, and each of these expressions can be applied to a part, component assembly or an entire system. They are Probability Function (PF), Failure Rate (FR) and Mean Time Between Failures (MTBF).

1.3.4 In-service stage

> *Evaluation of products and services performance during typical operating conditions and feedback of information gained through field use improves product.* (ISO)

During the in-service stage, the equipment user is, of course, principally concerned with system and equipment reliability. (See Figure 1.11)

Although reliability is based on the device's generic design (and can be easily proved by statistics), its practical reliability is often far less design dependent. This difference can be due to poor or faulty operating procedures, operating the system beyond its design capability or

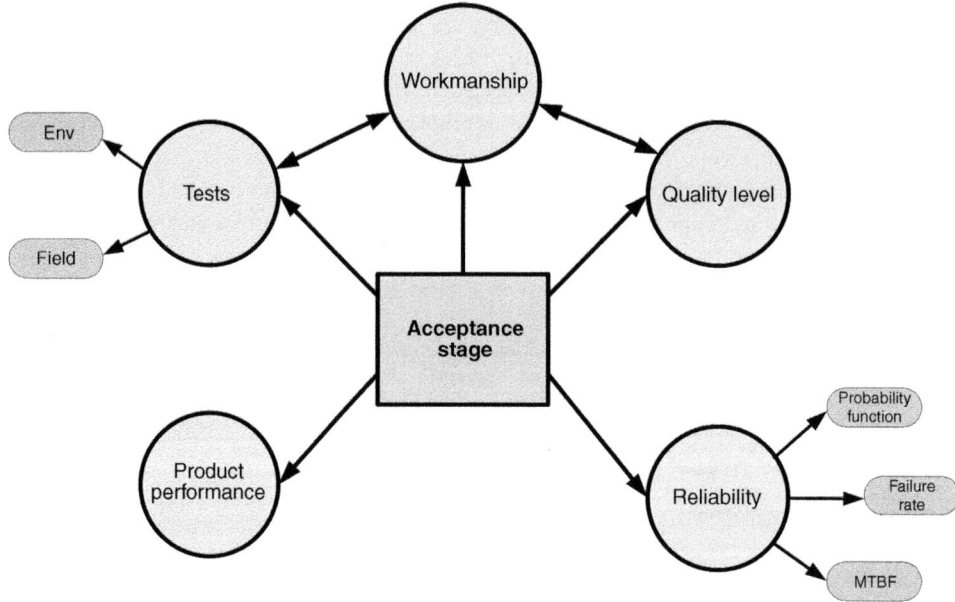

FIGURE 1.10   Quality during the acceptance stage

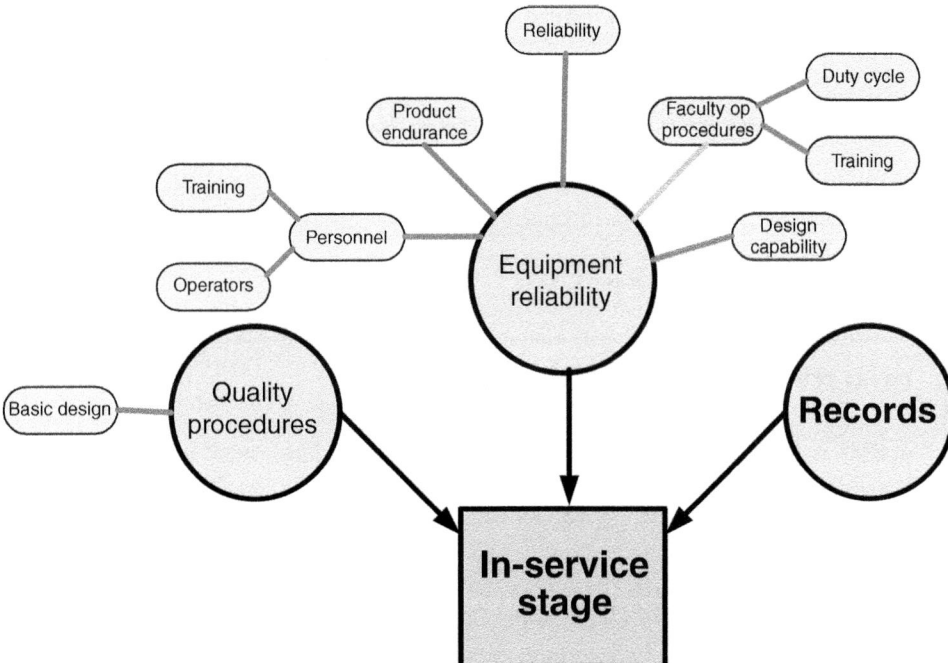

FIGURE 1.11   Quality during the in-service stage

operational abuses (e.g. personal, extended duty cycles, neglected maintenance, training etc.). Each of these hazards can damage individual components, subassemblies and soft- and/or firmware, and each will, in turn, reduce the device's dependability.

It is interesting to note that, according to studies previously completed by the British Chartered Management Institute (CMI) in 2008 (**and** reconfirmed by another survey in 2018), the maintenance technician (or engineer) **still** remains the primary cause of reliability degradations during the in-service stage. The problems associated with poorly trained, poorly supported or poorly motivated maintenance personnel with respect to reliability and dependability cannot be overemphasised and requires careful assessment and quantification.

The most important factor that affects the overall reliability of a modern manufactured device, nevertheless, is the increased number of individual components that are required in the device. Since most system failures are actually caused by the failure of a single component, the reliability of each individual component must be considerably better than the overall system reliability.

Information obtained from in-service use and field failures is enormously useful (always assuming that they are entirely accurate, of course!) in evaluating a device's performance during typical operating conditions. But the main reason for accumulating failure reports from the field is to improve the device. This can be achieved by carefully analysing the reports, finding out what caused the failure and taking steps to prevent it from recurring in the future.

Because of this requirement, quality standards for the maintenance, repair and inspection of in-service devices have had to be laid down in engineering standards, handbooks and local operating manuals (written for specific items and equipment). These publications are used by maintenance engineers and should always include the most recent amendments. It is **essential** that Quality Assurance personnel also use the same procedures for their inspections!

1.4 What is a Quality Management System?

> *A Quality Management System (QMS) is the organised structure of responsibilities, activities, resources and events that together provide procedures and methods of implementation to ensure the capability of an organisation meets the quality requirement of the client. (ISO 19011)*
>
> *An effective QMS should be designed to satisfy the purchaser's conditions, requirements and expectations whilst serving to protect the manufacturer's best interests. (ISO Annex SL)*

Or to put it another way, 'what is a QMS?'

QUALITY MANAGEMENT SYSTEM

A QMS is the organisational structure of policies, procedures, work instructions and resources that together provide processes focussed on achieving quality policy and quality objectives to meet customer requirements.

Thus a company controls its business through the application of a **business** management system **not** – as the previous 2008 edition of ISO 9001 and other similar Management System Standards suggested – through a Quality Management System. So one mustn't get too hung up on the word 'quality'!

 AUTHOR'S HINT

Some people generically refer to the group of documents as a QMS, but specifically it refers to the **entire system**. The documents just describe it.

An organisation's QMS defines the policy, organisation and responsibilities for the management of quality within that organisation. It ensures that all of your organisation's activities comply with an agreed set of rules, regulations and guidelines and that the end product and service (i.e. the deliverable) conforms to the customer's (i.e. the user's) contractual requirements. This is achieved by:

- accurately determining the needs and expectations of the customer;
- developing and maintaining the quality policy and quality objectives of the organisation;
- defining the processes and responsibilities necessary to attain the quality objectives;
- regularly reviewing the current effectiveness of each process;
- creating means of preventing non-conformities and eliminating their causes;
- completing a risk analysis programme;
- looking for opportunities to improve the effectiveness and efficiency of processes;
- planning the strategies, processes and resources to deliver the identified improvements;
- implementing these planned activities;

- monitoring the effects of improvements and modifications to the products and services;
- assessing the results against the expected outcomes;
- reviewing the improvement activities to determine appropriate follow-up actions.

Any organisation that adopts this sort of approach will create confidence in the capability of its processes and the reliability of its products and services. It will also provide a basis for continual improvement and can lead to increased customer satisfaction.

AUTHOR'S HINT

A Quality Management System is neither a manual (i.e. a document) nor a computer program (which is an information system as opposed to being a real quality system). It is a system that contains all the things used to regulate, control and improve the quality of your products and/or services. It is a network of interrelated processes with each process being made up of people, work, activities, tasks, records, documents, forms, resources, rules, regulations, reports, materials, supplies, tools, equipment etc. that are required to transform inputs into outputs.

So what actually is meant by having a successful QMS? To be effective, an organisation relies on a variety of interactions and inputs (as indicated in Figure 1.12) in order achieve their ultimate goals for QA and QC.

Together, these measures comprise the organisation's QMS and describe their capability for supplying products and services and services that will comply with the quality and other regulatory standards laid down.

Previously, this was contained in a document called the Quality Manual, which was a document setting out the quality policies, systems and practices of an organisation's QMS. However, the ISO Committee responsible for producing the new (i.e. year 2105) requirements for Management System Standards **left out** the requirement for an organisation to possess a formal Quality Manual – preferring to call everything associated with an organisations documents and records as '*documented information*'.

Whereas the previous editions of QMS used specific terminology such as '*document*' or '*documented procedures*', '*quality manual*' or '*quality plan*', the latest editions of the International Management Standards now contain requirements to '*maintain documented information*''. **However** – in acknowledging that now over 2 million companies worldwide are certified to a Management System Standard and are using a Quality Manual etc. – ISO's Technical Committees responsible for producing the latest version of these standards (e.g. ISO/TC 176 Quality Management and Quality Assurance) have obviously realised that this 'rule' could possibly cause a lot of problems (and possibly arguments!) and have now stated, '*There is no requirement in an International Standard for its structure and terminology to be applied to the documented information of an organization's Quality Management System*'!

So an organisation can choose whether to include their Quality Processes and Procedures and the like in an overall filing system called a Quality Manual or just retain them as 'documented information'. It's your choice, you won't be breaking any rules!

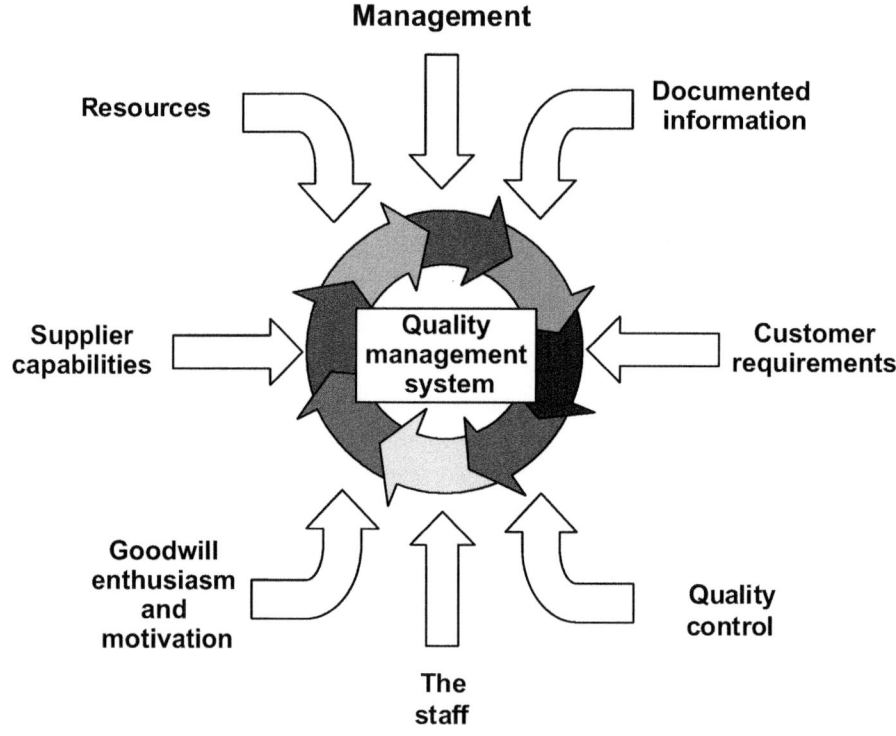

FIGURE 1.12 The ingredients of a successful Quality Management System

---

 **AUTHOR'S HINT**

With this in mind (and to avoid any confusion), I have continued to use the term 'Quality Manual' in this book and leave it up to my readers to choose what to call their 'database' – be it Quality Manual, Management Manual or simply the Company's Management Manual.

All that aside, in order to be successful, an organisation must be able to prove that they are capable of producing products and services that are to the customer's complete satisfaction and that not only conform to the customer's specific requirements but are always of the desired quality. An organisation's QMS is therefore the organisational structure of responsibilities, procedures, processes and resources for carrying out quality management. As such, it must be planned and developed so that it is capable of maintaining a consistent level of Quality Control.

The *'quality loops'* shown in Figures 1.13 and 1.14 should always be followed up by an organisation to ensure that all aspects of the production and supply cycles have been considered in the QMS.

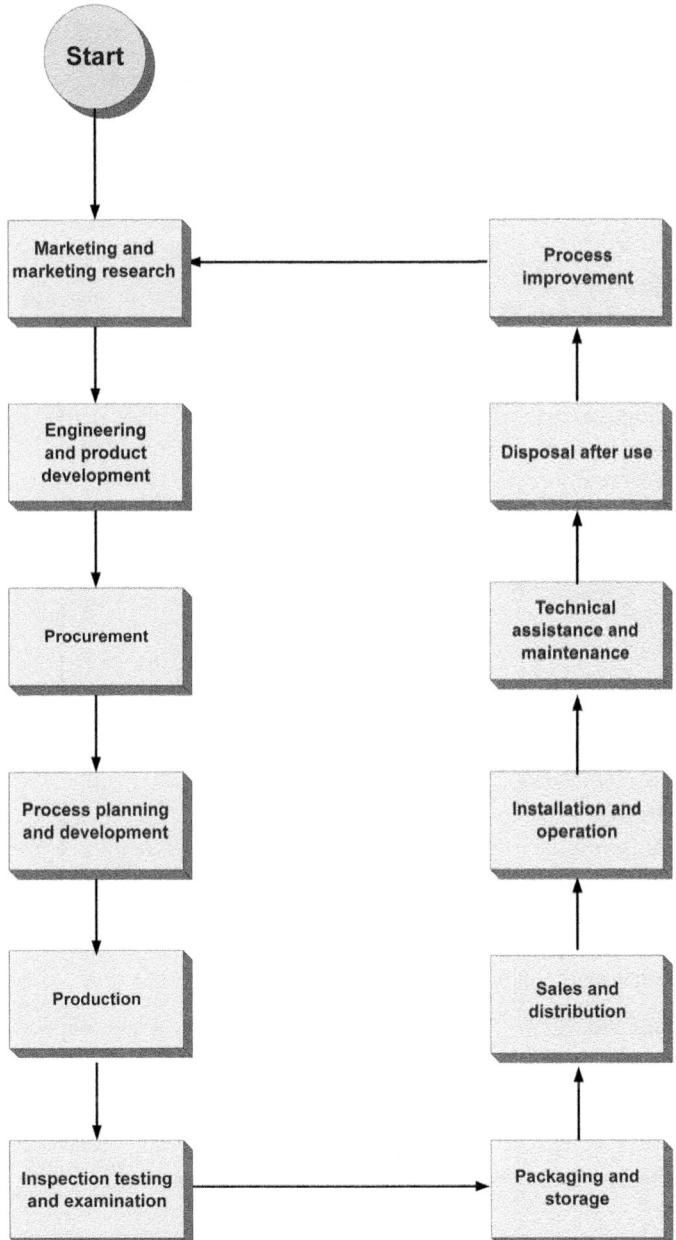

FIGURE 1.13 The quality loop for products

So whether you produce 'nuts and bolts' or design software or you provide a service such as public relations, a QMS is ideal for running your organisation.

However, to be effective, the QMS **must** be structured around the organisation's particular type of business and should be flexible enough to consider all functions such as customer liaison, design, purchasing, subcontracting, manufacturing, training, installation, updating of Quality Control techniques and the accumulation of quality records. As

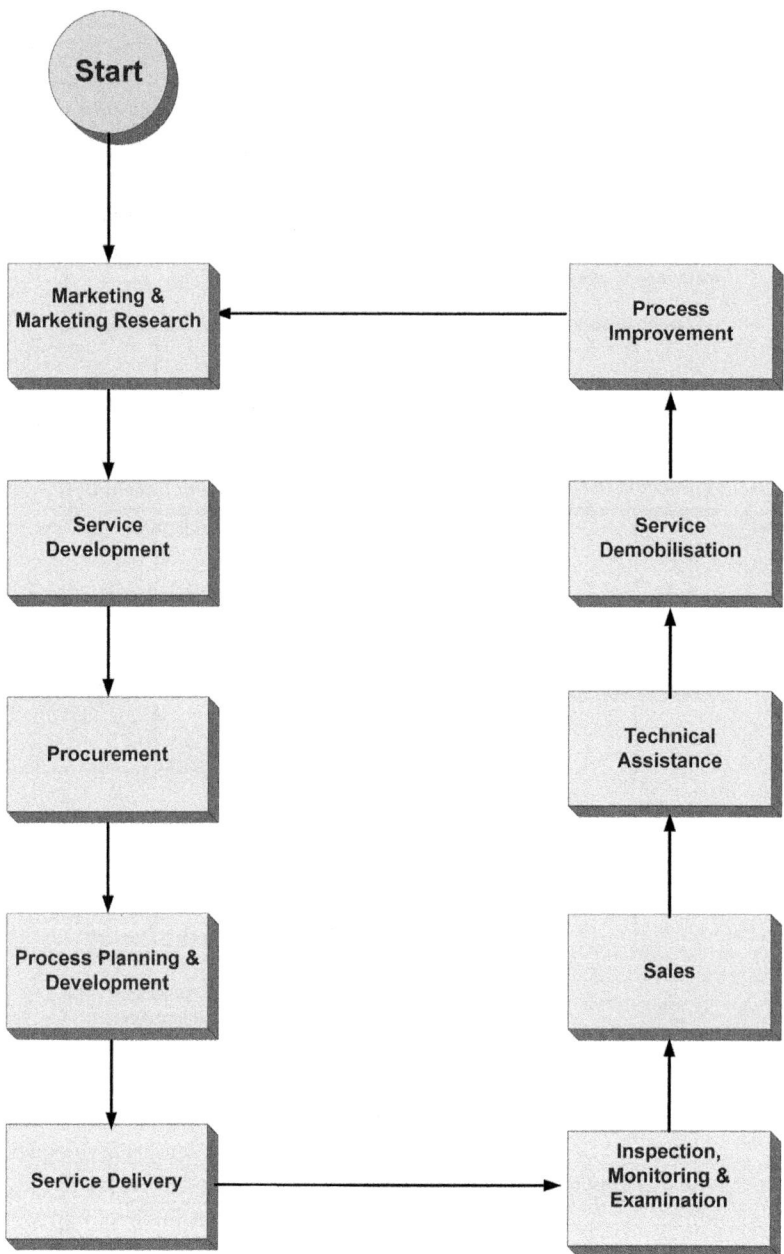

FIGURE 1.14   The quality loop for services

touched on before, in most organisations, this sort of information will normally be found in their Quality Manual.

The type of QMS chosen will, of course, vary from organisation to another, depending upon its size and capability. There are no set rules as to exactly how these documents should be written. Nevertheless, they should – as a minimum requirement – be capable of showing the potential customer exactly how the organisation is equipped to achieve and maintain the highest level of quality throughout the various stages of design, production, installation and servicing.

As an example, some of the determinants and measures of the quality of a products and services are shown in Figures 1.15 and 1.16.

Note: Figures 1.15 and 1.16 are extracts from BS 4778:1979, which have been reproduced with the kind permission of BSI. Although the 1979 edition has been superseded, these figures are included here since they still illustrate the concept.

1.5 QMS structure

A QMS defines the policy, organisation and responsibilities for the management of quality within an organisation. It ensures that all activities comply with an agreed set of rules, regulations and guidelines and that the end product or service (i.e. the deliverable) conforms to the customer's (i.e. the user's) contractual requirements.

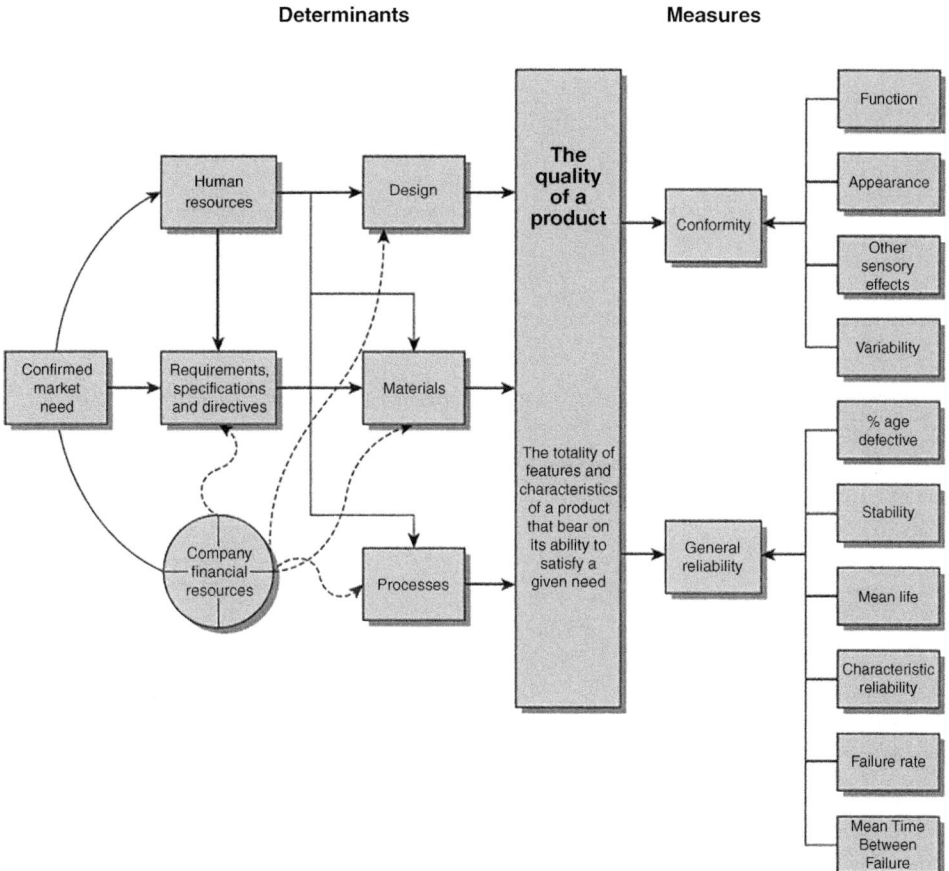

FIGURE 1.15   Some of the determinants and measures of the quality of a product

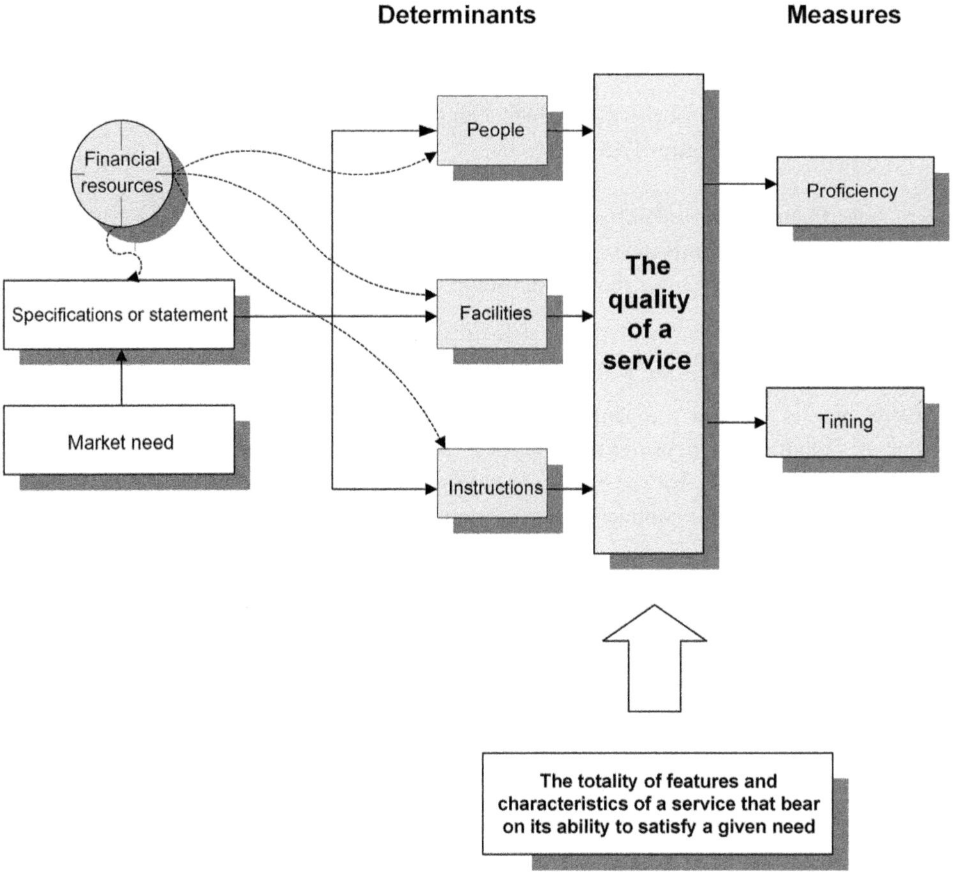

FIGURE 1.16 Some of the determinants and measures of the quality of a service

A QMS can be effective only if it is fully documented, understood and followed by all.

Within all Management System Standards, there are four levels of documentation (see Figure 1.17 and Table 1.3) and when trying to work out which processes should be documented, the organisation may wish to consider factors such as the:

- effect on quality;
- risk of customer dissatisfaction;
- statutory and/or regulatory requirements;
- economic risk;
- competence of personnel;
- complexity of processes.

Where it is found necessary to document processes, a number of different methods (such as graphical representations, written instructions, checklists, flow charts, visual media and/or electronic methods) can be used.

As previously mentioned, the latest editions of Management System Standards are all referred to as '*documented information*'.

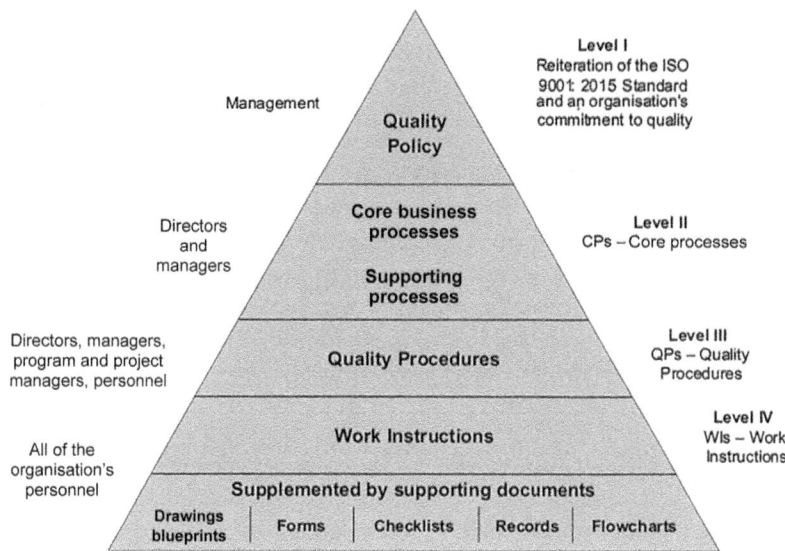

FIGURE 1.17   Quality Management System structure

TABLE 1.3 QMS documentation

Level 1 **Quality Manual**	A formal top management statement that establishes the QMS and how it meets the requirements of the chosen Management System Standards
Level 2 **Processes**	The core business process plus supporting processes that describe the activities required to implement the QMS and to meet the policy requirements shown in the Quality Manual
Level 3 **Procedures**	A description of the method by which quality system activities are managed
Level 4 **Work Instructions**	A description of how a specific task is carried out

1.5.1 Quality Manual

A Quality Manual shows how an organisation meets the requirements of a specific Management Systems Standard (or a number of associated standards) and defines:

- the overall quality policy adopted by that organisation;
- the organisation that has been developed to implement this quality policy;
- the documentation (i.e. Quality Processes, Quality Procedures and Work Instructions) that has been designed to enable that particular organisation to carry out that policy.

AUTHOR'S HINT

Organisational changes within a company or the environment in which it operates may necessitate modifications, amendments, insertions and/or deletions to the overall QMS adopted by that particular company and its associated documentation. The contents of this Quality Manual may therefore be altered on an as required basis – but, all changes **must** be subject to a Quality Procedure for the *Control of documented information*. Changes are deemed operational following approval by the authorised person(s) and published as updated sections of the Quality Manual.

The Quality Manual is a statement of the managerial policy and the objectives for each clause of ISO Annex SL (and/or an associated Management System Standard), and, as such, it provides a statement of commitment to customers (or external approval and/or regulatory bodies when required. The Quality Manual describes a number of systematic controls and procedures for the Staff in fulfilling their duties and responsibilities. It defines the lines of traceability, accountability and responsibility and exists primarily as an internal management control document. The Quality Manual also provides a definitive statement of the policy, objectives, operating systems, processes and procedures established by the organisation, and the system recognises the established elements of modern formalised quality management as expressed in national and international standards and as appropriate to the nature of the work undertaken. (See Figure 1.18)

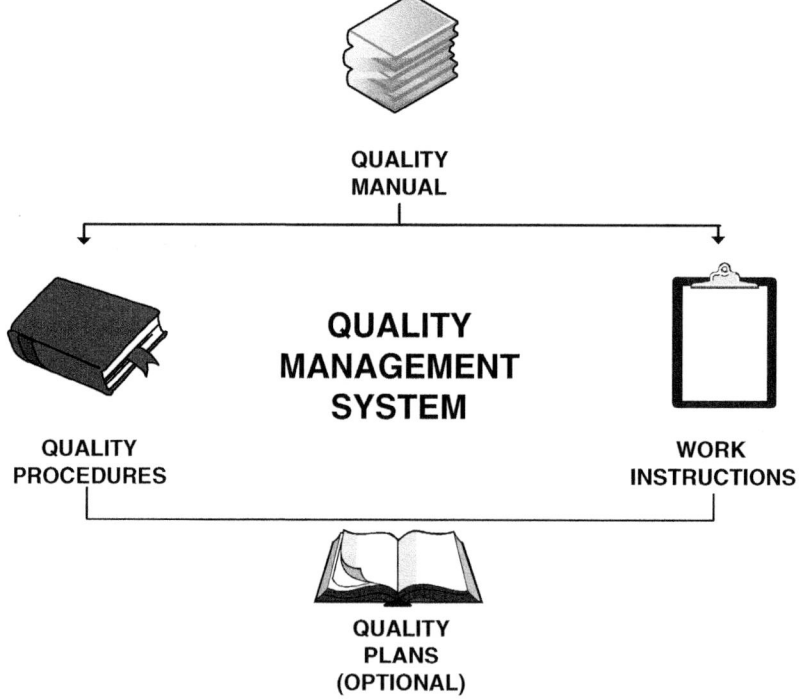

FIGURE 1.18   Quality Management System structure

Uncontrolled copies of the Quality Manual (including Quality Procedures and Work Instructions) should be made available to all Staff. Uncontrolled copies (stamped "**Uncontrolled copy**" across the title page; these copies will *not* be automatically updated) may also be provided to outside organisations or individuals for publicity or information purposes.

Since the first edition of a Management System Standard, it has been an accepted fact that a Quality Manual is '*a document specifying the quality management system of an organisation*'. A typical Quality Manual will include the company's quality policy and goals, as well as a detailed description Staff roles and relationships, procedures, systems and any other resources that relate to producing high-quality goods or services.

AUTHOR'S HINT

As mentioned earlier in this chapter, with the introduction of Annex SL, the ISO Committee responsible for updating the standard, removed the actual requirement for an organisation to possess a formal Quality Manual.

As the Quality Processes and Procedures etc. of an organisation are all interrelated, there must be some sort of centralised library for these documents (be they hard or digitised copies). These documents are normally combined in the Quality Manual – a document that has existed and has been used by auditors and quality managers for more than 50 years!

At the time of writing this book, the 'jury' still appears to be out on this 'ruling', and many organisations (particularly those who are already certified to a previous Management System Standard) intend to continue using their **existing**, albeit slightly modified Quality Manual so as to include the changes made by Annex SL.

Whatever the final ruling regarding the title of this document, it will become the formal record of its Quality Management System, and it will be:

- a rule book by which an organisation functions;
- a source of information from which customers may derive confidence;
- a means of defining the responsibilities and interrelated activities of every member of the organisation;
- a medium for defining the level of quality that an organisation wishes to consistently deliver;
- a vehicle for auditing, reviewing and evaluating the organisation's QMS.

There is no set specific rules concerning what format and structure you should use to produce your Quality Manual, provided that it:

- includes a statement of your organisation's policy towards Quality Control;
- contains details of your organisation's quality management structure and organisation, together with job descriptions and responsibilities;
- describes your organisation's Quality Control requirements, training programmes etc.

You can use one or many formats, from simple checklists and flow charts to descriptive text. You can use any type of media, and so a Quality Manual can be in hard copy, soft copy, online (via your business website or cloud- based), as an intranet help file or via one of many types of other currently available IT systems.

There is no limit to the size of the Quality Manual. It can be a simple pamphlet with a reference index to other stored documents (as indicated in the previous paragraph), or it can be a complete library.

Whatever the size and format of your Quality Manual, it still remains the single point of reference required to run all aspects of your organisation to consistent quality levels.

The Quality Manual is the heart of a QMS and is essential for anyone considering applying for certification to ISO 9001:2015 and/or other Management System Standards.

1.5.1.1 What goes into a Quality Manual?

The answer to 'What goes into a Quality Manual' is virtually anything and everything and depends on what you need in order to run your business efficiently. (See Figure 1.19) For example, a Mercedes sort of organisation, with many different departments, might have more than one Departmental Quality Manual supporting a company-wide Quality Manual, but a small to medium-sized business will probably only need a small manual for their QMS.

Whatever the size of your organisation and whether you produce, install or merely provide a product or service, the overall purpose of the Quality Manual is to act as your organisation's overarching policy 'bible'. It will identify (if required) subsets of Quality Processes, Quality Plans, Quality Procedures and Work Instructions and provide templates of the various forms and documents used by your organisation – such as production control forms, inspection sheets and documents used to purchase components from your subcontractors. (See Figure 1.20)

Quality Procedures (QPs) and Work Instructions (WIs) will include details of the specifications that must be complied with.

CONTENT

The Organisation's Policy towards Quality Control
Quality management structure and organisation
Job descriptions and responsibilites
Quality Control requirements
Training programmes
Quality Processes
Quality Plans
Quality Procedures
Work Instructions

FIGURE 1.19 What goes into a Quality Manual?

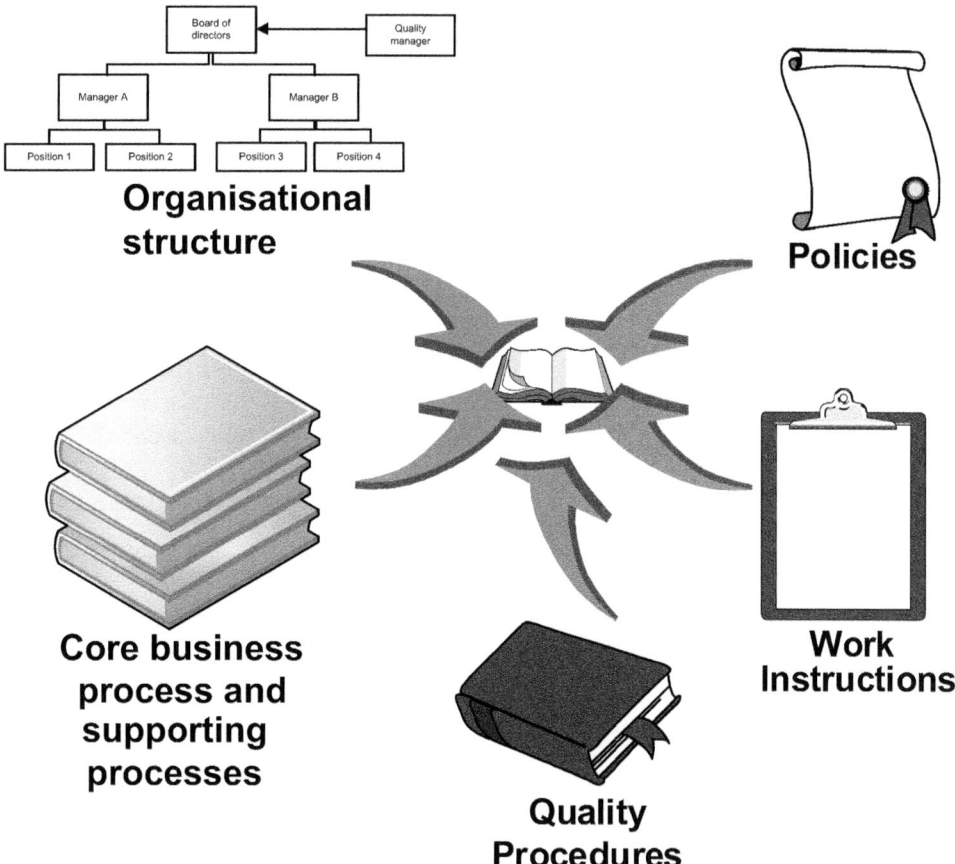

FIGURE 1.20 The basic contents of a Quality Manual?

For a producer, these may include:

*   particulars of drawings;
*   supporting documentation;
*   tools and gauges that are going to be used;
*   sampling methods;
*   any tests that have to be made;
*   test specifications and procedures;
*   the acceptance/rejection criteria, etc.

For organisations providing a service, the following may be found in their Quality Manuals:

*   response time criteria;
*   service standards;
*   customer satisfaction and complaints procedures;
*   courtesy requirements (e.g. acceptable telephone manner).

Note: For a complete description and guidance on how to develop a Quality Manual, the reader is referred to ISO 10013 Guidelines for Quality Management System Documentation.

1.5.1.2 What does each part of the Quality Manual do?

Each part of a Quality Manual has a specific role to play, as shown in Figure 1.21.

CASE STUDY

Most organisations use their Quality Manual to address each section of their chosen Management System Standard. Although this is not an ISO requirement, it is not a bad idea as it will assist internal and external auditors when they come to evaluate an organisation's QMS for compliance with the standard.

1.5.2 Quality Procedures

Quality Procedures (QPs) form the bulk of the QMS and describe how the policy objectives of the Quality Manual can be met in practice and how these processes are controlled. They detail **what** has to be carried out to meet the requirements of these primary and secondary processes and their associated Quality Policies. Without procedures, an organisation's best intentions will not always be met.

QPs need to:

- cover all the applicable elements of ISO 9001:2015 (and/or chosen Management System Standard), as well as detailing procedures that concern an organisation's actual method of operation;
- cover an easily identifiable and separate part of the quality system:
- be easily traced back to the policies dictated by senior management.

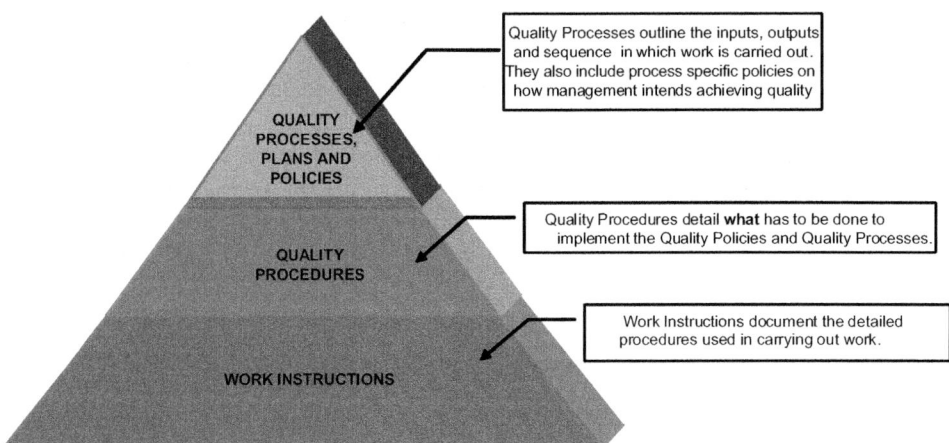

FIGURE 1.21 What each part of a Quality Manual does

QPs should **not** normally include technical requirements or specialist procedures for the manufacture of a product. This type of detail is generally included in a Work Instruction.

In addition to a descriptive title and a file number, each procedure needs to be dated and subjected to regular reviews and internal audits for possible updating. These documented procedures can be made available as uncontrolled copies and used as separate documents outside the Quality Manual in places of work.

The generation and control of a QP will need to be defined in a separate QP (e.g. 'Control of Documented Information').

Some procedures may contain data or information, the knowledge of which **must** remain restricted to that particular organisation. These particular procedures **shall not** be included in the Quality Manual, beyond their title and reference number. If these procedures are required for contractual purposes, the Managing Director *must* authorise their release.

1.5.2.1 What is the best way to write a Quality Procedure?

A simple rule is don't bother unless you really have to! A degree of common sense must prevail when writing procedures, and you should always consider the known competency and knowledge of the personnel performing them.

If you employ highly skilled professionals, it would be foolish to spend hours writing a procedure on something that they are already qualified to do or for which standards and guidelines already exist. For example, you would **not** tell a civil engineer how to design a beach hut. (See Figure 1.22)

On the other hand, you will probably want to write a procedure where you use untrained Staff to perform it. But a degree of common sense must prevail when writing procedures, and due consideration must be given to the competency of the personnel performing them.

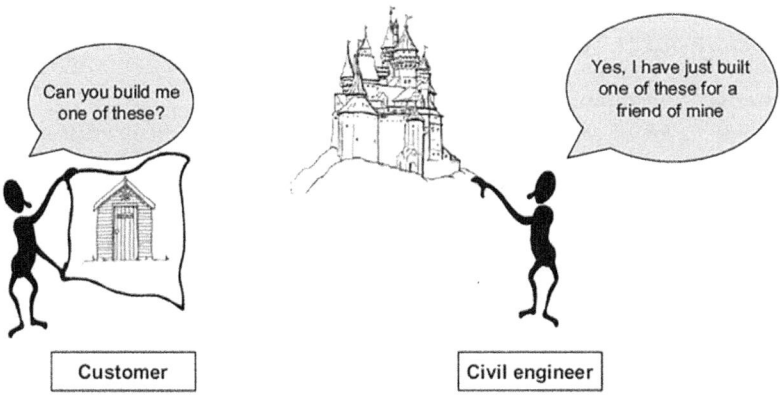

FIGURE 1.22   Can you design this?

The example in Figure 1.23 shows part of a typical procedure for resolving issues (such as some of the problems with providing a service).

This easy to follow flow chart can be enhanced with explanatory text so that the entire process is clearly understood and easily trained. The benefit of flow charts is that they can be stuck up on notice boards so that the people who have to implement the procedure can readily see what they are expected to do.

Procedures can take any suitable form. They can be a narrative, a flow chart, a process map or indeed any other suitable format. If you can do **without** a lengthy written procedure, then do so and use a simple process map instead. As long as the procedure is effective, it really doesn't matter what it looks like.

1.5.2.2 What should go into a Quality Procedure?

QPs form the basic documentation used for planning and controlling all activities that impact on quality. They detail how an organisation's core policy is to be implemented by adding the meat to the process-specific policies. They should cover all the applicable elements of ISO Annex SL, as well as your chosen Management System Standard, and detail procedures that concern the organisation's actual method of operation. These will normally remain relatively constant, regardless of the product, services, system or process being supplied.

Each QP should cover a specific part of the Core Business Process or one of its supporting processes – e.g. contract review, document control, audit procedures, training – and should be easily traced back to the process-specific policies dictated by senior management. (See Figure 1.24)

QPs should **not** normally include technical requirements or specialist procedures required for the manufacture of a product or delivery of a system/service. These sorts of details are generally explained in Work Instructions. QPs can (and usually do) form a large bulk of the QMS.

The layout and format of QPs should be consistent so that Staff can become accustomed to a familiar structure. This also helps to ensure systematic compliance with the ISO Annex SL requirements and the associated management standard chosen (e.g. ISO 9001:2015).

QPs will mainly include (but are not limited to) the following:

Document data sheet   all the salient information about the document: file name, who wrote it, a summary of the contents, when it was approved, who approved it, etc.

Distribution list   a record of everyone who has a controlled copy of the document

Amendments   a record of all changes made to the document

Contents list   a list of all the chapters, sections, parts and annexes, etc. that make up this document

List of annexes   all parts of a document should be traceable, especially when they are in separate volumes.

List of illustrations/tables   a list of all the figures and tables included in the document

Abbreviations and acronyms   an explanation of any abbreviations or acronyms used in the document

Terminology   an explanation of any technical and/or confusing terminology used in the document

References   any reference material that is specifically mentioned to in the document

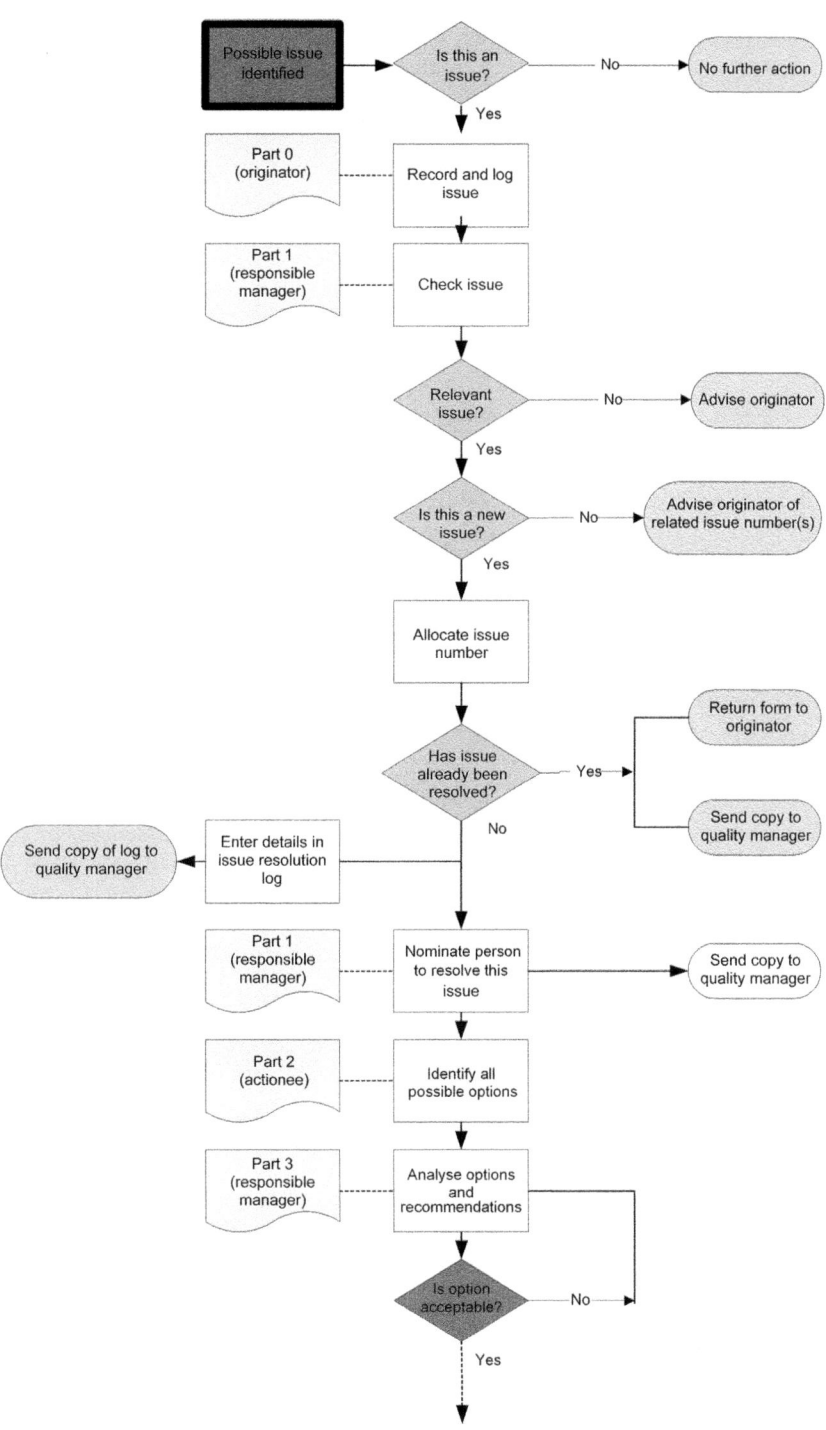

FIGURE 1.23 — Part of a typical Quality Procedure flow chart

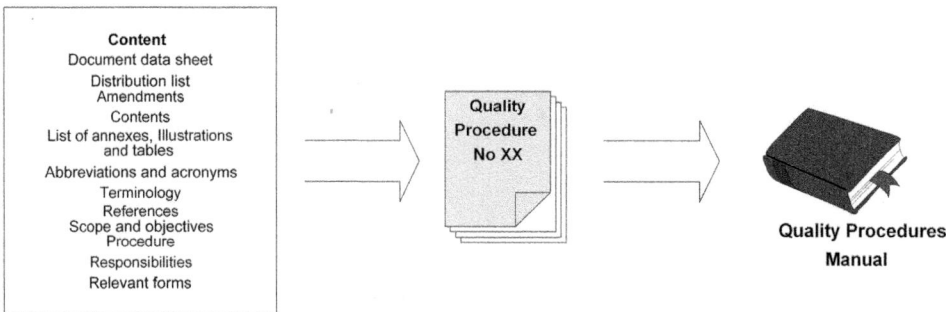

FIGURE 1.24 What goes into a Quality Procedure?

Scope and objectives a list of why you need the procedure, what it is for, the area covered and any exclusions

Procedure overview and the procedure itself this is the main part of the document and details in clear, concise and unambiguous terms the actions and methods to be used (ideally the procedure should be detailed in a logical order with the aid of flow charts)

Responsibilities clear specifications of who is responsible for implementing the procedure and who can carry it out, including (if necessary) minimum training requirements

Relevant forms the identification of any forms, paperwork or computerised forms required to implement the procedure

Think of QPs as a set of clear concise instructions. For example, if management has stipulated that all problems found within the organisation must go through a problem-solving process, then those dealing with the situation need clear instructions on how and what to do about it.

It is therefore essential that **all** QPs are written down so that everyone knows what to do.

However, beware of falling into the trap of writing a book for each procedure as human nature puts us off reading masses of text! It is **not** mandatory to write procedures for everything.

1.5.2.3 What documented procedures are required for Management Systems?

There is no restriction on the number of QPs that an organisation can use for quality management, but if you are going to seek ISO certification, then **the following six QPs are mandatory** and should be included in your QMS:

- Control of documents (4.2.3)
- Control of records (4.2.4)
- Internal audit (8.2.2)
- Control of nonconforming product (8.3)
- Corrective action (8.5.2)
- Preventive action (8.5.3)

AUTHOR'S HINT

Obviously, the extent of documented information for a QMS can differ from one organisation to another due to:

* the size of the organisation and its type of activities, processes, products and services;
* the complexity of processes and their interactions;
* the competence of persons.

Other QPs could therefore include:

* the approval procedure;
* budget and finance;
* change control;
* customer awareness and training;
* customer feedback;
* customer satisfaction;
* design control;
* gap analysis;
* health and safety
* human resources;
* inspection and test;
* internal quality audits;
* manufacture and build;
* marketing;
* notes and reports;
* press releases;
* product numbering;
* production of a quality document;
* purchasing;
* quality management system review;
* risk management;
* training;
* software quality plans;
* stores;
* subcontractors and suppliers;
* vigilance system.

In accordance with Annex SL, Quality Procedures are used to implement the Quality Processes of an organisation. QPs detail **what** has to be carried out to meet the requirements of these primary and secondary processes and their associated Quality Policies. Without procedures, an organisation's best intentions will not always be met.

Think of QPs as clear concise instructions. For example, management decrees that all problems found within the organisation must go through a problem-solving process (i.e. management sets a policy). A member of Staff couldn't be expected to know how to do this without clear instructions. Even worse, the entire work force would have their own ideas about solving problems and further problems would arise as a result.

It is, therefore, essential that **all** QPs are written down – and most importantly are freely available – so that everyone knows what to do.

1.5.3 Work Instructions

AUTHOR'S HINT

Although ISO Annex SL states that Work Instructions (WI) are no longer required (they now refer to them as *'documented information that defines the activities to be performed and the results achieved'*), it seems nowadays (well it certainly does to me!) that whenever you purchase something, you will need to assemble yourself (e.g. a fruit cage) or use (e.g. a simple car hoover), a WI is included in the packing box. So whatever you call this – a WI or 'written guidance' – it is still part of the overall Quality Assurance chain – in my opinion.

WIs describe, in detail, how individual tasks and activities are to be carried out. For example:

- what is to be done, by whom and when it has to be completed);
- the physical operating practices and controls within each process; and
- how individual tasks and activities are to be carried out.

They will normally also provide examples of the various forms and documentation used by the organisation; for instance:

- production control forms;
- inspection sheets; and
- documents used to purchase components from subcontractors.

Work Instructions, similar to the remainder of the QMS documentation, can take any appropriate form. However, one of the best ways to document a WI is probably to use a flow chart associated with a form that can then become a record once it is filled in.

So, in a nutshell:

- **Procedures** tell you who does **what** and **when**.
- **Work Instructions** tell you **how** to do something at a more granular level.

Work Instructions provide the nitty-gritty detail required to carry out a specific job in an exact manner and to a predetermined standard. It details how an organisation manufactures a product or supplies a process or service – as well as the controls that it has in place to ensure that the quality of that product and service etc. is consistent. (See Figure 1.25)

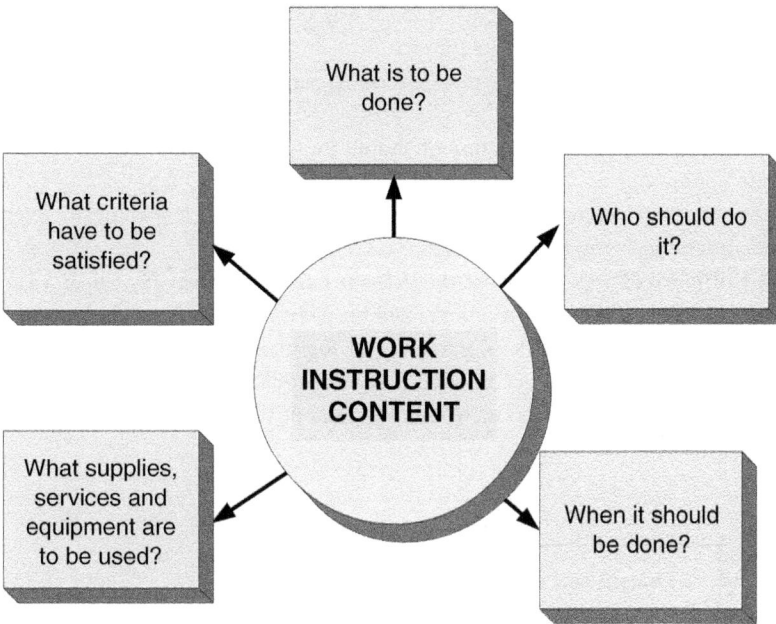

FIGURE 1.25 Written instructions should leave no room for error

WIs describe, in detail, the procedures that need to be adopted. Such as what is to be done, who should do it, when it should be done, what supplies, services and equipment are to be used and what criteria have to be satisfied. These WIs should be regularly reviewed for their continuing acceptability, validity and effectiveness.

Inferior or poor design, ambiguous specifications, incomplete or inaccurate WIs and methods, non-conformance etc. are the most frequent causes of defects during the manufacture or delivery of a product or service. In order that management can be sure that everything is being carried out under the strictest of controlled conditions, it is crucial that all WIs (in fact, any written instruction) are clear, accurate and fully documented.

Good WIs avoid confusion, show exactly what work has to be done or what services are to be provided. They also delegate authority and responsibility.

Without a written guide, differences in policies and procedures can easily arise, and these variations can result in confusion and uncertainty.

As ISO reminds us, '*Instructions provide direction to various ISO 9000 levels of personnel. They also provide criteria for assessing the effectiveness of control and the quality of the material, ensure uniformity of understanding, performance and continuity when personnel changes occur. They provide the basis for control, evaluation and review.*' (See Figure 1.26)

1.5.3.1 What should go into a Work Instruction?

In summary, a WI should ideally contain:

Document data sheet all the salient information about the document: file name, who wrote it, a summary of the contents, when it was approved, who approved it and a record of all changes made to the document etc.

Contents list a list of all the chapters, sections, parts and annexes etc. making up this document.

List of annexes all parts of a document should be traceable, especially when they are in separate volumes.

References a clear reference to any material or technology that is specifically referred to in the document (also any associated QPs etc.).

Scope and objectives exactly what the WI is needed for (Normally this is a very simple statement because a Work Instruction would usually be limited to one process

Procedure A procedure provides a statement of the manner of production, installation or application where the absence of such controls would adversely affect the quality and safety implications that may exist when carrying out the process.

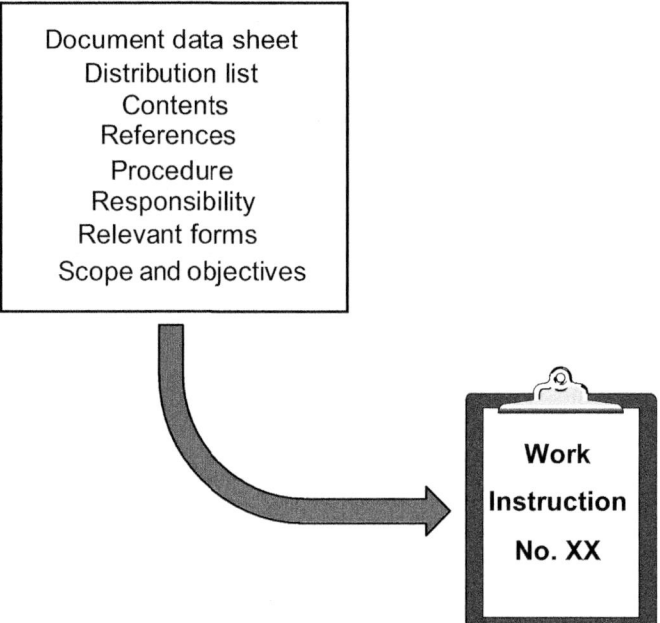

FIGURE 1.26 What goes into a Work Instruction?

Responsibility   a clear statement of who can carry out the process.
Relevant forms   the identification of forms, paperwork or computerised forms required
    to implement the WI.

1.5.3.2 How many Work Instructions can I have?

The manufacture of a device or the delivery of a process or service may require the completion of more than one WI. It is perfectly acceptable, indeed desirable, to separate processes into
a number of WIs because:

- it would be very difficult to write a single WI for large items, such as building an aircraft
  or laying on the catering services for the Royal Wedding;
- each WI may require Staff with different levels of training and qualifications;
- a particular contract may require the completion of only certain WIs;
- small concise WIs are more easily revised.

1.5.3.3 What is the difference between a Work Instruction and a record?

Work Instructions describe how tasks should be done and are used before the task is performed. Records document how tasks **were** completed and are used after the task has been
performed. Work Instructions come before the fact, while records come after the fact.

1.5.4 What goes into a Quality Plan?

When complex assemblies or multi-part contracts are required, separate instructions may have
to be included in order to cover individual parts of the contract. These types of instruction are
called Quality Plans – which by definition is '*a document specifying which procedures and associated
resources shall be applied, by whom and when to a specific project, products, service, process or contract*'.

Quality Plans will normally describe how the QMS is applied for a specific deliverable, but
they may also be used to demonstrate how the quality requirements of a particular contract
will be met and to monitor and assess adherence to those requirements.

A Quality Plan can be used in conjunction with a QMS or, in certain circumstances,
as a stand-alone document.

Quality Assurance for the supply of complex products and services can be very difficult to
stipulate in a contract especially if (in the case of manufactured products) the most important
inspections have to be left until the assembly is almost complete and, by which time, many
of the subassemblies and components will have become almost inaccessible! In these cases,
it is essential for the organisation to develop and produce a Quality Plan that details all the
important information that has to be provided to the 'shop floor management'.

The Quality Plan will cover all of:

- the quality practices and resources that are going to be used;
- the sequence of events relevant to those particular products or services;
- the specific allocation of responsibilities, methods, QPs and WIs; together with
- the details of the testing, inspection, examination and audit programme stages.

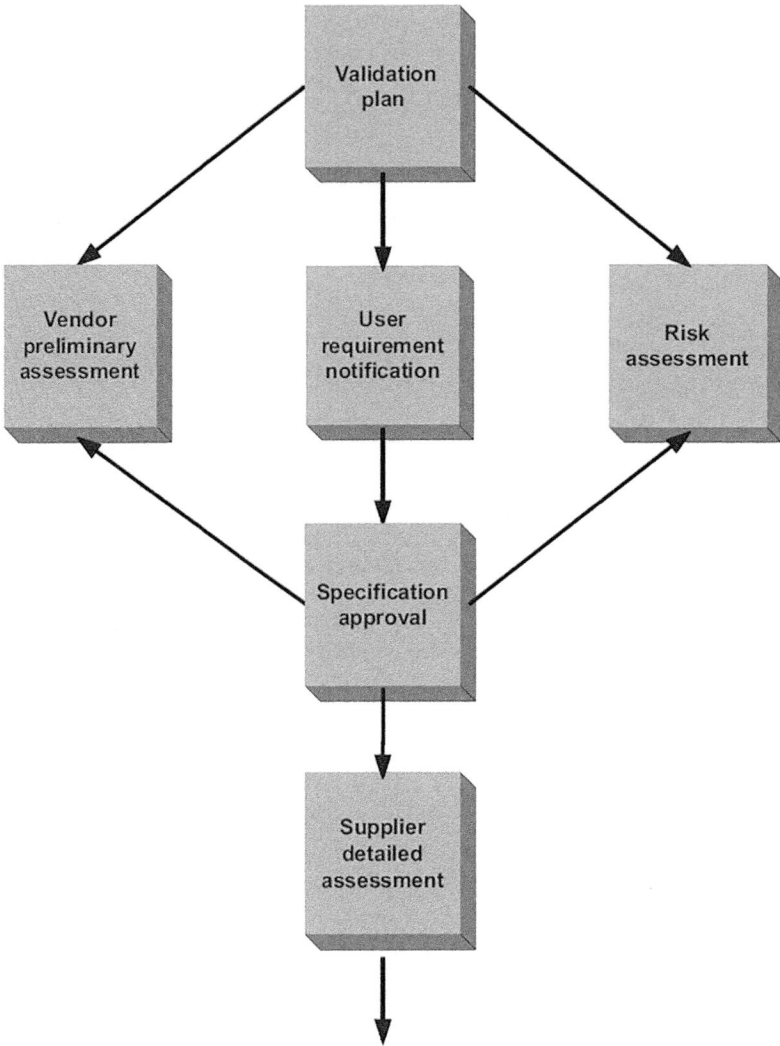

FIGURE 1.27 What goes into a Quality Plan?

It should be planned and developed in conjunction with all the business stages (be they design, development, manufacture, supply, subcontracting and/or installation or after-sales work) to ensure that all functions have been fully catered for. (See Figure 1.28)

One of the main objectives of quality planning is to identify any special or unusual require-ments, processes and techniques — including those requirements that are unusual by reason of newness, unfamiliarity, lack of experience and/or absence of precedents. As ISO point out, if the contract specifies that Quality Plans are required, then these Quality Plans should fully cover the following areas and ensure that:

- design, contract, development, manufacturing and installation activities are fully docu-mented and adequate;

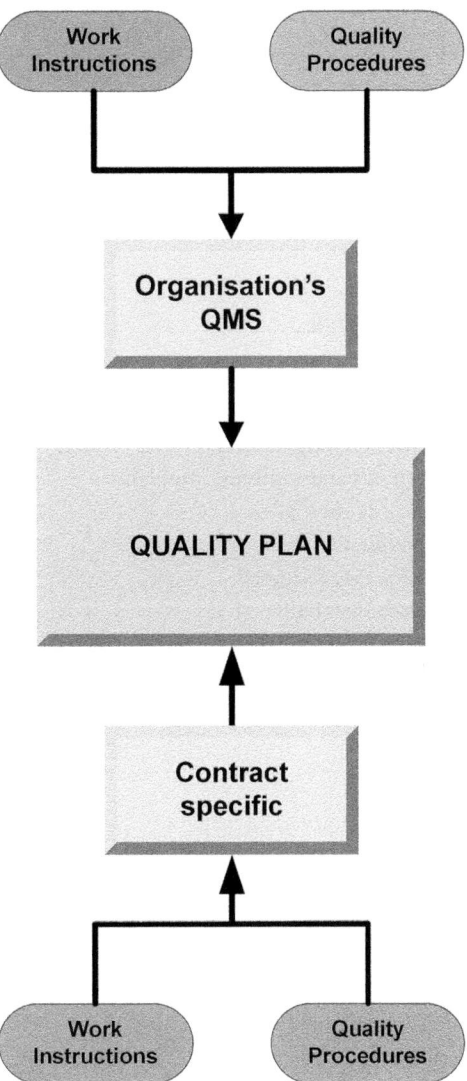

FIGURE 1.28 Quality Plan

- all controls, processes, inspection equipment, fixtures, tooling, manpower resources and skills that an organisation must have to achieve the required quality have been identified;
- Quality Control, inspection and testing techniques (including the development of new instrumentation) have been updated;
- any new measurement technique (or any measurement involving a measurement capability that exceeds the known state of the art) that is required to inspect the products or service has been identified and action taken to develop that capability;
- standards of acceptability for all features and requirements have been clearly recorded;
- compatibility of design, manufacturing process, installation, inspection procedures and applicable documentation has been assured well before production begins;

- as each special requirement is identified, the means for testing and being able to prove successfully that products or service is capable of successfully complying with the requirements has to be considered.

The integration of special or unusual requirements into the QMS must be carefully investigated, planned and documented.

The following briefly describes how each of the Quality Management elements is covered in a Quality Plan.

1.5.4.1 Management responsibility

The Quality Plan should show who is responsible for:

- ensuring activities are planned, implemented, controlled and monitored;
- communicating requirements and resolving problems;
- reviewing audit results;
- authorising exemption requests;
- implementing corrective action requests.

Where the necessary documentation already exists under the present QMS, the Quality Plan need only refer to a specific situation or specification. (See Figure 1.29)

1.5.4.2 Contract review

Contract review should cover:

- when, how and by whom the review is made;
- how the results are to be documented;
- how conflicting instructions or ambiguities are resolved.

1.5.4.3 Design control

Design control should indicate:

- when, how and by whom the design process, validation and verification of the design output is carried out, controlled and documented;
- any customer involvement;
- applicable codes of practice, standards, specifications and regulatory requirements.

1.5.4.4 Document and data control

Document and data control should refer to:

- what is provided and how it is controlled;
- how related documents will be identified;
- how and by whom access to the documents can be obtained;
- how and by whom the original documents are reviewed and approved.

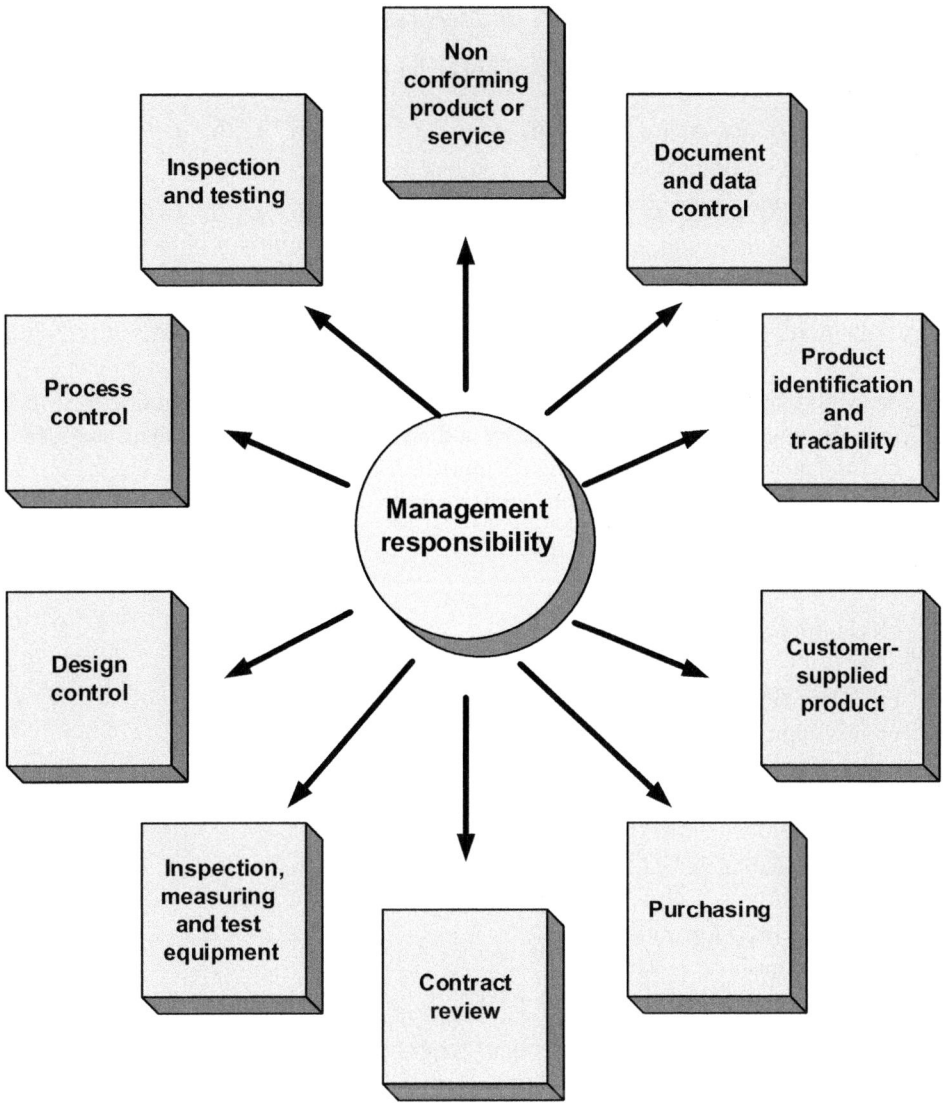

FIGURE 1.29 Management responsibility

1.5.4.5 Purchasing

Under the heading of purchasing, the following should be indicated:

- the important products and services that need to be purchased;
- the source and requirements relating to them;
- the method, evaluation, selection and control of subcontractors;
- the need for a subcontractor's Quality Plan in order to satisfy the regulatory requirements applicable to purchase products and services.

1.5.4.6 Customer-supplied products and services

Customer-supplied products and services should refer to:

- how they are identified and controlled;
- how they are verified as meeting specified requirements;
- how non-conformance is dealt with.

1.5.4.7 Identification and traceability

If traceability is a requirement, then the Plan should:

- define its scope and extent (including how products and services are identified);
- indicate how contractual and regulatory authority traceability requirements are identified and incorporated into working documents;
- indicate how records are to be generated, controlled and distributed.

1.5.4.8 Process control

Process control may include:

- procedures/instructions;
- process steps;
- methods to monitor and control processes;
- characteristics of products and services.

The Plan could also include details of:

- reference criteria for workmanship;
- special and qualified processes;
- tools, techniques and methods to be used.

1.5.4.9 Inspection and testing

Inspection and testing should indicate:

- any inspection and test plan;
- how the subcontractors' products and services (if used) shall be verified;
- the location of inspection and test points;
- procedures and acceptance criteria;
- witness verification points (customers as well as regulatory);
- where, when and how the customer requires third parties to perform:
  - type tests;
  - witness testing;
  - service/products verification;
  - material, service/products, process or personnel certification.

1.5.4.10 Inspection, measuring and test equipment

Inspection, measuring and test equipment should:

- refer to the identity of the equipment;
- refer to the method of calibration;
- indicate and record calibration status and usage of the equipment;
- indicate specific requirements for the identification of inspection and test status.

1.5.4.11 Nonconforming products and services

Under the heading of nonconforming products and services, an indication should be given of:

- how such products and services are identified and segregated;
- the degree or type of rework allowed;
- the circumstances under which the supplier can request concessions.

Details should also be provided with respect to:

- corrective and preventive action;
- handling, storage, packaging, preservation and delivery.

1.5.4.12 Other considerations

Quality Plans should also:

- indicate key quality records (i.e. what they are, how long they should be kept, where and by whom);
- suggest how legal or regulatory requirements are to be satisfied;
- specify the form in which records should be kept (e.g. paper, microfilm, disc, hard drive, cloud etc.);
- define liability, storage, retrievability, disposition and confidentiality requirements;
- include the nature and extent of quality audits to be undertaken;
- indicate how the audit results are to be used to correct and prevent recurrence of deficiencies;
- show how the training of Staff in new or revised operating methods is to be completed.

Where servicing is a specified requirement, suppliers should state their intentions to assure conformance to applicable servicing requirements, such as:

- regulatory and legislative requirements;
- industry codes and practices;
- service level agreements;
- training of customer personnel;
- availability of initial and ongoing support during the agreed time period;
- statistical techniques, where relevant.

AUTHOR'S HINT

For further information, I would recommend looking at ISO 10005:2005, which provides the reader with guidance on how to produce a Quality Plan as well as including helpful suggestions on how to maintain an organisation's quality activities.

1.5.5 Quality Processes

The success of a QMS relies on the universally adopted process approach of monitoring the quality of products and services. Summarised, '*[A] process is an integrated set of activities that uses resources to transform inputs into outputs*' **and** '*it is quite normal for processes to be inter-connected because the output from one process frequently becomes the input for another process*'. (See Figure 1.30)

A QMS is therefore a collection of management processes that are made up of people, work, activities, tasks, records, documents, forms, resources, rules, regulations, reports, materials, supplies, tools and equipment etc. – in other words, all those things that are required to regulate, control and improve in order to enhance the quality of an organisation's products and services. For organisations to function effectively, they will have to identify and manage a number of interlinked processes, and this identification and the associated management of the processes (and particularly the interactions between these processes) are referred to as the '*process approach*'. (See Figure 1.31)

Any activity that receives inputs and converts them to outputs can therefore be considered as a process, and often the output from one process becomes the input for another process.

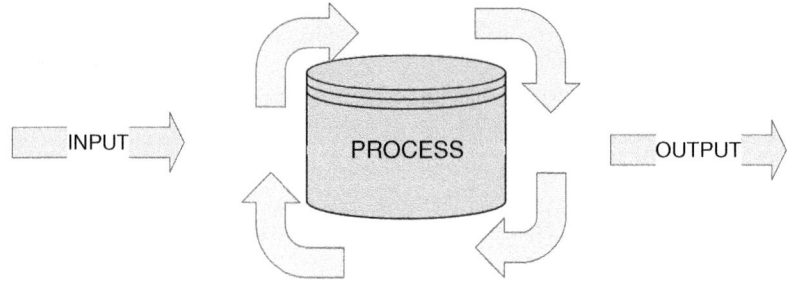

FIGURE 1.30 What is a Quality Process?

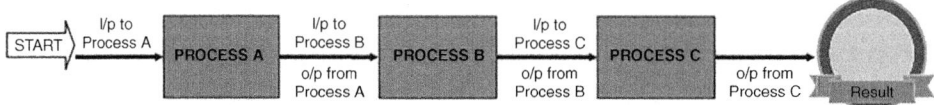

FIGURE 1.31 ISO 9001:2015's basic process approach

As the process approach is now central (indeed, **mandatory**!) for all Management System Standards, ISO's Committees have identified 12 primary processes that are an integral part of Management System Standards (see Figure 1.32):

1   Quality Management Process
2   Resource Management Process
3   Training and Awareness Process
4   Purchasing Process for Products and Services
5   Design and Development Process
6   Production Management Process
7   Service Provision Process
8   Management Process for Products and Services

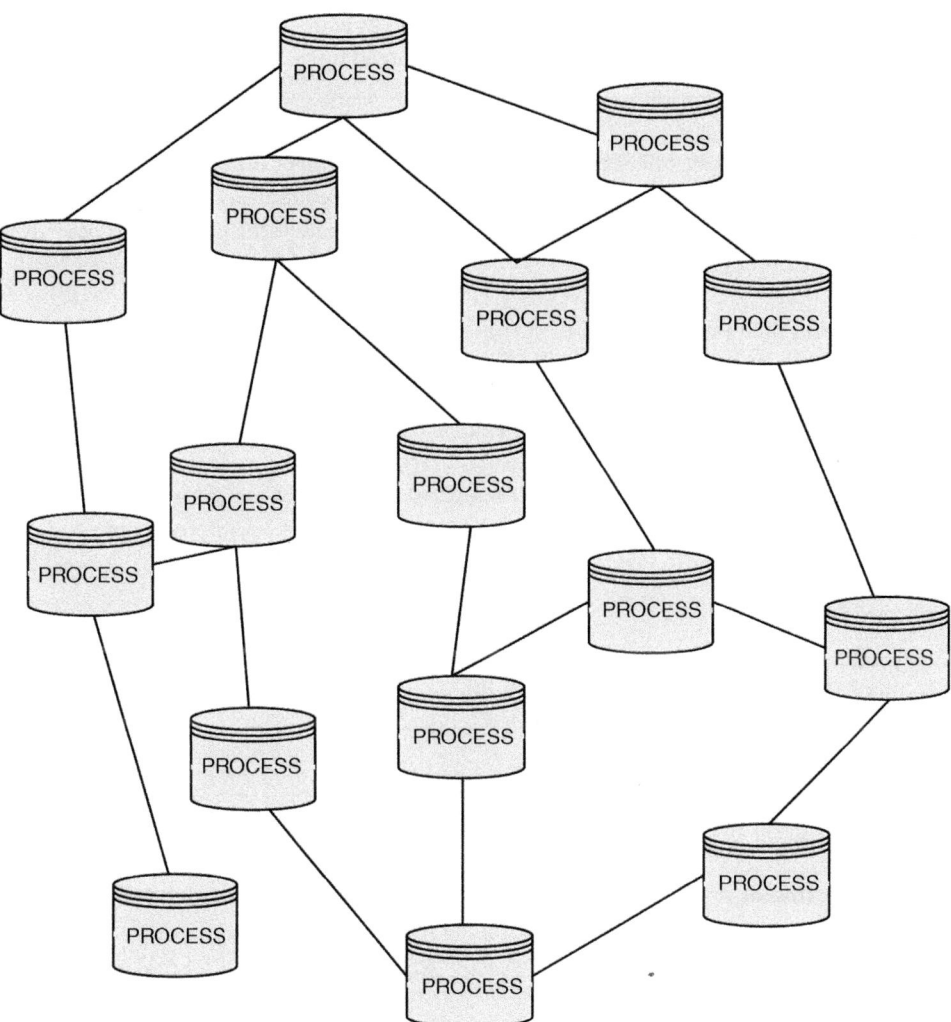

FIGURE 1.32   The interrelationship of processes

9 Customer Relationship Management Process
10 Internal Quality Management Audit Process
11 Monitoring and Measuring Process
12 Management Review Process

 AUTHOR'S HINT

Obviously this does not include a list of **all** possible processes that you could use to establish your own QMS, nor does it exhaust the many ways in which your processes can be grouped into larger processes or subdivided into smaller ones.

Your own particular organisation's list of processes will probably be different from the ones ISO have listed, and that is perfectly OK, as long as **your** QMS meets your organisation's needs and complies with the requirements agreed by ISO.

Throughout ISO Annex SL, the requirement for improvement is frequently (and heavily) emphasised, and so an organisation needs to concentrate on continually increasing the effectiveness and efficiency of its business processes whilst carrying out the policies and objectives of that organisation by:

- identifying their processes;
- deciding the order in which they should be carried out;
- ensuring that appropriate resources are provided; and
- establishing appropriate methods to operate and control them.

Annex SL (using ISO 9001:2015 as their template) requires that each of your processes will need to be designed, fully documented, implemented, supported, monitored, controlled and subject to continual improvement. (See Table 1.4)

When designing an internal organisational process, the most efficient way of completing a process map is to either walk through the process or get someone from that particular department or section to walk **you** through the process describing the various steps and how they interact.

1.5.5.1 Example of a simple process flow chart

When producing or supplying a service for other organisations (e.g. customers), one of the following steps would normally be required (see Figure 1.33):

In accordance with Section 7.5 of ISO Annex SL, an organisation's QMS system shall include:

- documented information required by this standard;
- documented information considered by the organisation to be necessary for the effectiveness and implementation of their QMS.

TABLE 1.4 Process design and content

For a small manufacturing business	For a small business providing a service (e.g. selling or installing products and services)	For a small business designing software or providing IT products and services
Receive enquiry	Receive enquiry	Receive enquiry
Identify specifications and standards	Provide quotation	Identify specifications and standards
Cost and identify material suppliers	Receive order	Complete initial breadboard design
Provide quotation	Purchase materials	Provide quotation
Receive order	Goods receipt	Receive order
Complete design	Goods-in stores	Complete design
Provide sample	Test	Provide sample
Receive sample approval	Goods-out stores	Receive sample approval
Purchase materials	Despatch	Produce software package
Goods receipt	Install (but not always)	Write manual and user instructions
Goods-in stores	Provide training	Purchase materials
Manufacture	Customer after care	Goods receipt
Test		Goods-in stores
Goods-out stores		Assemble package
Despatch		Test
Provide training		Goods-out stores
Customer after care		Install (but not always)
		Provide training
		Customer satisfaction

The extent of documented information can differ from one organisation to another due to:

- the size of organisation and its type of activities, processes, products and services;
- the complexity of processes and their interactions;
- the competence of persons.

In addition, the organisation is required to develop and maintain documented information that:

- supports the operation of its processes;
- provides confidence that the processes are being carried out as planned.

The Quality Management System is therefore **not** in itself a quality **system**; it is more just a series of actions that contain outline details of how all your processes inter-react and how they are documented and recorded. (See Figure 1.34)

With a well structured, planned process, continual improvement will respond to the growing needs and expectations of customers and ensure a dynamic evolution of the organisation's QMS.

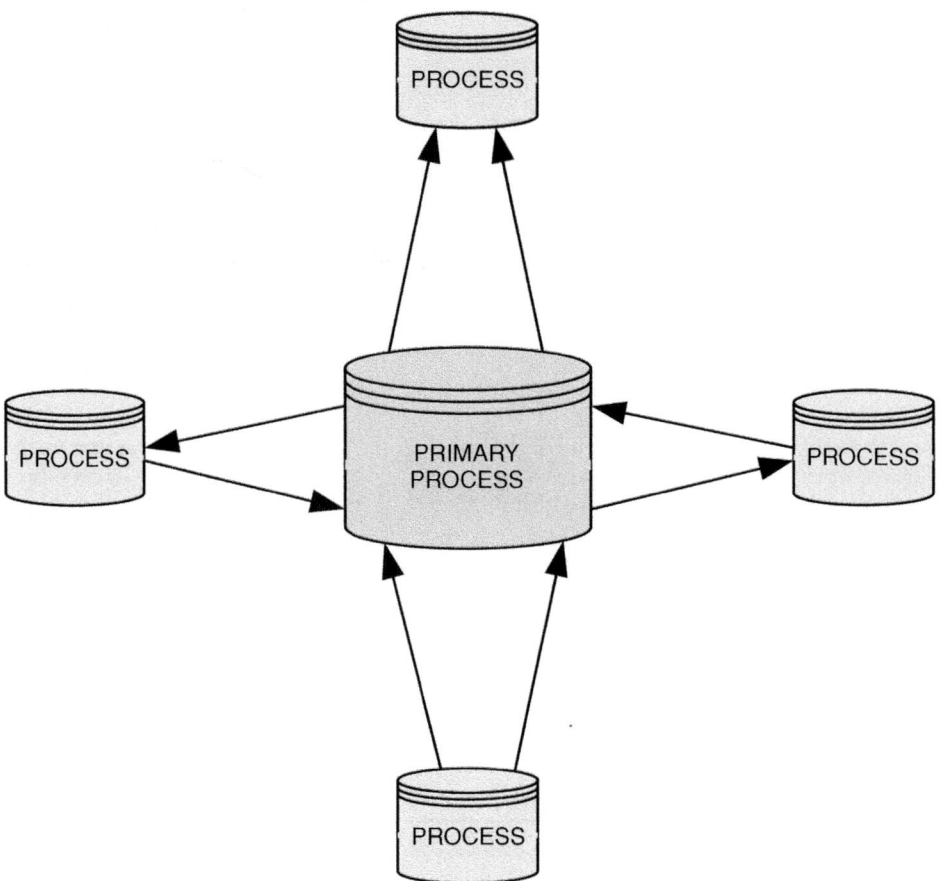

FIGURE 1.33 Initial process diagram

Note: Continual improvement is assured by utilisation of the PDCA model that was developed by the US mathematician Dr Walter Shewart (1891–1967), reinforced and used by the American statistician, professor, author, lecturer and consultant William Deming (1900–1993) and eventually adopted by ISO as the **plan–do–check–act (PDCA) cycle**. (See Figure 1.35)

This is a very simple four-step management method used in business for the control and continuous improvement of processes. The steps are:

1 **Plan** – determine what needs to be done, when, how, and by whom;
2 **Do** – carry out the plan, on a small scale first;
3 **Check** – analyse the results of carrying out the plan;
4 **Act** – take appropriate steps to close the gap between planned and actual results.

The following process model seeks to show how the four major sections of quality management (i.e. leadership, operation, performance evaluation and improvement) interrelate and

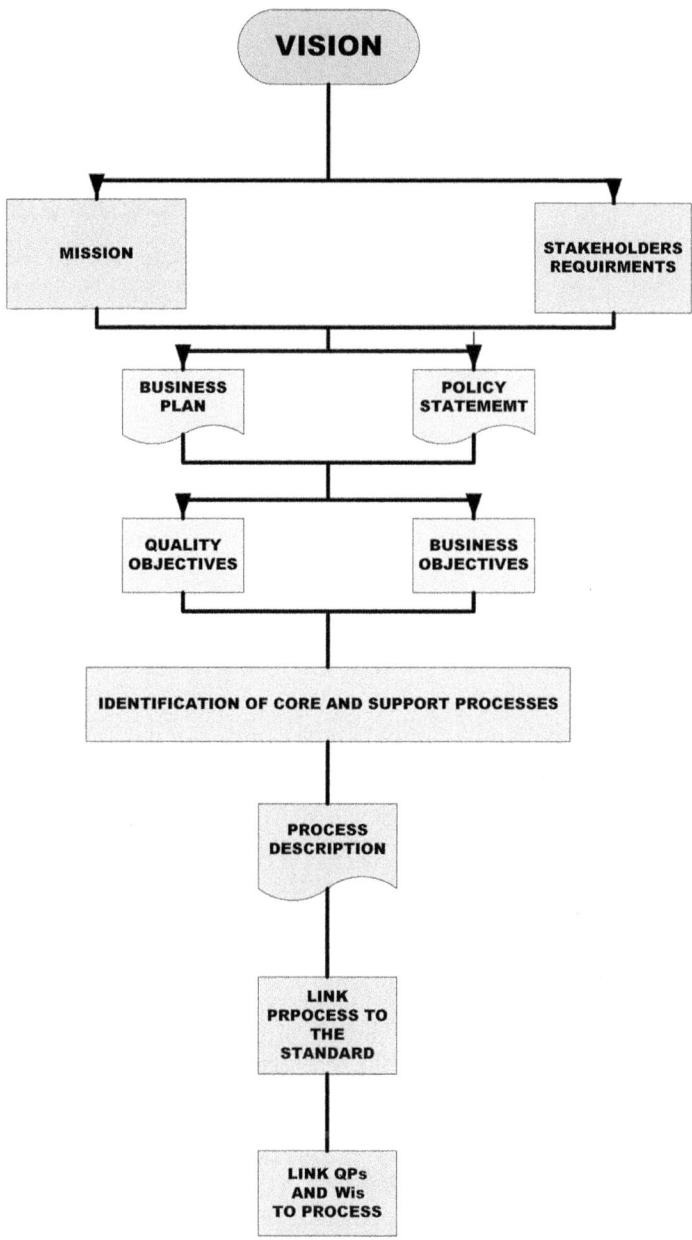

FIGURE 1.34   The integration of business and quality

how the improvement processes continuously revolve around all other aspects of quality management. (See Figure 1.36)

For clarity, the QMS requirements and management responsibilities can be combined, as shown in Figure 1.37.

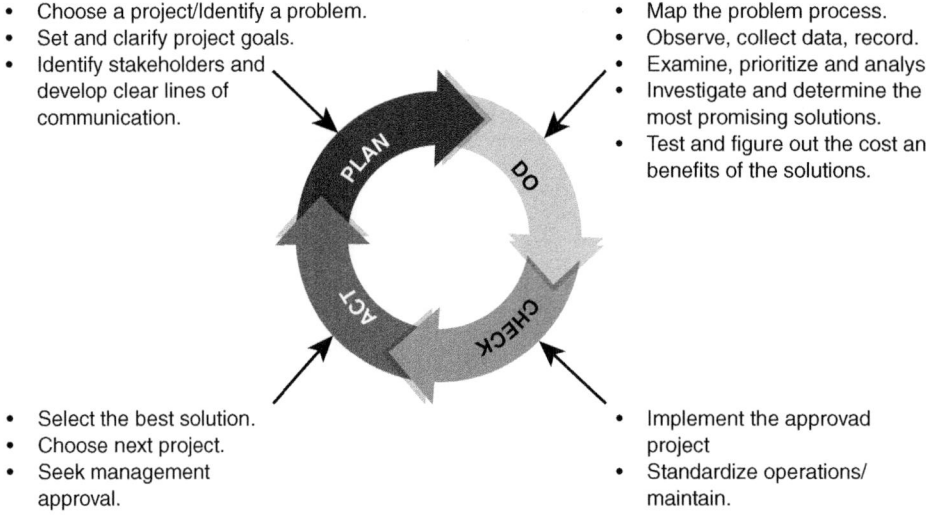

- Choose a project/Identify a problem.
- Set and clarify project goals.
- Identify stakeholders and develop clear lines of communication.

- Map the problem process.
- Observe, collect data, record.
- Examine, prioritize and analyse.
- Investigate and determine the most promising solutions.
- Test and figure out the cost and benefits of the solutions.

- Select the best solution.
- Choose next project.
- Seek management approval.

- Implement the approvad project
- Standardize operations/ maintain.
- Plan the next project.

FIGURE 1.35 ISO's concept of continual improvement

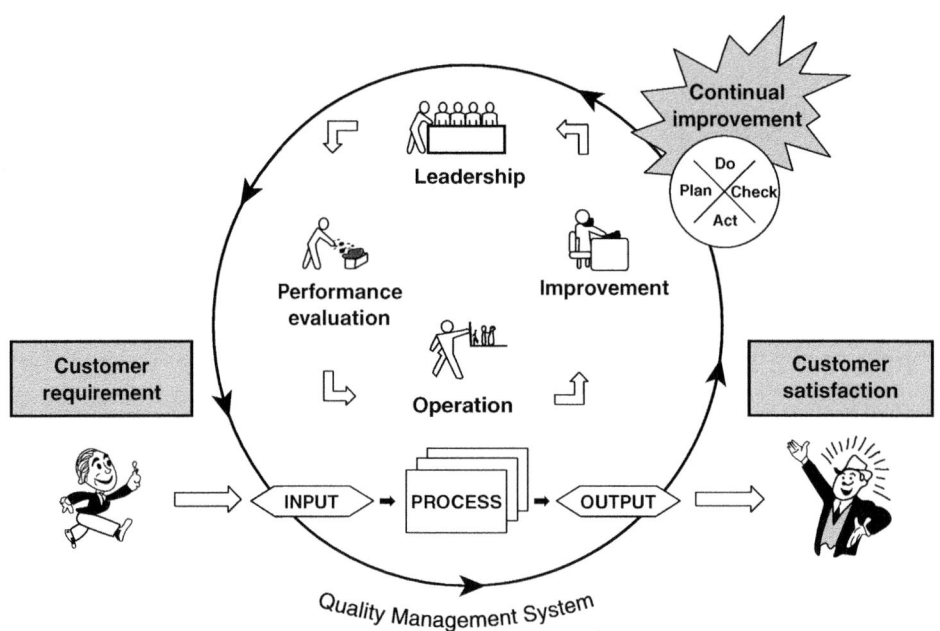

FIGURE 1.36 The basic process model

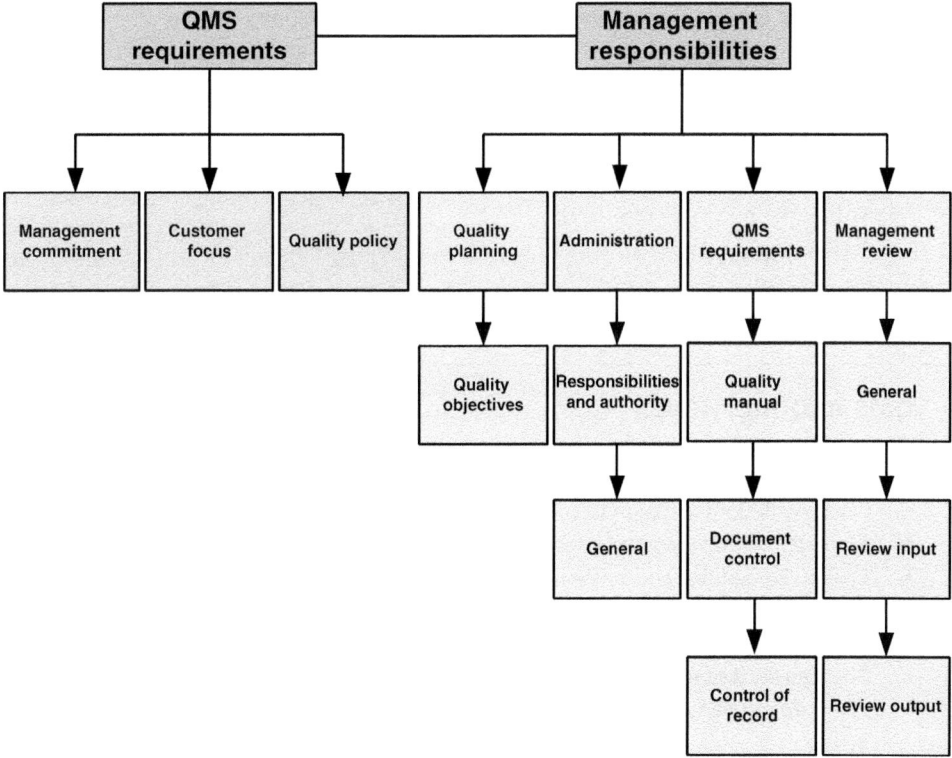

FIGURE 1.37 Quality Management System requirements and management responsibilities

 AUTHOR'S HINT

If your current QMS is successfully implemented, satisfies the needs and objectives of your organisation, reflects the way your organisation works and addresses all of the requirements detailed in the applicable management standard, then, other than addressing risk management and paying more attention to the increased responsibility of top management to demonstrate Leadership, very few changes will be required.

However, if your current documented system does not address all of these requirements, additional documentation may be necessary.

Organisations need to establish, implement, maintain and continually improve a Quality Management System that includes the processes needed for its implementation throughout our company by:

* addressing risks and opportunities that need to be tackled;
* assigning responsibilities and authorities;

- defining the inputs required and outputs expected from the processes;
- determining the internal and external issues that are relevant to our purpose;
- determining the sequence and interaction of these processes;
- ensuring that these processes achieve their intended results;
- establishing and applying the methods required to ensure the effective operation and control of these processes;
- providing the necessary resources;
- understanding the expectations and requirements of interested parties.

Summarised, an organisation's QMS shall ensure everything shown in the following box.

QMS REQUIREMENTS

- Responsibilities have been assigned for all activities and tasks.
- Documented information to support the operation of its processes is assured.
- Management reviews and internal audits are carried out on a regular basis.
- Quality Procedures and/or Work Instructions have been defined for all activities.
- Staff are fully trained.
- The needs and expectations of interested parties have been clearly established.
- The Quality Manual, Quality Procedures, Work Instructions and Contract Quality Plans are regularly reviewed.

Quality management contents

Processes describe the activities required to implement the QMS and to meet the policy requirements set out in top management's Quality Policy.

Typically, the organisational processes making up a company's QMS will normally comprise a core business process supplemented by a number of supporting processes that describe the infrastructure required to produce the contract deliverable (or market opportunity) on time and within budget.

 AUTHOR'S HINT

A process owner with full responsibility and authority for managing the process and achieving process objectives should be nominated. In many organisations, one person might be responsible for a number of processes or even all of them. This is particularly so in the case of an extremely small business or a 'one-man-band' sort of organisation.

For each process, there will be an organisational document detailing:

Objective   what the process aims to achieve;
Scope   what the process covers;

Responsible owner who is ultimately responsible for implementing the process;
Policy what the organisation intends doing to ensure quality is controlled;
Key performance indicators items of objective evidence that can be used as a way of
monitoring performance of the process plan;
Cross-references to supporting system documentation (QPs and WIs).

1.5.5.2 Core Business Process

The QMS is based on a common structure formed around a Core Business Process (CP)
that describes the end-to-end activities involved in an organisation's project management and
the production of contract deliverable. The CP is supplemented by a number of supporting
processes (SPs) that describe the infrastructure required to complete projects on time and
within budget.

The Core Business Process commences with the definition of corporate policy and ends
when the product or service is manufactured and/or marketed or the service completed. (See
Figure 1.38)

Within reason, anything can be added to make the process more efficient, but nothing can
be eliminated and when the Core Business Process states that certain tasks must be performed
in sequence; then it must be reflected in the implementation. In the same manner, any specified formulas or steps associated with a task must also be reflected within the implementation

1.5.5.2.1 What types of core processes would a business require?

If you are a small or medium-sized business, then probably five core processes will suffice (see
Figure 1.39):

1 Sales and marketing
2 Accounting and technology
3 Quality and product or service delivery
4 Management, HR and finance
5 Product or service development

When your business starts to grow, however, this will introduce new complexities that
might require more employees and more focus, and these five processes will have to be
expanded (e.g. sales and marketing might have to become two separate entities), and the
number of core processes required could increase to ten or even more. There is no restriction
to how many primary business processes an organisation can have, but you will find that the
following ten are the most used today (see Figure 1.40):

1 Customer acquisition (*Sales*)
2 Customer strategy and relationships (*Marketing*)
3 *Accounting* management
4 *Technology* management
5 *Quality,* process improvement and change management
6 Products/service *delivery*
7 *Management responsibility*

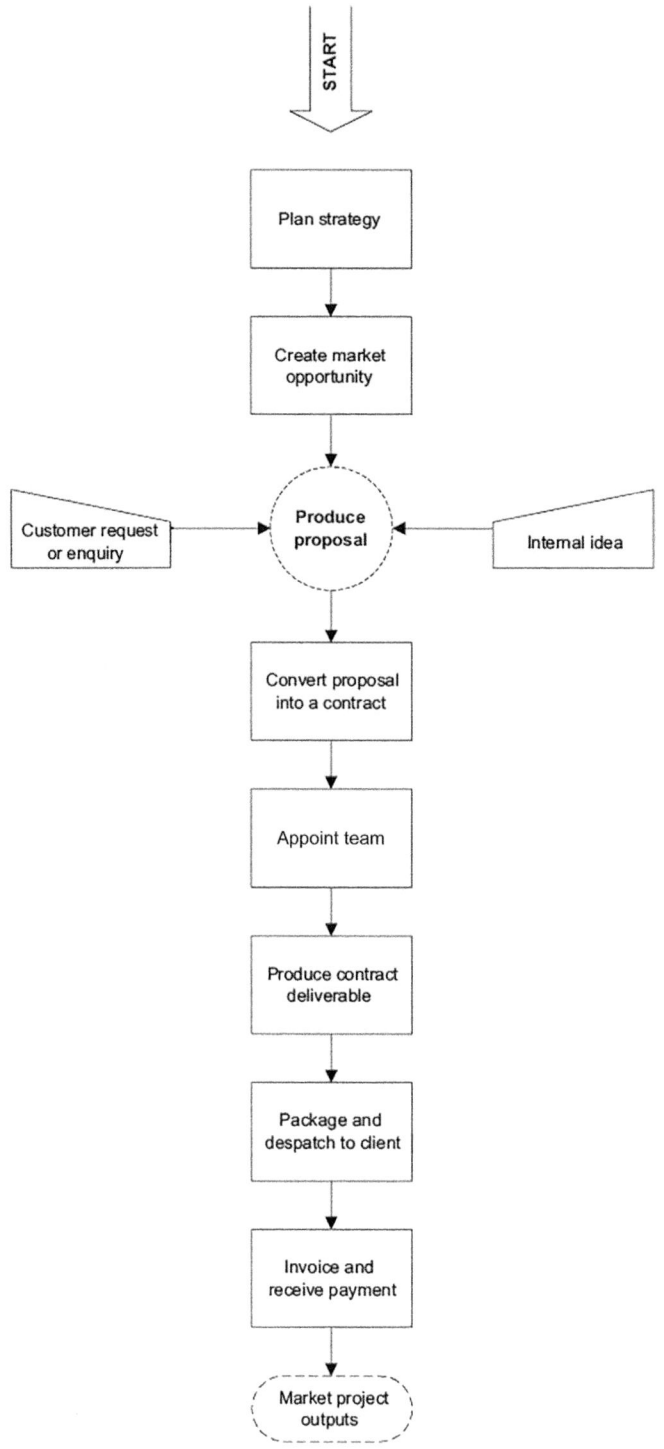

FIGURE 1.38 An example of a Core Business Process

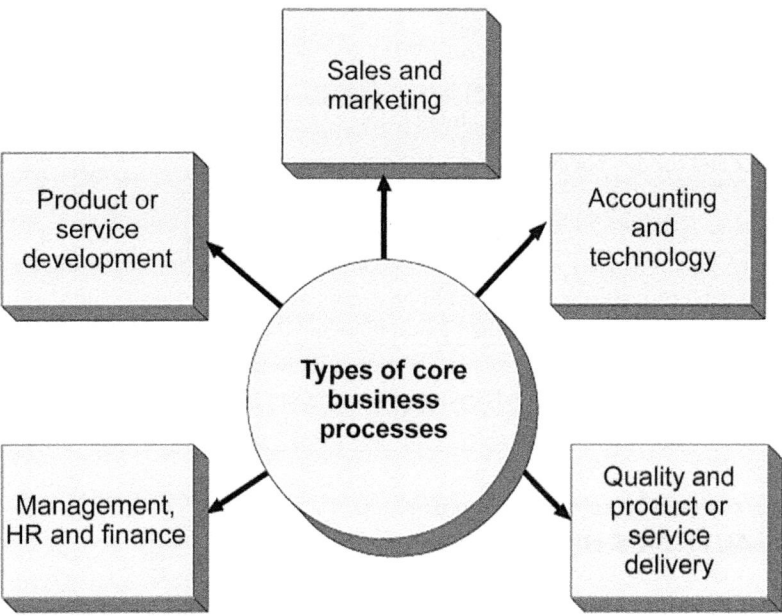

FIGURE 1.39   Types of Core Business Processes

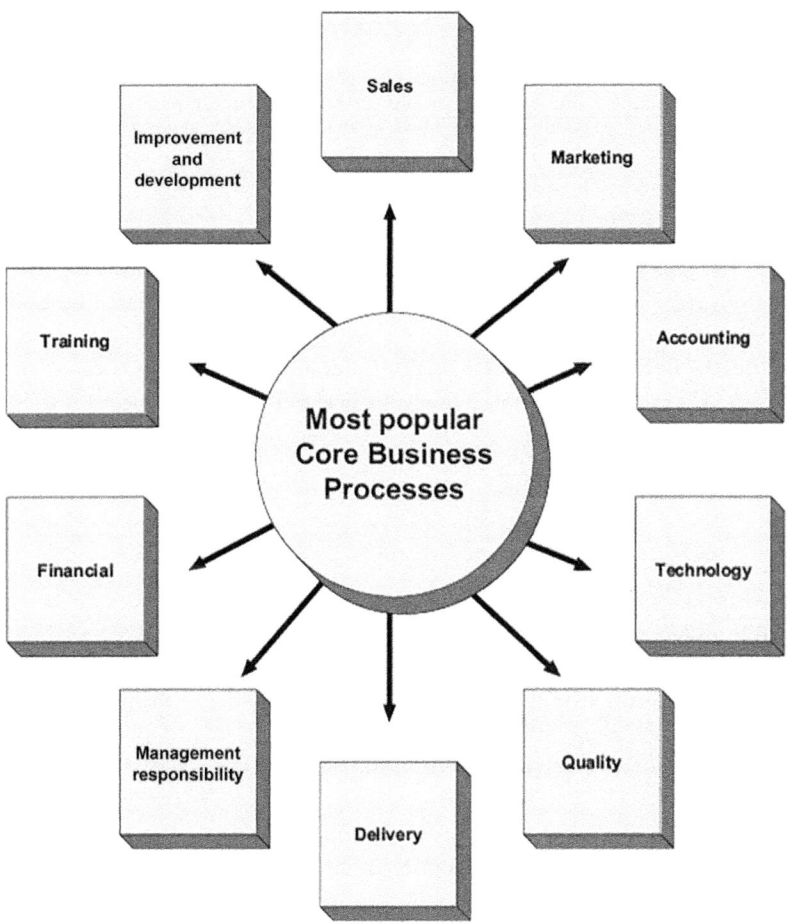

FIGURE 1.40   – Most popular Core Business Processes

8 *Financial* analysis, reporting, and capital management
9 *Training*
10 Product and service *improvement and development*

 Note: A process owner with full responsibility and authority for managing each process and for achieving process objectives should be nominated.

The Core Business Process may then be supplemented (depending on the size of the business) by a number of supporting processes that describe the infrastructure required to manufacture (or supply) the products and services on time. (See Figure 1.41)

💡 **AUTHOR'S HINT**

All businesses revolve around taking inputs and putting them through a series of activities that turn them into useful outputs, be that a product or service. These activities are the supporting processes.

Note: The managing director is normally responsible for managing the Core Business Process.

1.5.5.3 Primary supporting processes

Supporting processes are a basic set of activities that, when combined into a logical sequence, takes you from receipt of an order (or marketing opportunity) through to the realisation of the finished product or service.

Of course, the only way for an organisation to ensure repeat orders is to control quality. Consequently, it is essential that you define your quality policy and objectives for each supporting process

Thus, for each process within the flow chart, there will be accompanying documentation detailing:

Objective   what the process aims to achieve;
Scope   what the process covers;
Responsible owner   who is ultimately responsible for implementing the process;
Policy   what the organisation intends doing to ensure quality is controlled;
Key performance indicators   those items of objective evidence that can be used as a way of monitoring performance of the process;
Reference to supporting system documentation   (i.e. QPs and WIs).

All businesses revolve around taking inputs and putting them through a series of activities that turn them into useful outputs, be they products or services. These activities are the supporting processes.

A flow chart of a typical supporting process is shown in Figure 1.42.

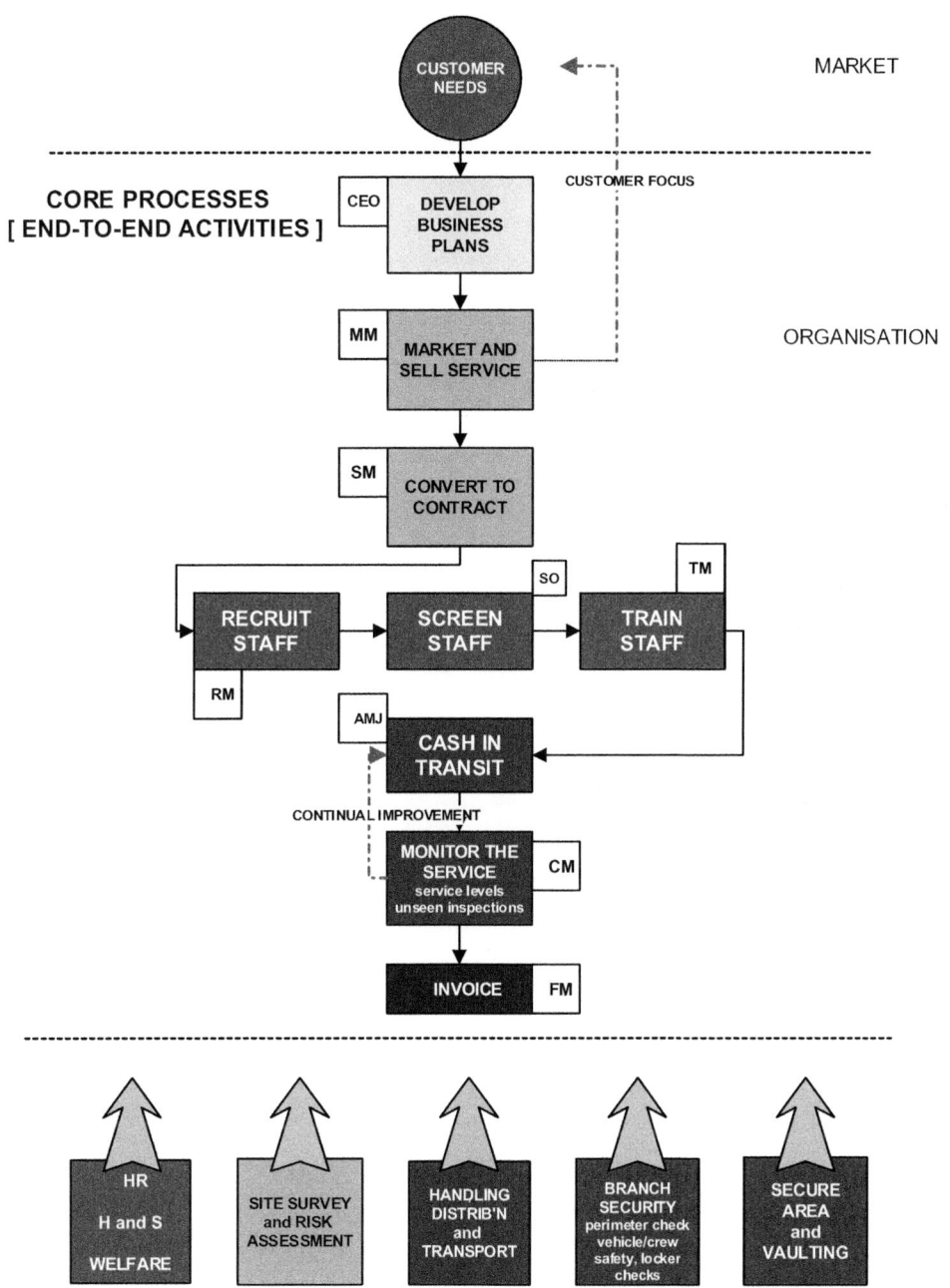

FIGURE 1.41 Typical Core Business Process

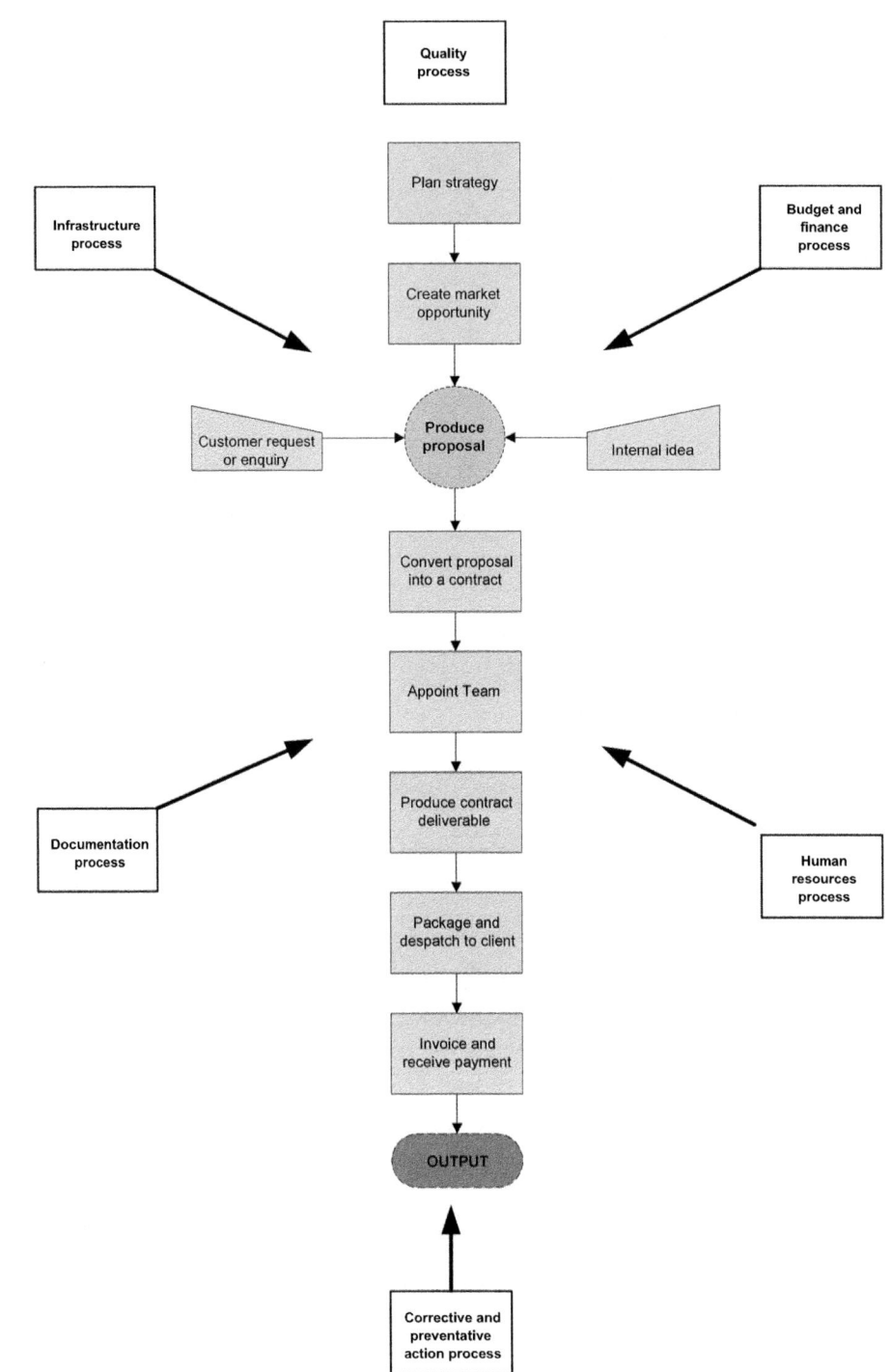

FIGURE 1.42 Example of a supporting process

1.5.5.4 Secondary supporting processes

In addition to primary supporting processes, there will be **secondary supporting processes** that run in parallel with and support the primary supporting processes. These secondary supporting processes are equally important as they control all other activities that may influence the quality of products and services – as well as supporting and achieving the primary supporting processes.

The purpose of secondary supporting processes is to document those activities that are essential for supporting and achieving the primary supporting processes. (See Figure 1.43)

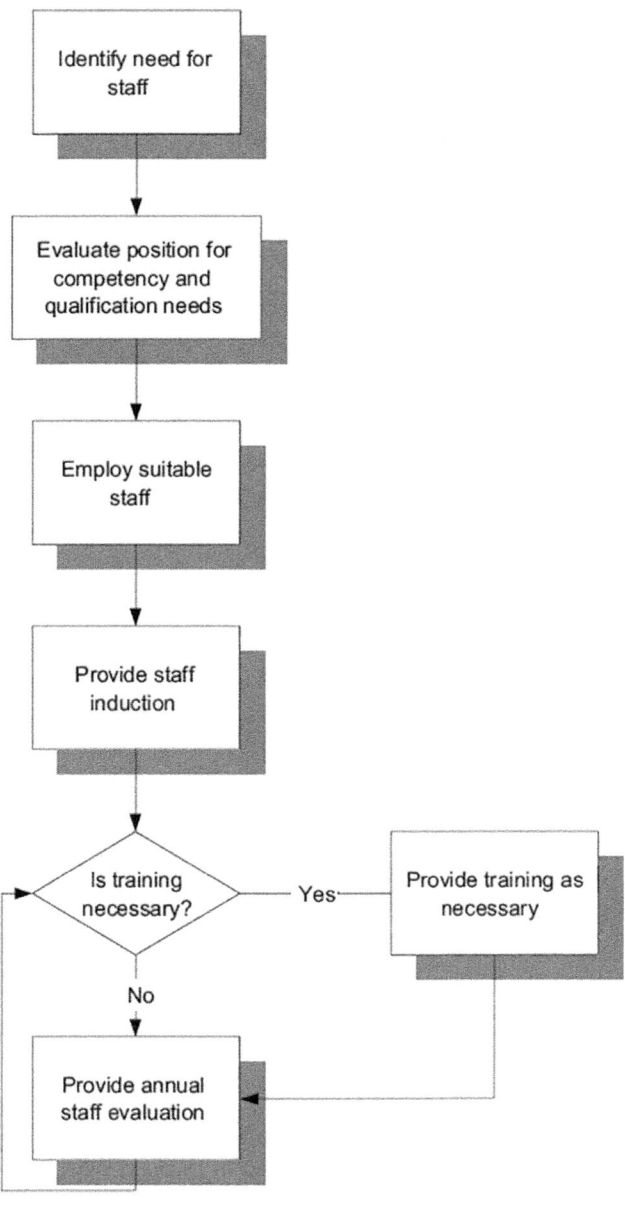

FIGURE 1.43 Example of a secondary supporting process flowchart

Secondary supporting processes will have an identical structure to the primary supporting processes and will also have their own associated supporting documentation (e.g. QPs and WIs). Secondary supporting processes may include such things as:

* identification and provision of suitable Staff;
* management and support of Staff;
* identification and provision of information;
* identification and provision of materials;
* identification and provision of equipment and facilities;
* management of the QMS;
* continual improvement.

These secondary supporting processes will have an identical structure to the primary supporting processes and will also have their own associated supporting documentation (i.e. Quality Procedures and Work Instructions). (See Figure 1.44)

All processes should be thoroughly documented so as to provide a complete picture of how to perform the activity to a consistent level of quality – depending on whether it is a process, procedure or a work instruction.

1.5.5.4.1 An example of a compliance and approval supporting process

See Figure 1.45.

Before an organisation can market an electronic device, it must comply with the applicable regulations and standards. In order to achieve approval, the organisation will put into practice the various steps shown in Figure 1.45.

1.5.5.4.2 An example of a subcontractor's and supplier's supporting process

From the selection process through to delivery and storage, all contract requirements will be monitored and assessed for compliance. (See Figure 1.46)

1.5.5.4.3 An example of a customer satisfaction supporting process

In all dealings with customers all Staff will ensure that customer satisfaction is their main aim. (See Figure 1.47)

1.5.5.4.4 The hierarchy of processes

CASE STUDY

Developing process maps can become very complex. It is therefore recommended that you develop a hierarchy of process maps, which will enable users to drill down through a number of levels to reach the desired level of detail.

Figure 1.48 shows one way in which this can be achieved.

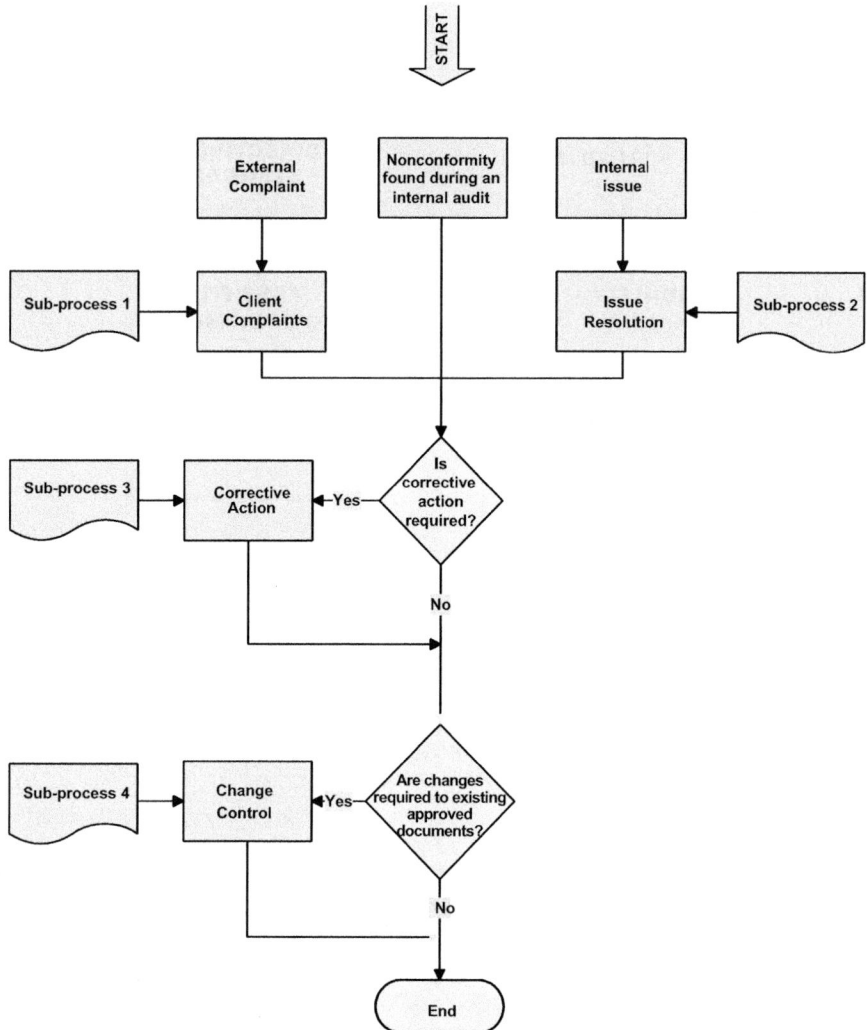

FIGURE 1.44 Flow chart showing a typical primary supporting process for corrective action

Level 1 *(Overview) does nothing but show a summary of the Core Business Process and the supporting processes.*

Should you wish to know more detail on a certain process, then by drilling down to the **Level 2** *maps, you can get more information on the activities making up that specific process.*

If more detail is required, then further levels can be added as shown, until you perhaps choose to supplement the maps with a written procedure.

This type of hierarchy is ideal for producing computer-based management systems, where the functionality offered by websites enables process maps to be linked, thereby simplifying navigation between maps.

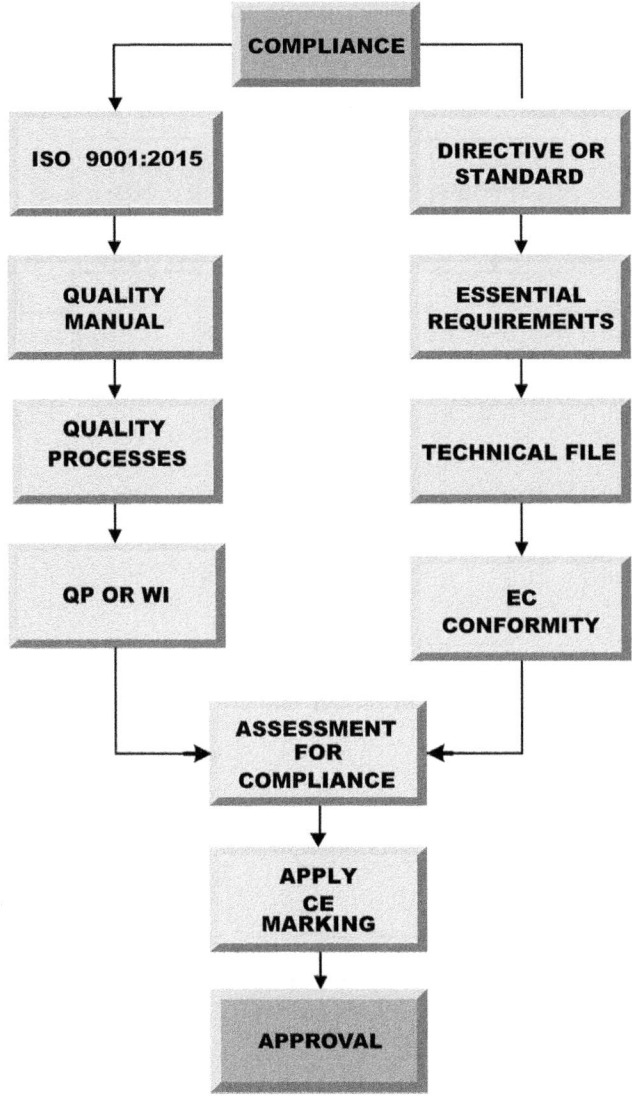

FIGURE 1.45 Example of compliance and approval supporting process

From the initial identification of the task through to final customer satisfaction, any number of interrelating primary and secondary processes may be part of the Core Business Process. These, in turn, are supported by Quality Procedures that ensure that all activities are fully understood, controlled and documented and that everyone knows exactly to do and how to do it.

 Note: An example of a typical medium-sized business is shown in Figure 1.49.

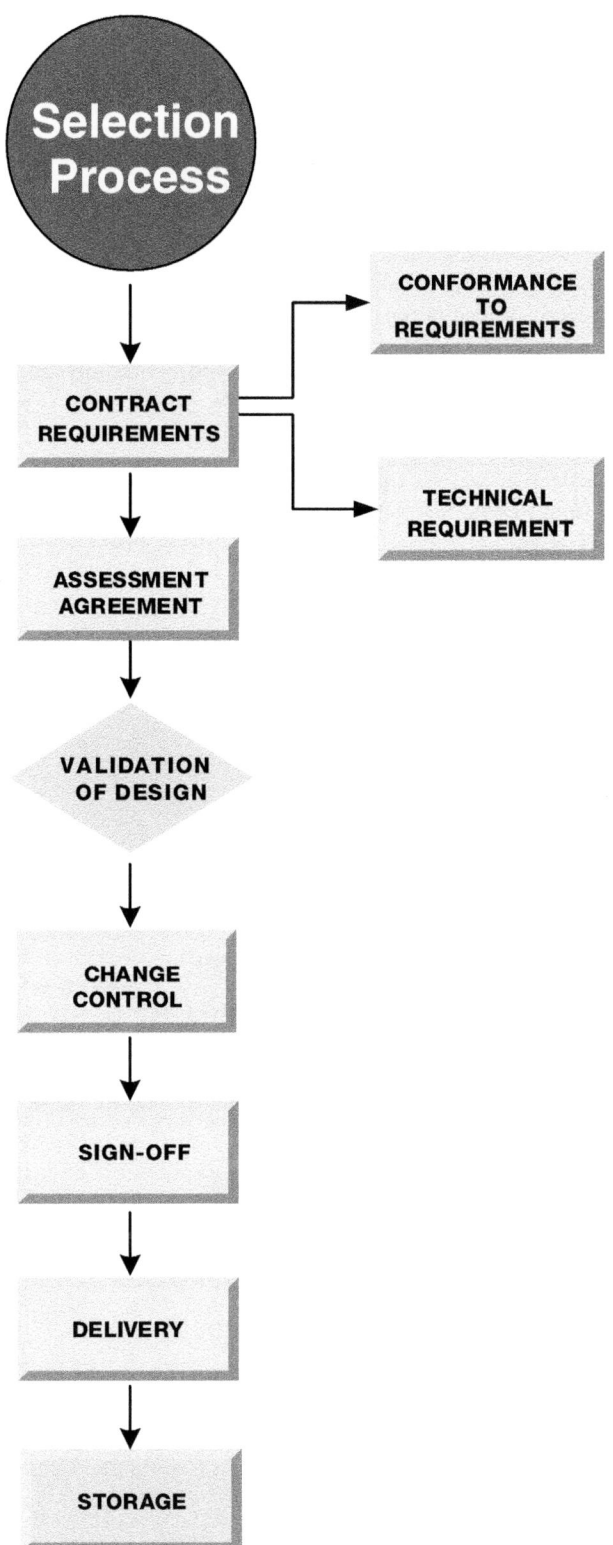

FIGURE 1.46   Example of subcontractors and suppliers supporting process

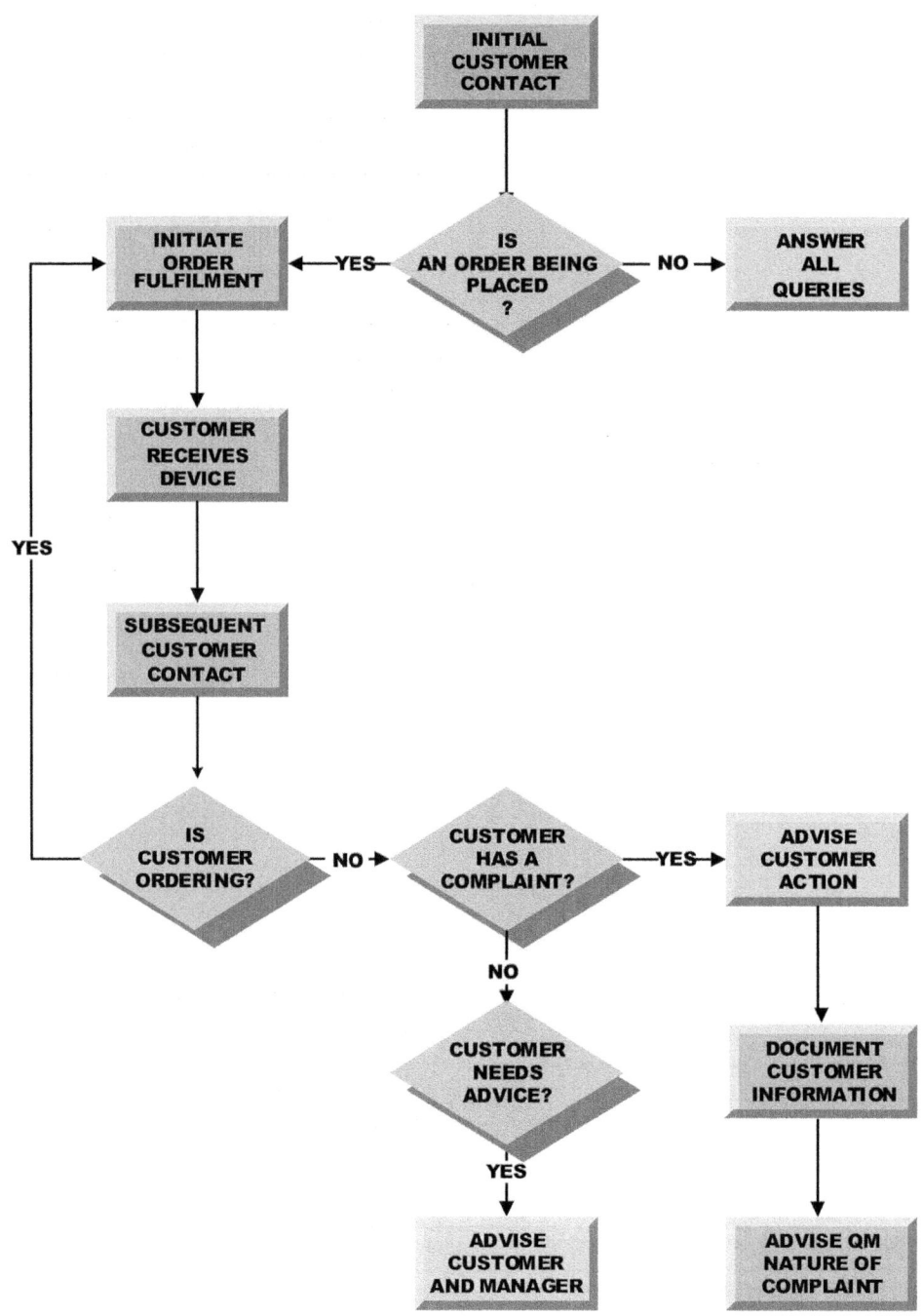

FIGURE 1.47 Example of customer satisfaction supporting process

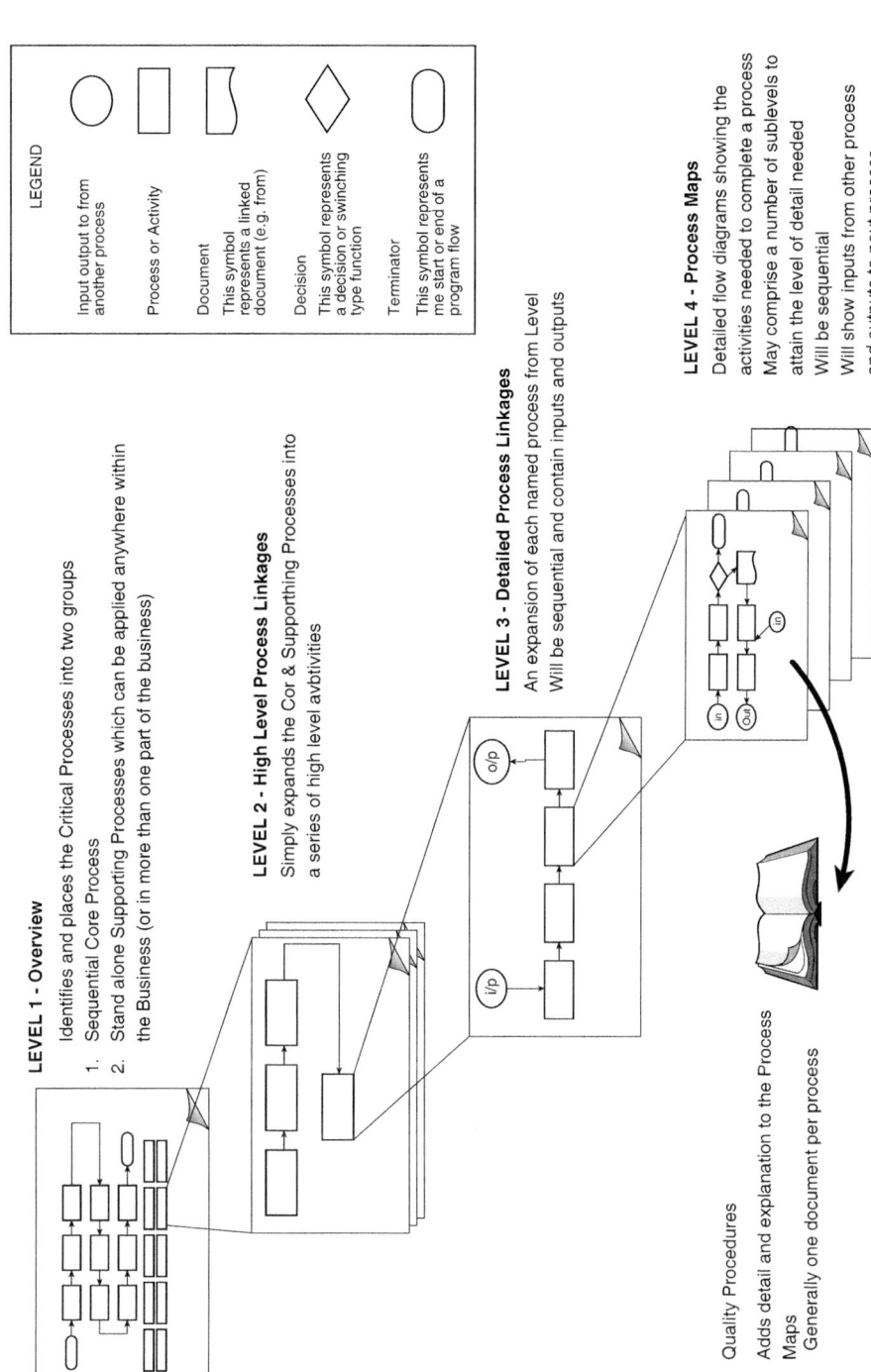

LEGEND

○ Input output to from another process

▭ Process or Activity

⧙ Document
This symbol represents a linked document (e.g. from)

◇ Decision
This symbol represents a decision or switching type function

▢ Terminator
This symbol represents me start or end of a program flow

LEVEL 1 - Overview

Identifies and places the Critical Processes into two groups

1. Sequential Core Process
2. Stand alone Supporting Processes which can be applied anywhere within the Business (or in more than one part of the business)

LEVEL 2 - High Level Process Linkages

Simply expands the Cor & Supporting Processes into a series of high level avtivities

LEVEL 3 - Detailed Process Linkages

An expansion of each named process from Level
Will be sequential and contain inputs and outputs

i/p   o/p

LEVEL 4 - Process Maps

Detailed flow diagrams showing the activities needed to complete a process
May comprise a number of sublevels to attain the level of detail needed
Will be sequential
Will show inputs from other process and outputs to next process

in   Out

Quality Procedures

Adds detail and explanation to the Process Maps
Generally one document per process

FIGURE 1.48   *Processes and their hierarchy*

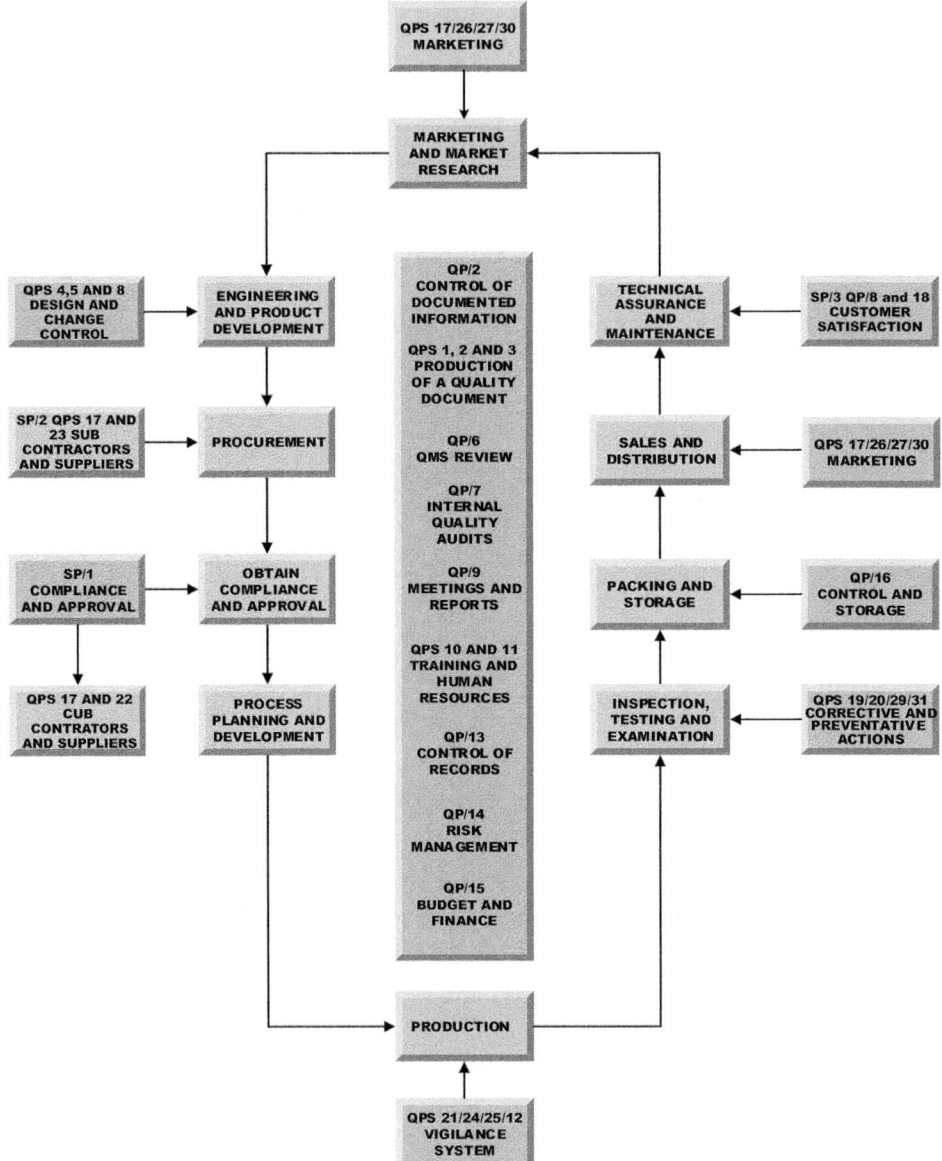

FIGURE 1.49 Example of the interrelationship of documented processes with QPs and WIs

1.6 How to manage quality in an organisation

Customers are interested in more than the level of quality 'intended' by the supplier. They are far more interested in the maintenance of the quality level and want an assurance that products (hardware or processed material) and services (software and information technology etc.) that they are buying truly meets the quality standard that they were initially offered and/or recommended. (See Figure 1.50)

The Chartered Quality Institute (CQI) have carried out extensive research on this point and have advised that the effective management of quality not only creates value for an

THE TOTALITY OF FEATURES AND CHARACTERISTICS OF A PRODUCT OR SERVICE THAT BEARS ITS ABILITY TO SATISFY STATED AND IMPLIED NEEDS

FIGURE 1.50   A definition of quality

Source: WorldAtlas.com

organisation and its stakeholders but also manages its exposure to risk and can make the difference between success and failure.

A properly implemented and effective business management system identifies and manages organisational risks to ensure that:

- the organisation consistently delivers the products and services that customers want, when they want them and to the quality they expect;
- customer satisfaction and loyalty is improved;
- organisational goals and objectives are achieved;
- organisational risk is identified and effectively managed;
- products and services and the processes that deliver them to customers are continually improved through innovation;
- waste throughout the organisation is identified and eliminated;
- partnerships and the supply chain deliver value to the parties involved.

1.6.1 Company requirements

The principal goal for any organisation is that they can maintain the quality of their products and/or services and be able to offer them so that they:

- comply with the customers' requirements and expectations;
- meet the need, use and purpose as defined in the approved product specifications; but also
- comply with applicable international, European and national quality standards and specifications.

In order to meet these objectives, the organisation needs to be organised so that all technical, administrative and human factors affecting the quality of our products and services are always under control and that this control is aimed at the reduction, elimination and the prevention of quality deficiencies.

A QMS therefore needs to be developed and implemented throughout the company for the purpose of accomplishing the objectives previously set out, and – in order to achieve maximum effectiveness – it has to be designed so that it is appropriate for all types of contract and/or services being offered by that particular organisation.

 AUTHOR'S HINT

In order to meet this commitment, organisations need to develop and maintain a QMS that meets the requirements of and the recommendations of their Management System Standard, and quality **must** become the responsibility of everyone, in every activity, throughout that organisation and regular management reviews and internal audits should be used to demonstrate the continued success of their QMS.

It is essential that everyone is involved and totally committed to observing the requirements of the organisation's QMS and to fully comprehending their quality responsibilities. Everyone connected with that organisation needs to be supported by top management according to their individual needs for personal development, training and facilities.

To be successful, an organisation (whether large or small) **must**:

- be able to offer products and services that satisfy a customer's expectations;
- agree with the relevant standards and specifications of a contract;
- be available at competitive prices;
- be able to supply products and services at a cost that will still bring a profit to that organisation.

Organisations must, above all, provide quality products and services that will promote further procurement and recommendations.

So how can your organisation become a Quality organisation?

Well, it is **not** just a case of simply claiming that you are a reliable organisation and then telling everyone that you will be able to supply reliable products and services! Nowadays, especially in the European and American markets, purchasers are demanding proof of these claims – proof that **you** are the organisation that **they** should be dealing with. (See Figure 1.51)

But how can you supply this proof? Well, the easiest and most recognised/usually accepted way is to work in conformance with the requirements of your particular Management System Standard as they provide guidelines for organisations wishing to establish their own QMS and thereby control the quality of their organisation – from within their organisation. (See Figure 1.52)

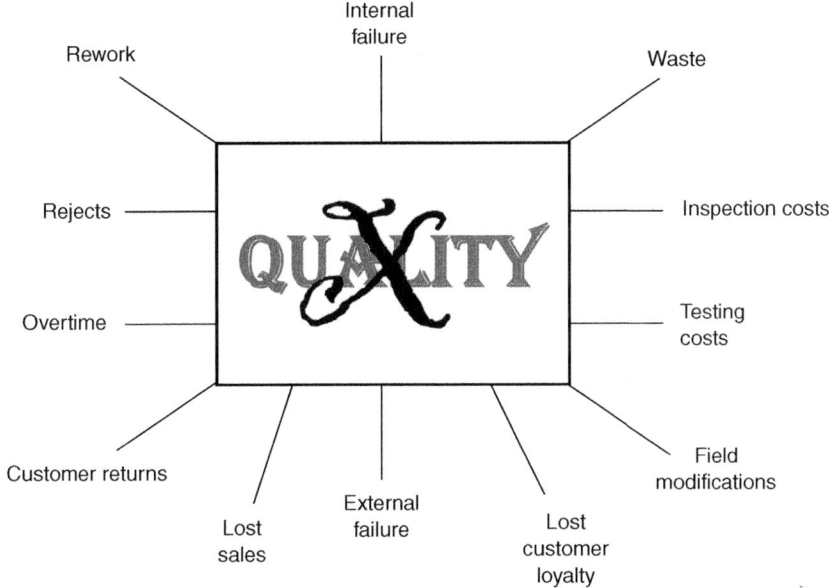

FIGURE 1.51   No proof of quality = no business!

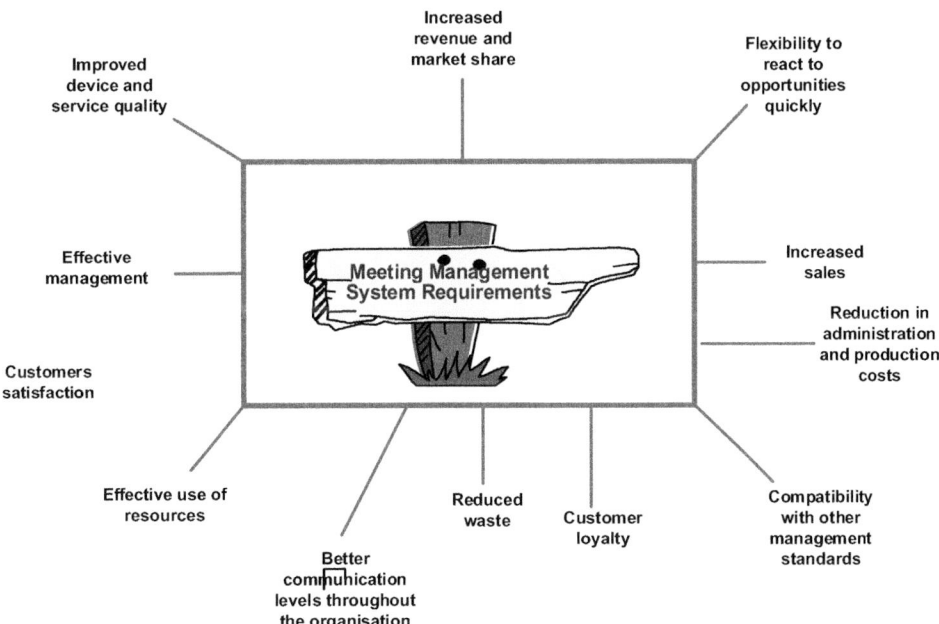

FIGURE 1.52   The benefits of quality management

But it doesn't stop there! Sometimes a contract will require an organisation to comply with the specifications of other standards. For example, a British semiconductor component manufacturer would be required to meet the mechanical standards contained in BS EN 60191–6–22, or for a dental laboratory it could be ISO 13485 [i.e. the European Medical Devices Regulation (MDR)], and so a well-structured QMS can prove extremely useful in dealing with these situations.

As previously mentioned, an organisation must **prove** their organisational capability by showing that they can operate to a fully auditable and compliant QMS. Figure 1.53 shows how a QMS benefits an organisation by providing both that organisation and their potential customers with the necessary proof.

To satisfy these requirements, an organisation's QMS has to encompass all the different levels of Quality Control and Quality Assurance that are required during the various stages of design, production and acceptance of a product or a service (i.e. system or process) and be capable of guaranteeing quality.

These requirements generally cover the following topics:

- After-sales service, contract-specification
- Design control
- Handling, storage, packaging and delivery
- Organisational structure
- Measurement of Quality Assurance
- Purchasing and procurement
- Production control
- Products and service testing and
- Risk analysis.

1.6.2 Meeting the customers' requirements

From the customer's (i.e. user's) point of view, an organisation's QMS must provide a level of confidence in the ability of delivering the desired quality as well as the consistent maintenance of that quality.

To be effective, their QMS will need to ensure that:

- consideration has been given to the risks related to deficient products and service;
- costs due to design deficiencies (including rework, reprocessing and loss of production) have been considered;
- consideration has been given to the risks pertaining to the health and safety of the user;
- objective evidence is provided (in the form of information and data) concerning the quality of the system and the quality of their products and service;
- the needs of interested parties has been taken in to consideration –'parties' such as:

  - customers;
  - suppliers and subcontractors;
  - consultants working alongside their company; and
  - relevant regulatory bodies etc.

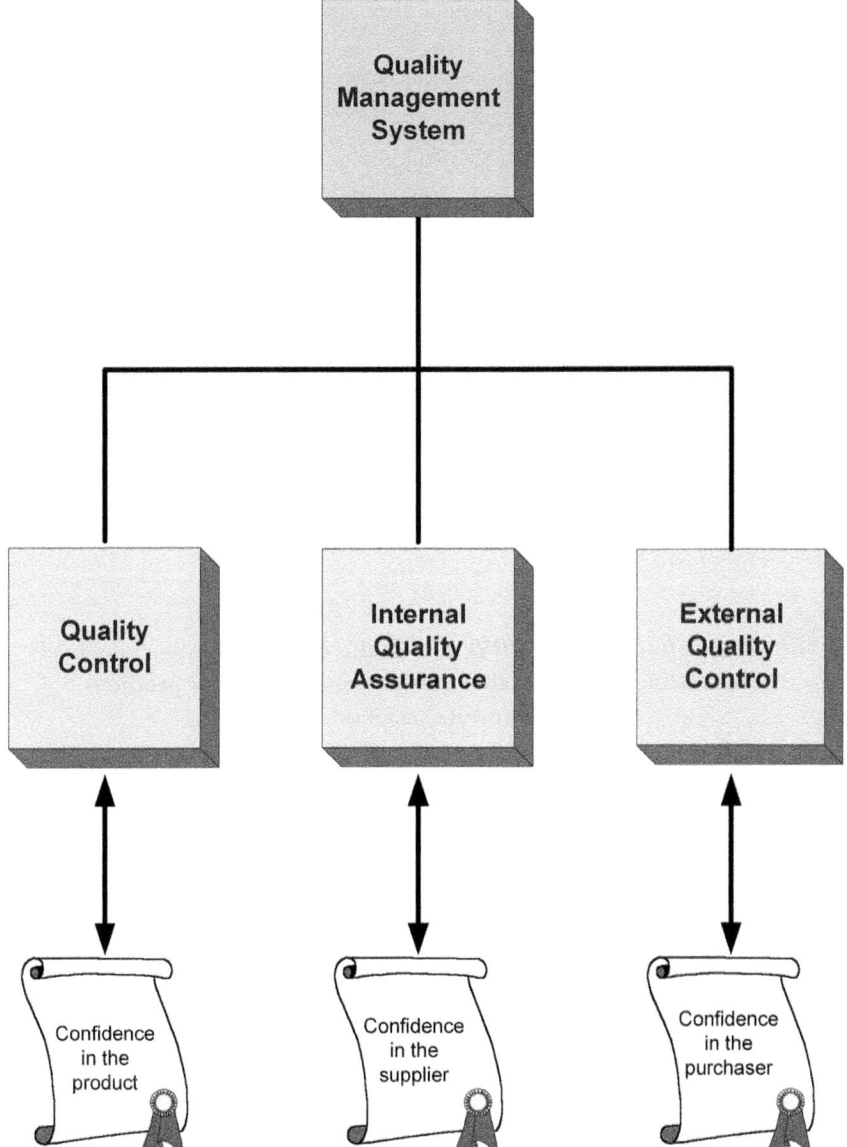

FIGURE 1.53 Benefits of a Quality Management System

An effective QMS therefore needs to be designed to:

* meet the customer's needs and expectations;
* provide an effective management resource in the optimisation and control of quality in relation to risk, cost and benefit considerations;
* be based around the recommendations and specifications contained in the organisation's selected Management System Quality Standard.

To provide this effectiveness, the QMS shall be structured so that:

- emphasis is placed on problem prevention rather than dependence on detection after occurrence;
- the system is fully understood and effective.

1.6.3 Who is responsible for quality within an organisation?

Quality management includes all the activities that organisations use to direct, control and coordinate quality. These activities include formulating a quality policy, setting quality objectives and establishing Quality Processes. They also include quality planning, Quality Control, Quality Assurance, and quality improvement. (See Figure 1.54)

Previously, the overall responsibility for an organisation's Quality Management System was the sole responsibility of the Quality Manager, who was often referred to as the Management Representative. The new Management System Standards ISO has removed the mandatory requirement for a single person (i.e. a Quality Manager) to be responsible for quality within an organisation.

Now, effectively, EVERYONE in the organisation is collectively responsible for the quality of the organisation, its products and its services!

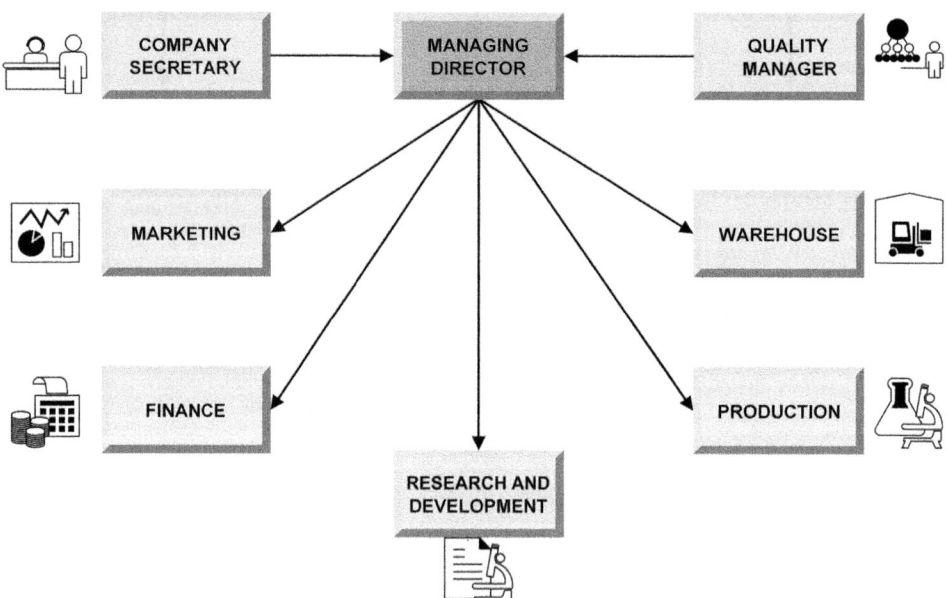

FIGURE 1.54 Typical organisational chart

Quality management ensures that an organisation's, products and services are consistent. It has four main components:

1   **Quality planning** – identifying which quality standards are relevant to the product or service and working out how to satisfy their requirements
2   **Quality control** – ensuring that products and services have achieved their highest standard and that their manufacture, installation, modification and/or repair have been completed in an efficient and timely manner
3   **Quality assurance** – providing assurance to a customer that the standard of workmanship within a contractor's premises is of the highest level and that all products and services leaving that particular organisation (or supplied by that organisation) are above a certain fixed minimum level of specification, and
4   **Quality improvement** – analysis of performance and systematic efforts to improve it.

Quality management is **not**, however, focussed just on product and service quality but also on the means to achieve it. Quality management therefore uses Quality Assurance and control of its processes to ensure that their products and services achieve more consistent quality.

But on the other side of the coin, ISO, in having decided to do away with the role and title of Quality Manager, rather confused matters (!) by clearly stating in ISO 9001:2015 that, although '*there is no longer a requirement for an organisation to have an identified Management Representative, the duties currently assigned to the Management Representative in ISO 9001:2008 must still be undertaken*', and so the question has to be, 'By whom?'!

There have been numerous thoughts and discussions about ISO's new 'ruling' within professional bodies and on social media. The general feeling appears to be that, as this is **not** conceived to be a mandatory requirement, an organisation may, if they so wish, continue to use the term 'Quality Manager' **but** with the proviso that top management will now have to play a far more important role in overseeing management within their organisation than before **and**:

Everyone within an organisation now has a part to play in quality!

So what responsibilities does each of the groups of people in Figure 1.55 have?

1.6.3.1 Top management

With the publication of Annex SL, '*management responsibility*' is replaced by '*leadership*'. Although *leadership* would seem at first glance to be just a reiteration of what's gone before regarding policy, organisational roles, responsibilities, authorities and so on, in the 2015 editions of Management System Standards, there is now much more emphasis on this being seen as a 'hands-on' leadership as opposed to just 'management'.

This now makes it mandatory for top management to demonstrate leadership and commitment with respect to the Quality Management System by establishing, implementing and maintaining a quality policy that is:

*   appropriate;
*   provides a framework for setting quality objectives;

Management

The Quality Control
Management Team   **The Staff**

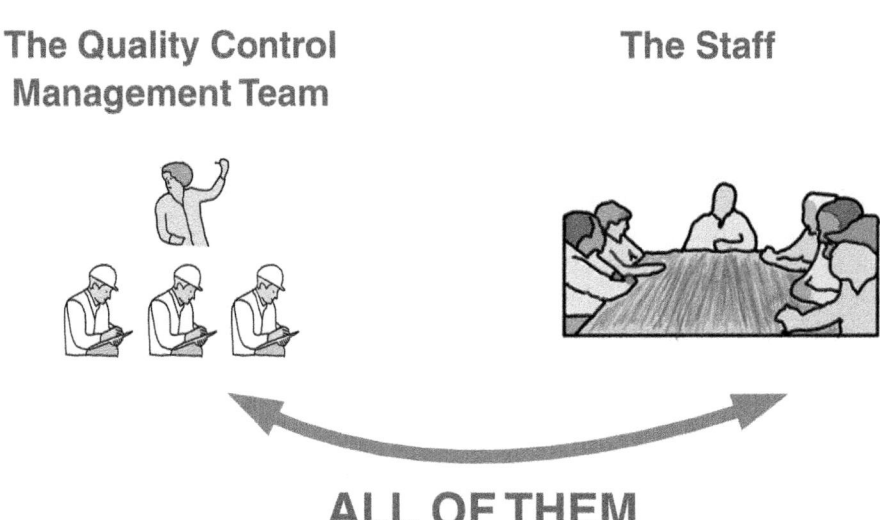

ALL OF THEM

FIGURE 1.55   Everyone has a control on quality

- includes a commitment to satisfy applicable requirements;
- includes a commitment for continual improvement of the Quality Management System.

Top management (i.e. the people who have overall responsibility for coordinating, directing, and controlling the organisation) need to:

- ensure that everyone within their organisation plays a role in being part of the effective implementation of the Quality Management System;
- define and communicate organisational responsibilities and authorities;
- establish (and use) internal communication processes;
- review the Quality Management System at planned intervals.

Having established their overall position, management will then have to:

- ensure that the organisation's QMS always meets the requirements of ISO 9001:2015 (and/or other associated Management System Standards) and, when this fails to happen, see that corrective actions are carried out;
- define objectives such as fitness for use;
- ensure that the performance, safety and reliability of their products and services are correct and that costs associated with these objectives are kept to a reasonable figure.

1.6.3.2 Quality Management Team

It is quite normal (especially for large organisations) that a completely separate and independent division, headed up by someone from top management to deal solely with quality matters. The organisation of this section 'could' look something like that shown in Figure 1.56.

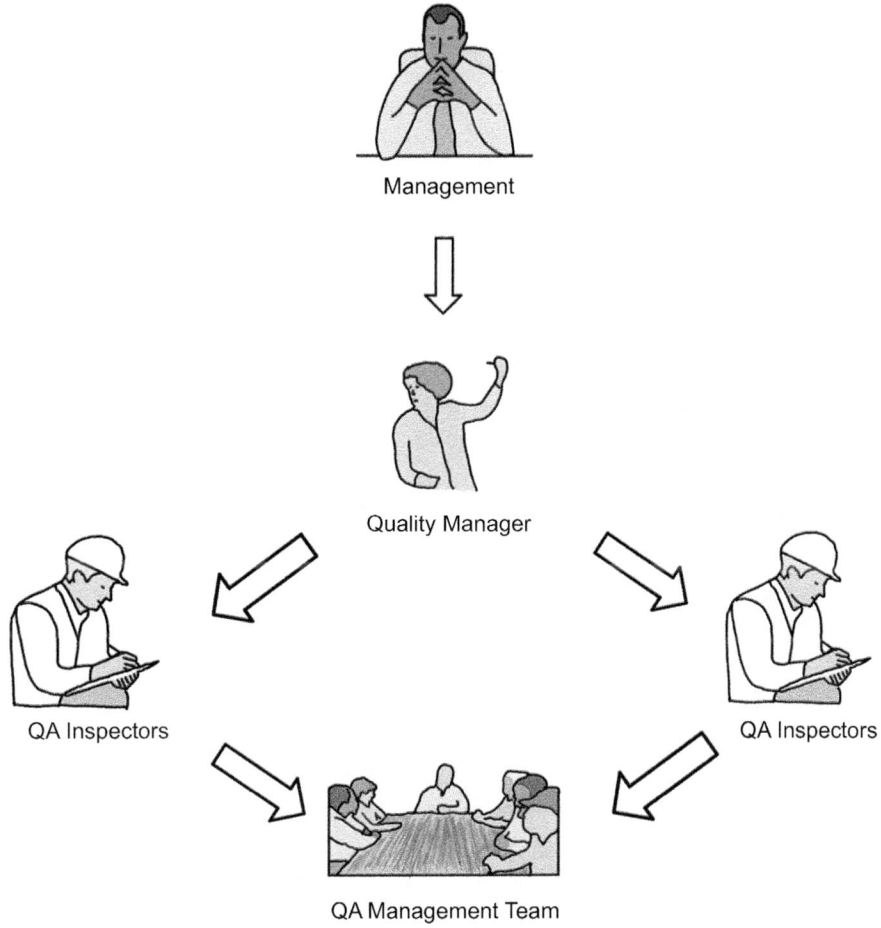

FIGURE 1.56 Quality management structure for a typical large organisation

For organisations that cannot justify the cost of employing full-time inspectors, other options are available, such as:

- selecting personnel from existing Staff who are not directly involved with a production process; they are then able to act as independent unbiased assessors;
- employing third-party quality consultants, on a temporary basis, to carry out fully independent Quality Controls.

The Quality Team (i.e. QA Inspectors), working under the Quality Manager, are members of an organisation judged competent to carry out Quality Assurance duties

1.6.3.3 Staff

Your Staff are at the sharp end of delivering quality. They are responsible for implementing the Quality Control processes (i.e. the previously described Quality Procedures and Work Instructions) to ensure that the desired level of quality is consistently applied to the product. Of course, they are not responsible for setting the level of quality, but, so long as they have been clearly briefed on what is required and have received the appropriate training to do the job, they will be capable of delivering that level of quality.

It is vital that a workforce is as committed to quality as the management. A committed workforce will look after your organisation. A workforce that is empowered to implement quality (and are allowed to have an input into defining and improving it) will be highly motivated. Morale will improve as Staff will feel that they are doing a good job that they can be proud of.

In summary, an organisation workforce has the responsibility for:

- working in accordance with the predefined QPs and WIs;
- refusing to accept anything that is substandard;
- having an active role in quality improvements;
- having an input into defining levels of quality (after all, they know better than anybody what can be achieved);
- delivering the level of quality specified in the QMS.

In short, your Staff are your greatest asset (Figure 1.57).

1.7 Staff training

1.7.1 Why is it important that staff receive training in ISO?

There are a number of very good reasons why it is important that Staff receive training on aspects of your Quality Management System.

1 It is important that everyone should have a broad understanding of why the organisation has a QMS and what benefits it brings to the organisation.
2 Staff need to fully understand the characteristics of the QMS that relate to their particular part in the organisation and why these are important. Only be understanding this relevance will Staff really engage with the system.

FIGURE 1.57   Recognise your greatest asset!

3   Through training, Staff can be made aware that the system is dynamic and can be adapted and altered to meet the needs of the business.

4   Having a robust QMS system in place can have a positive impact on moral. Knowing that the business is focussed on ensuring that a consistent and quality product is produced helps Staff to feel confident that the business is run professionally and is clear on its future.

Training is an important way of communicating these messages. A Staff presentation is okay, but training is the best way to ensure that the key aspects are fully understood. It gives Staff the opportunity to get involved and ask questions; it is the best way to ensure that these messages are clearly communicated to all.

A number of elements of all Management System Standards relate to Staff training and the importance of raising awareness and communicating with Staff. These include the following issues.

1.7.2 What are the essential requirements for staff training?

1.7.2.1 General

Top management **shall**:

- ensure that resources needed for the Quality Management System are available;
- communicate the importance of effective quality management and of conformance to Quality Management System requirements;
- engage, direct and support persons to contribute to the effectiveness of the Quality Management System;
- promote improvement;
- support other relevant management roles to demonstrate their leadership as it applies to their areas of responsibility'.

1.7.2.2 Organisational roles, responsibilities and authorities

Top management **shall** ensure that the responsibilities and authorities for relevant roles are assigned, communicated and understood within the organisation.

1.7.2.3 Competence

The organisation **shall**:

- determine the necessary competence of person(s) doing work under its control that affects the performance and effectiveness of the Quality Management System;
- ensure that these persons are competent on the basis of appropriate education, training, or experience;
- where applicable, take actions to acquire the necessary competence and evaluate the effectiveness of the actions taken; retain appropriate documented information as evidence of competence.

Note: Applicable actions can include, for example, the provision of training to, the mentoring of, the reassignment of currently employed persons or the hiring or contracting of competent persons.

1.7.2.4 Awareness

The organisation **shall** ensure that persons doing work under the organisation's control are aware of:

- the quality policy;
- relevant quality objectives;
- their contribution to the effectiveness of the Quality Management System, including the benefits of improved performance; and
- the implications of not conforming to Quality Management System requirements.

1.7.2.5 Communication

The organisation **shall** determine the internal and external communications relevant to the Quality Management System, including:

- on what it will communicate;
- when to communicate;
- with whom to communicate;
- how to communicate;
- who communicates.

1.7.2.6 Who should be trained?

As your QMS will touch every part of the business, then it follows that every member of Staff should receive training. However, it wouldn't be appropriate for everyone to receive the same level of training.

There are probably six levels of training that an organisation should consider:

1 **General awareness/induction** – for all Staff to understand the benefits of and the imperatives of the standard
2 **General guidance of the QMS in action** – for all Staff who need to follow the 'rules' of the QMS (levels 1 and 2 may well be run together depending on the size and complexity of the organisation)
3 **Specific training on relevant processes and procedures** – this might be done at a team level focussing only on the relevant procedures, Work Instructions etc. for that team
4 **Management training** – to help team leaders/managers and any member of Staff who might need to oversee the development of revisions and new procedures, Work Instructions etc.
5 **Quality team training** – a much more detailed look at the QMS from end to end
6 **Internal auditor training** – to ensure that any Staff undertaking an internal audit are fully aware of their responsibilities.

1.7.3 What needs to be included in the training?

1.7.3.1 General guidance

This session could well be run alongside the general awareness training (although a word of caution: it may be going into too much detail if used as part of an 'induction').

The guidance session should include:

* the different levels of documentation – what is a procedure, what is a work instruction etc.;
* how this documentation must be controlled;
* how documentation can be altered and amended;
* what audits entail from a user point of view;
* what is a nonconformity, how to report it, what to do.

1.7.3.2 General awareness training

General awareness should include:

* an overview of the standard;
* benefits that a QMS offers to the business;
* specific details of controls that are included in the QMS;
* why it is important to adhere to the 'rules' of the QMS;
* the importance of risk-based thinking.

This level of training is probably more appropriate for new employees as part of their induction. Whilst they are likely to require further training at a later date, this is probably enough for them to absorb in their first week!

1.7.3.3 Management training

Similar to team training, management training can be a good idea to ensure that those in charge of teams/areas of the business are fully aware of not only the detail their Staff are having to abide by but also their role in ensuring that it remains relevant at all times.

This training should include:

- how to make changes to a procedure or documentation;
- how to identify and rectify nonconformities;
- what to do if nonconformities are identified during an audit.

1.7.3.4 Quality Team training

The Quality Team need to understand the QMS from end to end.
This training should include:

- what the standard requires;
- how the QMS relates to the standard;
- the role of the Quality Team in ensuring that the QMS continues to be relevant;
- how to schedule internal audits, quality management reviews etc.

1.7.3.5 Team training

This session can focus specifically on the procedures and associated documents that are relevant to the day-to-day running of that team. Training a whole team together is the best way to ensure that everyone has received the same information.
This session should include:

- an overview of document control;
- a detailed look at all the procedures and related documents covering all aspects of their work;
- why it is important to keep to the procedures;
- what to do if procedures or Work Instructions etc. become irrelevant or out of date;
- how to identify a nonconformity and what to do – forms to use etc.;
- what will be expected of you in an internal audit.

1.7.3.6 Internal Auditors

It is advisable that at least *one* member of Staff has received an auditor training course from an accredited organisation to ensure that the audit procedure is thorough and appropriate. However, if you are planning to use a range of Staff to carry out internal audits, the following topics should be given:

- why audits are important;
- what is the procedure for conducting an audit;
- what documentation should be used;
- what to do if a nonconformity is identified;
- when it is appropriate to escalate issues identified;
- how to write up an audit report;
- how to monitor and track corrective actions.

1.8 Costs and benefits of having a Quality Management System

The main requirement of a quality management system is to possess a *system by 'which an organisation can aim to reduce and eventually eliminate non-conformance to specifications, standards and customer expectations in the most cost effective and efficient manner' (ISO).*

In practice, some Quality Assurance programmes can be very expensive to install and operate, particularly if inadequate Quality Control methods were used previously. If purchasers require consistent quality, then they must pay for it, **regardless** of the specification or order the organisation has accepted. Yet this expenditure must always be offset by the savings in scrapped material, rework and general problems arising from lack of quality. How much an organisation benefits from its QMS is directly related to the money it invests in quality.

However, it is always possible to put **too** much money into Quality Controls, and so the optimum benefit comes when the investment in Quality Control is balanced against the most significant reduction in the cost of poor quality. As can be seen from Figure 1.58, any further investment beyond this point will not result in substantial gains.

The main benefits of quality management are:

- an increased capability to provide products and services that consistently conform to agreed specifications;
- a reduction in administration and production costs because of less wastage and fewer rejects;
- a greater involvement and motivation within an organisation's workforce.
- for an organisation to derive any real benefit from a QMS, all Staff in the organisation must:

  - fully appreciate that QA is absolutely essential to their future;
  - improve customer relationship through fewer complaints, thus increasing sales potential;

- know how everyone can assist in achieving quality; and
- be stimulated and encouraged to do so.

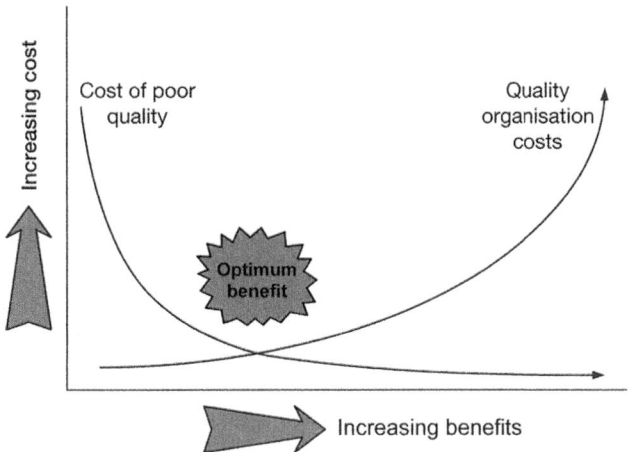

FIGURE 1.58 Quality Management System costs

With an effective QMS in place, the organisation will achieve increased profitability and market share, and the purchaser can expect reduced costs, improved products and services' fitness for role, increased satisfaction and, above all, growth in confidence. (See Figure 1.59)

But **without** an effective QMS, organisations will definitely suffer!

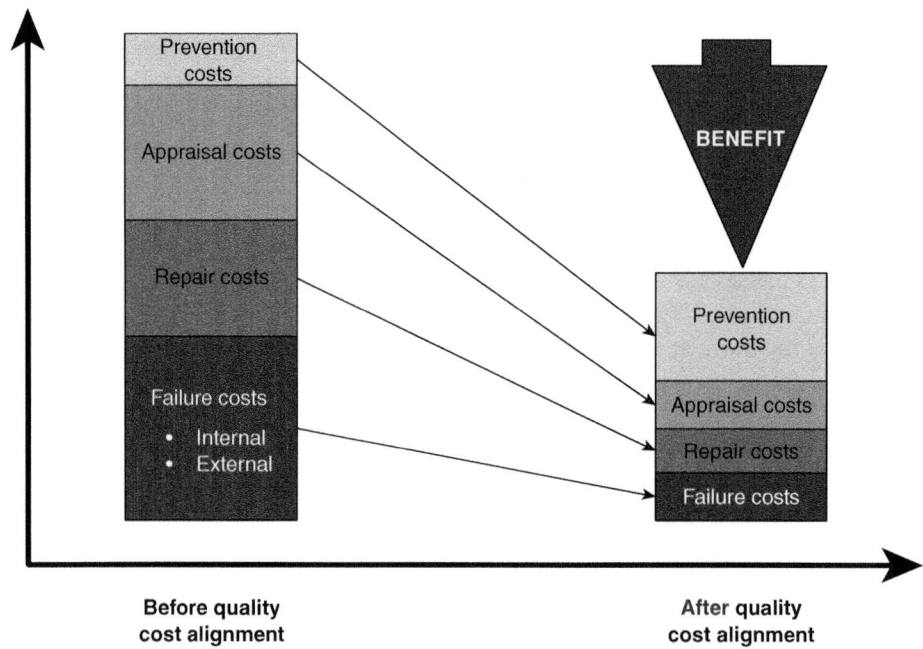

FIGURE 1.59   Preventing poor quality

1.8.1 What are the costs of quality failure?

1.8.2 What are the suppliers' responsibilities regarding costs?

The term 'supplier' relates to organisations that produce products or provide services. Their prime responsibility must always be to ensure that anything **and everything** prepared by their organisation conforms to the specific requirements of the purchaser – particularly with regard to quality. (See Figure 1.60)

The simplest way to be a 'responsible supplier' is to ensure that their particular office, production facility or manufacturing outlet fully complies with the requirements of the quality standards adopted by the country in which they are working and the country to whom they intend to supply products and services.

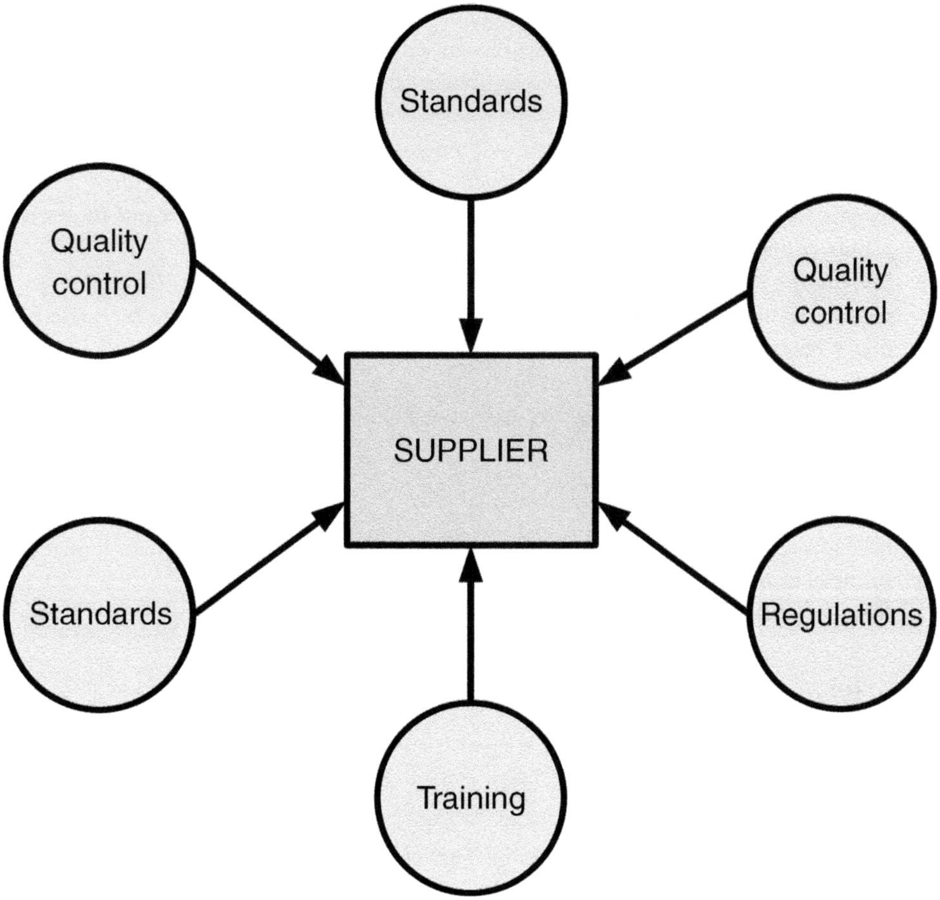

Standards

Quality control

Quality control

SUPPLIER

Standards

Regulations

Training

FIGURE 1.60   Supplier's responsibilities

To do this, they must, of course, first be aware of the standards applicable to that country, know how to obtain copies of the country's standards, how to adapt them to their own particular environment and how to get them accepted by the relevant authorities (for example, notified bodies).

Every country has its own set of recognised quality management standards to which suppliers can be assessed and certified. The following are the most frequently used certification and guideline standards used in the UK.

- **BS EN ISO 9001:2015** Quality Management Systems. Requirement
- **BS EN ISO 14001:2015** Environmental Management Systems. Requirements with Guidance for Use

 Note: This standard replaces OHSAS 18001:2007.

- **BS ISO 45001:2018** Occupational Health and Safety Management Systems. Requirements with Guidance for Use

Although an organisation can set out to abide by accepted standards, unless it achieves its aim. it will fail in its attempt to become a recognised supplier of quality products.

Lack of Quality Control and Quality Assurance can cause the supplier to:

- replace scrapped products or have to redo unsatisfactory services;
- re-inspect and reprocess products returned as unsatisfactory by the purchaser;
- lose money by having to send Staff to the purchasers' premises to sort out their complaints of unsatisfactory labour;
- lose money through a major quality failure halting production;
- lose money through field repairs, replacements and other work having to be carried out under warranty;
- lose money by having to carry out investigations into claims of unsatisfactory work;
- lose money by having to investigate alternative methods of producing a deliverable without quality failures;
- lose their image and reputation;
- lose market potential;
- have to acknowledge complaints, claims, liabilities and be subject to waste of human and financial resources; but most of all. . .
- **lose customers!**

1.8.3 What are the purchaser' responsibilities regarding costs?

CASE STUDY

By not insisting that the supplier abides by a set of recognised quality standards, the purchaser can be subject to:

- *delays in being able to use the products or services and the possibility of the purchaser losing orders because of it;*
- *possible increases in their organisation, operation, maintenance downtime and repair costs;*
- *dissatisfaction with products and services;*
- *health and safety aspects (now a mandatory requirement of ISO 13485:2016 for medical devices);*
- *lack of confidence in the supplier.*

 AUTHOR'S HINT

In the following examples, we look at each element that makes up a QMS and in what way they can combine to clearly define how a business achieves its goals.

Whilst the supplier must be firmly committed to the fundamental principle of always supplying the right quality product or service, equally, a purchaser must be committed to the fundamental principle of accepting only the right quality product – especially when quite a number of problems associated with a product's quality are usually the fault of the purchaser!

Obviously purchasers can expect to get only what they ordered. It is therefore extremely important that that the actual order is correct but also that the purchaser provides the product or service provider with all the relevant (and accurate) information required to complete the task (Figures 1.61 and 1.62).

There is little point in trying to blame the product or service provider when the finished deliverable doesn't come up to expectation because of an unsatisfactory design provided by the purchaser. In certain cases (for example, when the requirements of the item cannot easily be described in words), it could be very helpful if the purchaser is to provide a drawing as a form of graphic order (i.e. a Work Instruction!). In such cases, this drawing should contain all the relevant details such as type of material to be used, the materials' grade or condition and the specifications that are to be followed; where possible, the graphic order/drawing should be to scale.

FIGURE 1.61 Purchasers' request

FIGURE 1.62 Insufficient information provided to the seller

If this approach proves impractical, then the order has to include all the relevant dimensional data, sizes, tolerances etc. or refer to one of the accepted standards.

Having said all that, it must be appreciated that the actual specification being used is also very important for it sets the level of quality required and therefore directly affects the price of the article. Clearly, if specifications are too demanding, then the final cost of the article will be too high. If specifications are too vague or obscure, then the supplier will have difficulty in assembling or even designing the object or may even be unable to get it to work correctly.

The choice of product or service provider is equally important. It is an unfortunate fact of life that purchasers usually consider that the price of the article is the prime and (in some cases) even the **only** consideration. Buying cheaply is obviously **not** the answer because a purchaser who accepts the lowest offer all too often will find that delivery times are lengthened (because the manufacturer/supplier can make more profit on other orders), the article produced does not satisfy requirements and, worst of all, the quality of the article is so poor that the device has to be replaced well before its anticipated life cycle has been completed.

If a product or service provider has received official recognition that the quality of his work is up to a particular standard, then the purchaser has a reasonable guarantee that the article being produced will be of a reasonable quality – always assuming that the initial order was correct! Official recognition is taken to mean that an organisation has been assessed and certified to a recognised quality standard such as ISO 9001. In other words, he can **prove** his level of quality.

 AUTHOR'S END NOTE

Having now discussed what a basic Quality Management System consists of and how it can be used to support businesses, large or small, in Chapter 2 we will look at the history of quality standards, how they began and how they developed into a recognised, internationally accepted set of Management System Standards.

2

THE HISTORY OF QUALITY STANDARDS

 AUTHOR'S START NOTE

The history of quality management can be traced way back to medieval Europe, where work completed by journeymen and apprentices was evaluated and inspected by a skilled worker to ensure that the quality of the finished product was up to the required standard and, most importantly, ensured the satisfaction of the buyer. Although quality management has undergone a number of important changes since that time, the end goal has always been the same, but it wasn't until the 1920s that the Quality Management System, as we know it today, started to surface. This chapter is intended to give you a sort of ISO 9000 'time map' by providing you with a brief historical record of how quality management standards began, their interoperability and the basic requirements of ISO 9001:2015.

The quality movement can trace its roots back to thirteenth-century medieval Europe, where craftsmen began organising themselves into unions called guilds. These guilds were responsible for developing strict rules for product quality, and inspection committees enforced the rules by marking flawless goods with a special mark or symbol. Craftsmen themselves often placed a second mark on the goods they produced (Figure 2.1). At first this mark was used to track the origin of faulty items, but over time the mark came to represent a craftsman's good reputation and symbolized each guild member's obligation to satisfy customers and enhance the trade's reputation.

Until the early nineteenth century, manufacturers tended to follow this craftsmanship model until the Industrial Revolution when the factory system (with its emphasis on product inspection) became increasingly important. Gradually, manufacturers began to include quality processes in their quality practices.

In the 1920s, a Munitions Standard was developed by the UK Ordnance Board to guarantee that bullets used during the First World War were good (and safe!) enough to be fired. This standard is now known as Def Stan 13-131 and is the benchmark to which all munitions are still measured nowadays (Figure 2.2).

FIGURE 2.1   Guild of handicraft silver makers' mark. Photograph courtesy Stingray.

FIGURE 2.2   A successful quality check!

FIGURE 2.3   Vice Admiral Hyman G. Rickover: The founding father of quality?

Quite a lot of people have said that today's Quality Management System Standards originated from this 1920s munitions standard. I tend to believe, however, that the actual '*start*' of Quality Standardisation was probably during the US Navy Polaris submarine programme in the late 1950s. At that time, Admiral Hyman G. Rickover (Figure 2.3) – who was the head of the US Nuclear Navy and renowned for having a ruthless disposition and a very hot temper – became frustrated with the number of Polaris submarines that were unseaworthy and moored up at the dockyards mainly due to defects, errors and general quality breakdowns.

He took 30 fresh graduates from Harvard, gave each of them a list of subcontractors to visit and investigate, a time scale, and a report format – and then sent them out into the industrial jungle!

When they returned and the results were analysed, Rickover discovered that a number of major and semi-major items were the most common or root cause to all of the problems being experienced. The main ones are shown in Figure 2.4 and Table 2.1.

The points that emerged from the survey were then used as the cornerstone for quality in the American Space Research Programme and eventually became the basis of the first NATO

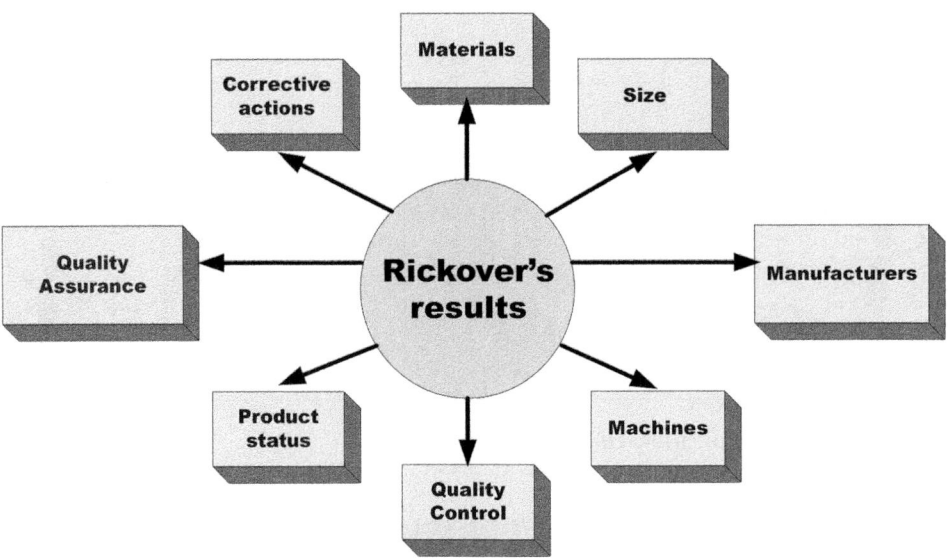

FIGURE 2.4 Admiral Rickover's major survey results

TABLE 2.1 Admiral Hyman G. Rickover's findings

Wrong materials	Wrong materials obtained – failure to specify totally and exactly what was required on the purchase orders
Wrong dimensions	Items made to wrong dimensions – failure to withdraw obsolete drawings when essential design changes had been made
Different manufacturers	Items from different manufacturers would not fit together at the quayside – failure to calibrate measuring instruments to reliable reference standards that differed among organisations and districts
Inefficient machines	Machines operated incorrectly – defects made in products through lack of skill and failure to train operators in performing vital tasks
Quality Control	Lack of Quality Control and defective items dispatched – failure to inspect effectively
Product status	Status of products unknown – no records available to show what had or had not been done
Quality Assurance	Products in doubt and no corrective actions taken – no appointed person to ensure that operations were conducted properly
Corrective action	Corrective actions not recognised or at best delayed, etc. – top management unaware of what was and was not happening

Allied Quality Assurance Publications (AQAP) specifications, which define the Quality Management System requirements to be adopted by all military subcontractors for all defence products. (See Figure 2.5 and Table 2.2)

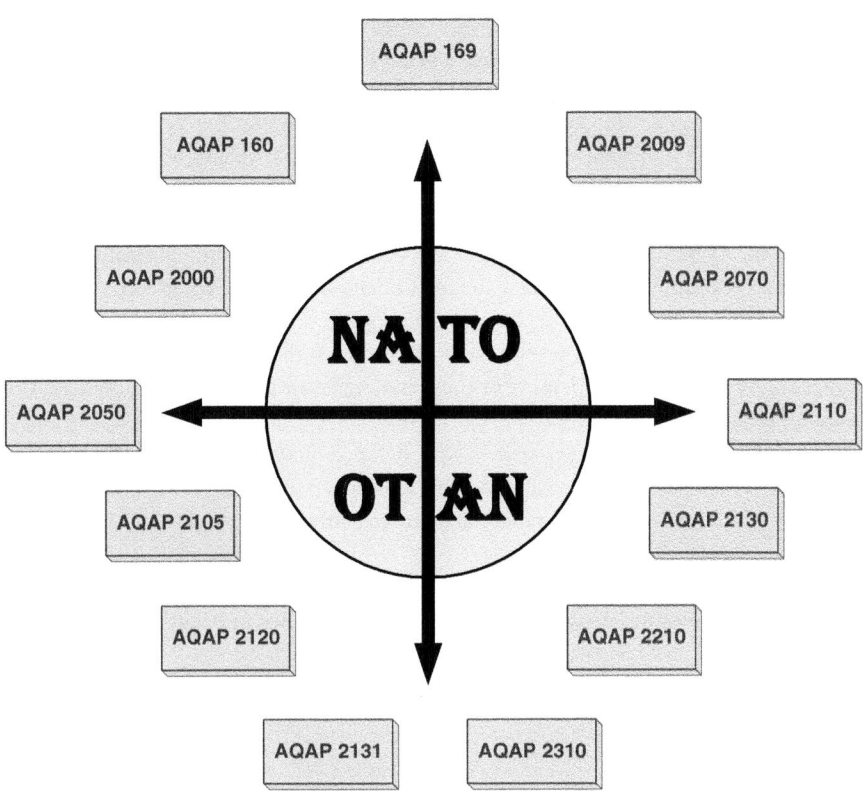

FIGURE 2.5 List of current AQAP publications

TABLE 2.2 List of current AQAP publications

AQAP 160	NATO Integrated Quality Requirements for Software throughout the Life Cycle
AQAP 169	NATO Guidance on the Use of AQAP 160 Ed.1
AQAP 2000	NATO Policy on an Integrated Systems Approach to Quality through the Life Cycle
AQAP 2009	NATO Guidance on the Use of the AQAP 2000 Series
AQAP 2050	NATO Project Assessment Model
AQAP 2070	NATO Mutual Government Quality Assurance (GQA) Process
AQAP 2105	NATO Requirements for Deliverable Quality Plans
AQAP 2110	NATO Quality Assurance Requirements for Design, Development and Production
AQAP 2120	NATO Quality Assurance Requirements for Production
AQAP 2130	NATO Quality Assurance Requirements for Inspection and Test
AQAP 2131	NATO Quality Assurance Requirements for Final Inspection
AQAP 2210	NATO Supplementary Software Quality Assurance Requirements to AQAP 2110
AQAP 2310	NATO Quality Management System Requirements for Aviation, Space and Defense Suppliers

2.1 1979 – BS 5750:1979 Parts 1, 2 and 3

The year 1979 was important for quality standards in the United Kingdom. The British Standards Institution (BSI) had already published a number of guides on Quality Assurance (such as BS 4891:1972 A Guide to Quality Assurance), but with increased requirements for some sort of auditable Quality Assurance, BSI set up a study group to produce an acceptable document that would cover all requirements for a two-party manufacturing and/or supply contract.

This became the BS 5750 series of standards on quality systems, which were first published in the UK during 1979 and (incidentally, that is when I wrote my first book on Quality Management!). These standards supplied guidelines for internal quality management as well as external Quality Assurance. They were quickly accepted by manufacturers, suppliers and purchasers as being a reasonable minimum level of Quality Assurance that they could be expected to work to. The BS 5750 series thus became the cornerstone for national quality.

But in the meantime, the United States had been working on their American National Standards Institute (ANSI) 90 series, and other European countries were also busily developing their own sets of standards. Quite naturally, however, as the BSI had already produced and published an acceptable standard, most of these national standards were broadly based on BS 5750. (See Figure 2.6)

The concept was further developed by the defence, power generation, automobile and textile industries and gradually expanded from Admiral Rickover's initial points to 20 basic elements applicable to a very wide range of industries producing products of many kinds:

1 **Management responsibility** – Management should define and document a quality policy, an organisation structure, including responsibility and authority. Management

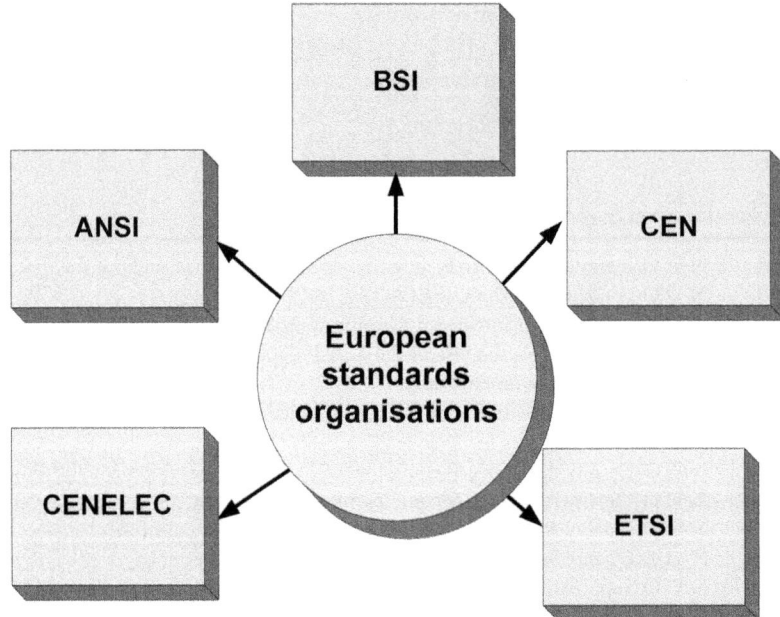

FIGURE 2.6 The main parties involved in the transition to ISO 9000

should make available verification resources (inspectors), appoint a management representative and carry out management reviews.

2 **Quality system** – The quality system must be documented, including a manual, procedures and work instructions.

3 **Contract review** – A procedure for performing contract review – documenting what was agreed with the customer – should be written, stating clearly the criteria for contractual obligations to be met.

4 **Design control** – Procedures should define how the organisation designs its product and controls any design changes.

5 **Document control** – Procedures and work instructions must be approved before issue and upon subsequent changes. Control of documents should encompass availability, distribution, issue level, revision and obsolescence.

6 **Purchasing** – Suppliers should be assessed and monitored, incoming product should be verified.

7 **Customer supplied stock** – Customer-supplied stock should be subject to procedures for identification, inspection, storage and periodic maintenance. There should also be a procedure for reporting and recording lost or damaged stock.

8 **Product identification and traceability** – A company-wide procedure should detail how items and equipment are to be identified at all stages from receipt to despatch. Where traceability is required, a unique identification should be used and recorded.

9 **Process control** – Work instructions, defining when, how and what should be done, need to be documented and made available.

10 **Inspection and test** – Inspections should be performed upon receipt of a product, and documented procedures should define the appropriate tests. Tests should be performed on all products that were repaired or serviced before they were released to demonstrate the restoration of operative condition. Records should provide evidence to demonstrate the equipment and/or device met the necessary inspection or test criteria.

11 **Inspection, measuring and test equipment** – These must be controlled, calibrated and maintained.

12 **Inspection and test status** – This must be identified by using markings, stamps, labels, routing documents, inspection/test record sheets, physical location or other suitable means.

13 **Control of nonconforming product** – Procedures must define the controls used to prevent the use of nonconforming product. Items should be identified and segregated and the authority for disposition made clear.

14 **Corrective action** – A corrective action procedure must be documented defining what is to be analysed, how corrective actions are to be initiated and obtained to prevent reoccurrence. Corrective action procedures should also be documented for dealing with customer complaints.

15 **Handling, storage, packaging and delivery** – There must be procedures for all of these. Additionally, inventories must be controlled, and procedures for warranty must be written and communicated to customers.

16 **Quality records** – Procedures for the identification, collection, indexing, filing, storage and maintenance must be written, and records must be kept.

17 **Internal quality audits** – These must be planned and scheduled to verify the effectiveness of the quality system. Audits must be performed by staff independent of the

authority responsible for the area being audited. The procedures for audits, follow-up actions and reporting must be documented.

18 **Training** – Procedures should be established to identify training needs. Training must be conducted on a formal basis and records kept.

19 **Servicing** – If there is a requirement to service equipment, the servicing procedures should be documented and maintained.

20 **Statistical techniques** – Statistical techniques should be used where appropriate to estimate key parameters.

2.2 1981–1986

In 1981, the UK Department of Trade and Industry (DTI) formed a committee called FOCUS to examine areas where standardisation could benefit the competitiveness of British manufacturers and users of high technology – for instance, local area network (LAN) standardisation. Owing to the wider international interest concerning Quality Assurance, ISO then set up a Study Group during 1983 to produce an international set of standards that all countries could use.

This initiative, the Open Systems Interconnection (OSI), ensured that products from different manufacturers and different countries could exchange data and interwork in certain defined areas. In the United States, the Corporation of Open Systems (COS) was formed in 1986 to pursue similar objectives. (See Figure 2.7)

2.3 1987 – ISO 9000:1987 Parts 1, 2 and 3

Similar to quality standards from other countries, the new **ISO 9000 (1987)** set of standards were very heavily based on BS 5750:1979 Parts 1, 2 and 3 (i.e. Part 1 Model for Quality Assurance in Design, Development, Production, Installation, and Servicing, Part 2 Model for Quality Assurance in Production, Installation, and Servicing and Part 3 Model for Quality Assurance in Final Inspection and Test) and followed the same sectional layout except that an additional section (ISO 9000 Part 0 Section 0.1 1987) was introduced to provide further guidance about the principal concepts and applications contained in the ISO 9000 series.

When ISO 9000 was first published in 1987, it was immediately ratified by the United Kingdom and republished by the BSI (without deviation), as the new **BS 5750 (1987)** standard for Quality Management Systems.

Similarly, on 10 December 1987, the Technical Board of the European Committee for Standardisation [Commission Européen de Normalisation (CEN)] approved and accepted the text of ISO 9000 (1987) as the European Standard – without modification – and republished it as **EN 29000 (1987)**.

So at that time official versions of EN 29000 (1987) existed in English, French and German. Other CEN members were allowed to translate any of these versions into their own language with the same status as the original official versions.

BS 5750:1987 was therefore identical to ISO 9000:1987 and EN 29000:1987 except that BS 5750 had three additional guidance sections. Consequently, BS 5750 was not just the British Standard for Quality Management Systems, it was also **the** European and **the** international standard!

But the question had to be, 'If all of these titles referred to the same quality standard, why not call the standard by the same name?'! (See Figure 2.8)

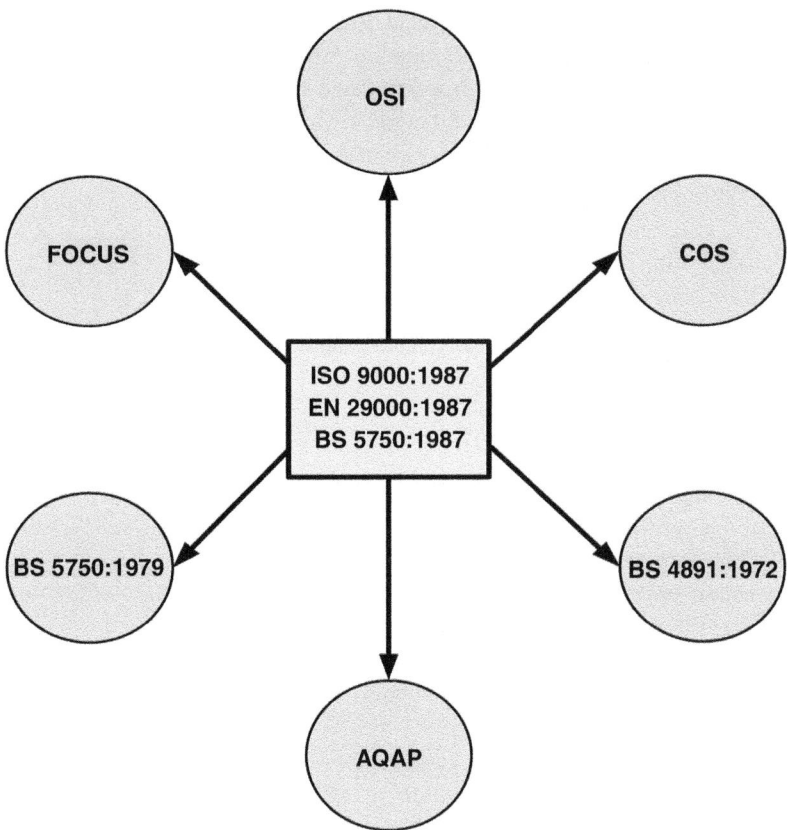

FIGURE 2.7 The background to the first ISO 9000 Study Group

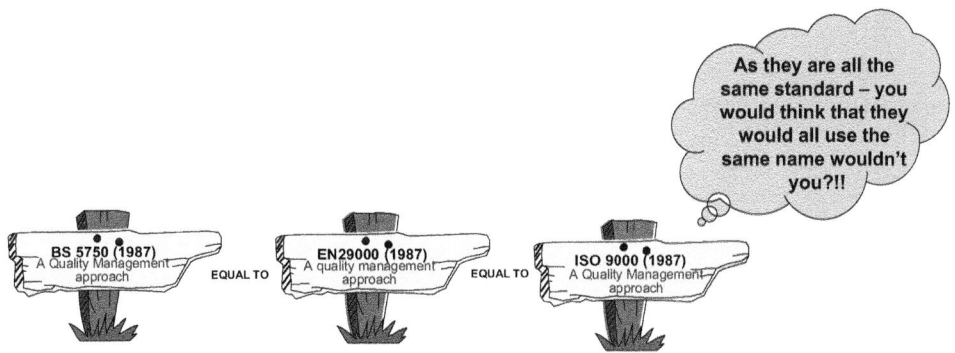

FIGURE 2.8 – Identical 1987 Quality Standards

2.4 1994 – BS EN ISO 9000:1994

Well, that is exactly what happened. ISO, realising the problems of calling the same document by a variety of different names was confusing (even a bit ridiculous!), reproduced (in March 1994) the ISO 9000:1994 series of documents. This series included ISO 9001 (Model for Quality Assurance in Design, Development, Production, Installation, and Servicing), ISO 9002 (Model for Quality Assurance in Production, Installation, and Servicing) and ISO 9003 (Model for Quality Assurance in Final Inspection and Test). (See Figure 2.9)

And by the end of 1999, more than 60 countries had ratified ISO 9000 as their accepted quality management standard, and the majority of all national quality standards were (and still are) equivalent to the ISO 9000 series.

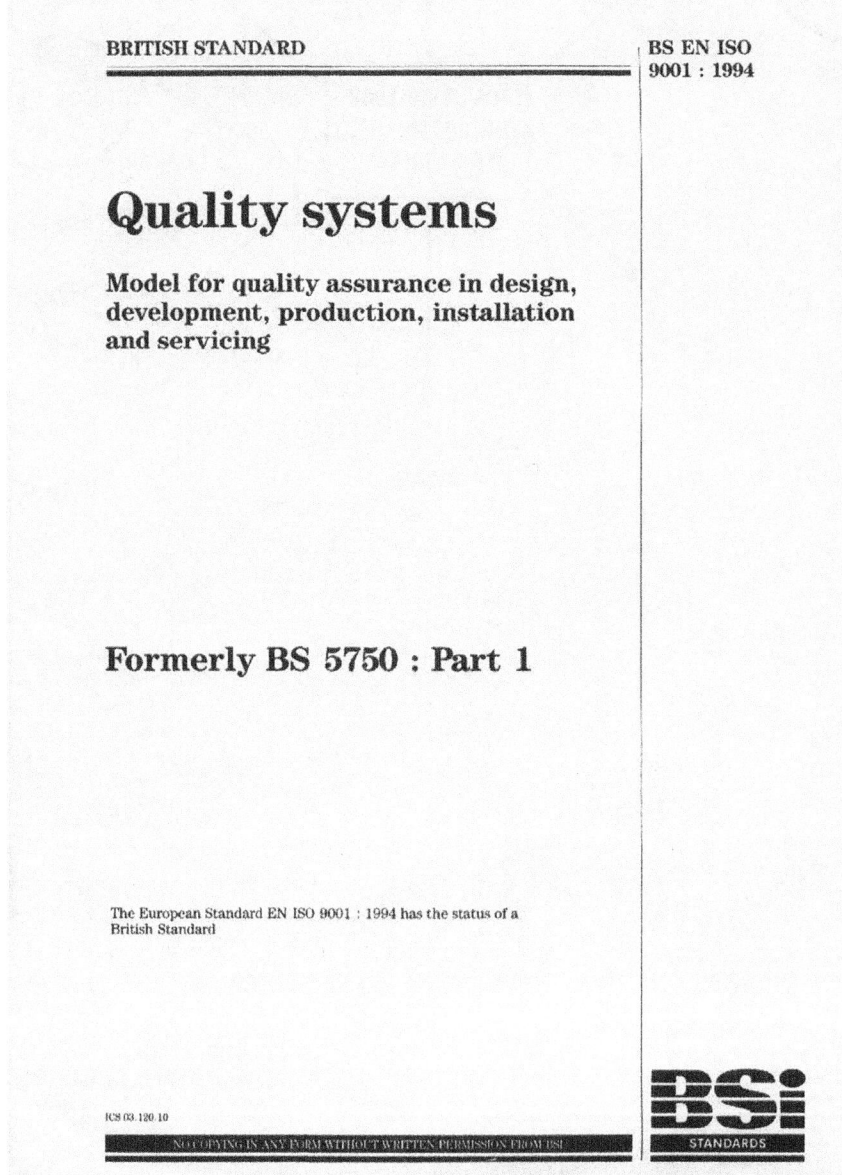

BRITISH STANDARD

BS EN ISO 9001 : 1994

Quality systems

Model for quality assurance in design, development, production, installation and servicing

Formerly BS 5750 : Part 1

The European Standard EN ISO 9001 : 1994 has the status of a British Standard

ICS 03.120.10

NO COPYING IN ANY FORM WITHOUT WRITTEN PERMISSION FROM BSI

BSi STANDARDS

FIGURE 2.9 ISO 9001–1994

Although the most notable change between the 1987 and the 1994 versions of the ISO 9000 standard was the streamlining of the numbering system, there were also around 250 other changes, the main ones being that:

- it became an explicit requirement that all members of an organisation (down to supervisory level at least) must have job profiles (descriptions) to define their authority and responsibility;
- design reviews became compulsory throughout the work package lifetime;
- documentation control was extended to ensure that all data was up to date.

Most of these 250 changes were intended to clarify the standard, making it easier to read. However, they did not significantly alter the way in which most organisations were running their businesses, merely seeking to improve it.

2.5 2000 – ISO 9001:2000

When ISO 9000 was first released in 1987, it was recognised as being **mainly** aimed at manufacturers, and it was largely incomplete, requiring auditors to fill in many gaps. The first revision of ISO 9000 in 1994 got rid of many of these problems. However, an organisation could still conform to the standard **but** at the same time produce substandard products that were of a consistently poor quality! There was clearly a major 'tick-in-the-box' loophole that enabled organisations to comply with the requirements of ISO 9001:1994 – without having to **improve** the quality of their product or service!

Some managers also found it extremely difficult to see the real benefit of having to commit more and more manpower and finance to maintaining their ISO 9000 certification, and whilst most organisations accepted that the initial certification process was worthwhile (and could result in some very real benefits), these were mainly one-offs, and it was felt that once ISO 9000 had been fully adopted within an organisation, these savings could **not** be repeated.

The ISO 9000 certificate had been hanging on the wall in the reception office for many years, and but there was little or no actual benefit to be gained from having to continually pay out for re-certification and surveillance fees.

On the other hand, however, a considerable number of organisations who initially sought ISO 9000 registration (because it was a requirement to continue doing business with a client), having used and seen the benefits of this qualification, they, in turn, had pushed it on down their own supply chain, thus **increasing** the requirement for ISO 9000 certification. (See Figure 2.10)

So as the 1990s progressed, more and more organisations started reaping benefits from the existing ISO 9001:1994 requirements, but as the standard became more popular the inadequacies of ISO 9001:1994 became more apparent. For example:

- some organisations were not manufacturers and did not need to carry out all the 20 elements making up ISO 9000:1994 in order to be a quality organisation;
- the standard was too biased towards manufacturing industries, thus making it difficult for service industries to use;
- there was growing confusion about having three quality standards available for certification (i.e. ISO 9001, ISO 9002 and ISO 9003), and there was a need for the requirements for all three standards to be combined into one overall standard;

FIGURE 2.10 The ever increasing demand for ISO 9000 quality management certification

- the ISO 9001:1994 requirements were reproduced in quite a lot of other management systems (e.g. ISO 14001 Environmental Management and OHSAS 18001 for Occupational Health and Safety), which resulted in duplication of effort (see Figure 2.11);
- many organisations wanted to progress beyond the confines of ISO 9001 towards Total Quality Management (TQM);
- the documents were viewed by many as not being very user-friendly;
- the language used was not clear and could be interpreted in many different ways;
- the standard was very inflexible and could not be tailored to specific industries, etc.;
- the standard did not cater for continual improvement;
- the standard did not fully address customer satisfaction.

The reasons went on and on, and there was clearly a need for revision with the overall aim of making a new ISO 9001:2000 that was:

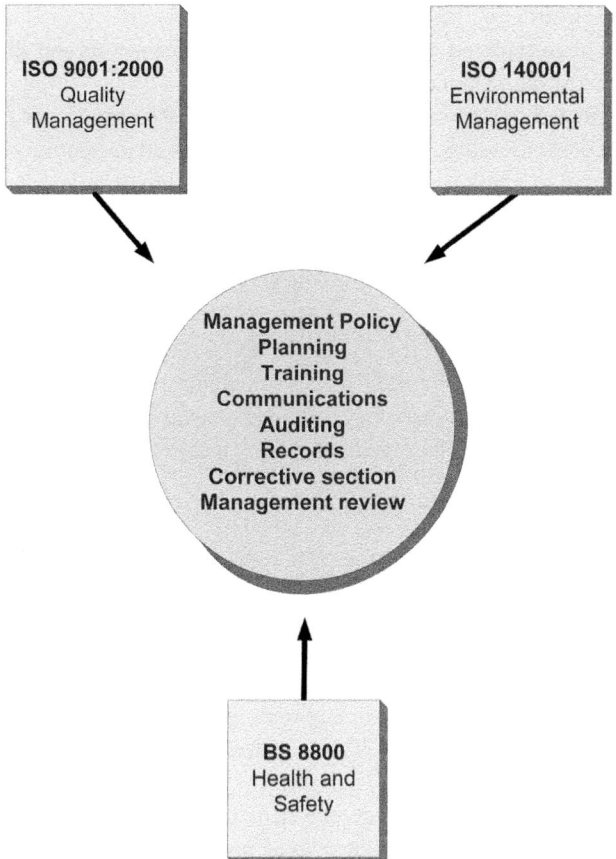

FIGURE 2.11   Common elements from Quality, Environmental and Safety Management Standards

- more compatible with the other management systems;
- more closely associated to business processes;
- easier to understand;
- capable of being used by all organisations, no matter their size;
- capable of being used by all types of industry and profession (i.e. manufacturers and service providers);
- a means of continually improving quality; and, above all,
- future proof.

A decision was made, therefore, to provide a revised standard that would:

- be split, so that one standard (i.e. ISO 9001:2000) would address requirements, whilst another standard (ISO 9004) would address the gradual improvement of an organisation's overall quality performance;
- be simple to use, easy to understand and use only clear language and terminology (a definite plus for most readers of current international standards!);

- have a common structure based on a 'process model';
- be capable of being 'tailored' to fit all product and service sectors and all sizes of organisation (and not just the manufacturing industry);
- be more orientated toward continual improvement and customer satisfaction;
- be capable of demonstrating continuous improvement and prevention of nonconformity;
- provide a natural stepping stone towards performance improvement;
- have an increased compatibility with other Management System Standards;
- provide a basis for addressing the primary needs and interests of organisations in specific sectors such as aerospace, automotive, medical devices, telecommunication and others.

ISO emphasised, however, that this revision of the ISO 9000 standards should **not** require the rewriting of the organisation's current QMS documentation! They pointed out that the only real change had been from a '*system based*' to a more '*process orientated*' management approach, which could be easily addressed by organisations on an as-required basis.

2.6 2008 – ISO 9001:2008

According to the rules of ISO (and like all other ISO standards), ISO 9001 is required to undergo review and revision every five years. The ISO 9001 standard was first revised in 1994 and then underwent a major revision in 2000 and a further one in 2008. Thankfully, however, the changes made in ISO 9001:2008 were relatively minor and of little concern to most companies. The new standard did **not** contain any **new** requirements, nor did it contain changes to any of the requirements of ISO 9001:2000, and, more importantly, it did not change the objective of ISO 9001:2000.

For all intents and purposes, therefore, the structure and outline of ISO 9001:2008 was identical to that of ISO 9001:2000 and introduced only clarifications to the existing requirements based on eight years of experience of implementing the standard worldwide with over 1 million certificates issued in over 175 countries. It also introduced some changes to the wording intended to improve consistency with the other Safety (OHSAS 18001) and Environmental (ISO 14001) Management Systems.

According to ISO, the benefits of the changes to the wording in ISO 9001:2008 were as follows:

- Easier to use
- Clearer language
- Easier to translate into other languages
- Better compatibility with the environmental and safety management standards.

In November 2008, ISO published their latest revision, which was called (you won't be surprised to hear!) ISO 9001:2008.

2.7 2015 – Annex SL

As well as ISO 9001 for Quality Management Systems, ISO also publishes a number of other Management System Standards (MSS) (e.g. safety and security, general management, health and medical, environmental and energy, industry, services, occupational health and safety, risk, business continuity, asset management systems etc.), and, of course, many other standards are actually based on ISO 9001 (such as ISO/IEC 27001:2013 for Information Security Management). However, the structure and format of each of these standards vary considerably, and so it is not surprising therefore that these variations continue to cause problems for organisations who have to become certified against multiple schemes.

ISO realised the problems associated with these dissimilarities, and in an attempt to produce some form of consistency across the standards, they agreed that in future all new revisions to existing Management System Standards **will have to** have the same high-level structure as detailed in Appendix 3 of ISO/IEC Directives, Part 1 Annex SL (previously known as *ISO Guide 83* but now usually referred to as just Annex SL), which has been created to form the basis of a generic management system with identical core text, common terms and definitions (where suitable), with the overall aim of making them easier to read and understand and thus making it easier to integrate more than one standard into an overall business management system.

Note: Whilst the high-level structure cannot be changed, subclauses and discipline-specific text can be added. This commonality requires less maintenance and audit resources, meaning that it can be changed more easily to meet evolving business needs.

By adopting Annex SL (named SL simply because it happens to appear after SK and before SM!), ISO considered that new standards could be designed to be much less 'fussy', allowing organisations greater freedom to design their own management system and the scope to create organisation-specific manuals and procedures.

2.8 2015 – ISO 9001:2015

Following the publication of Annex SL, the ISO Committee responsible for looking after ISO 9001 carried out extensive research aimed at developing a specific Quality Management System Standard that could be used as a template (i.e. customised) for **all** Management Standards.

The main result of ISO's research indicated that whilst there was still significant satisfaction with the 2008 version of the standard, most people considered that, in order to keep ISO 9001 relevant and reflect changes in its environment, this revised standard should (among other things):

* remain generic and relevant to all sizes and types of organisation regardless of whether they are designers, manufacturers, suppliers or end users;
* maintain the current focus on effective process management to produce cost-effective and desirable end results;
* take account of changes in Quality Management Systems practices and technology since the last major revision in 2000;
* reflect changes in the increasingly complex, demanding and dynamic environments in which organisations operate;
* enhance compatibility and alignment with other ISO Management System Standards;
* facilitate effective organisational implementation and effective conformity assessment by first, second and third parties;

- use simplified language and writing styles to aid understanding;
- emphasise the importance of leadership;
- introduce risk and opportunity management;
- use simplified language and writing styles to aid understanding and consistent interpretations of its requirements; but, above all,
- provide a stable core set of requirements for the next ten years or more.

ISO 9001:2015 therefore not only supports the development of continual improvement, customer satisfaction and traceability through the implementation of various management system processes; it also enables an organisation to:

- increase profits – owing to a reduction in wastage and errors;
- increase sales – new clients sourced and a reduction in lost orders;
- increase management efficacy – less time wasted;
- increase business prospects – opening doors restricted to ISO 9001:2015 Certified Suppliers; and
- by demonstrating compliance to ISO 9001's requirements, organisations are actively advertising their commitment to quality and, in doing so, evidencing why potential clients could rely on the organisation's products and services. See Figure 2.12.

The new 2015 version of this standard helps to maintain consistency, align different Management System Standards, match sub clauses against the top-level structure and apply common language across all standards.

With the new standard in place, organisations will find it easier to incorporate their Quality Management System into their Core Business Processes and gain greater business benefit.

Quality **used to be** about making sure that a product was right, with an emphasis on the manufacturer being required to produce something that could be inspected against a specific dimension or criterion. The product was then considered acceptable, or had to be reworked to become acceptable, or had to be scrapped (which could be very expensive). When things went wrong, it was usual to blame the craftsmen (e.g. designers, software engineers, construction engineers, etc.!). (See Figure 2.13)

But that was in the past, and we are now on the threshold of Integrated Management Systems (IMS)!

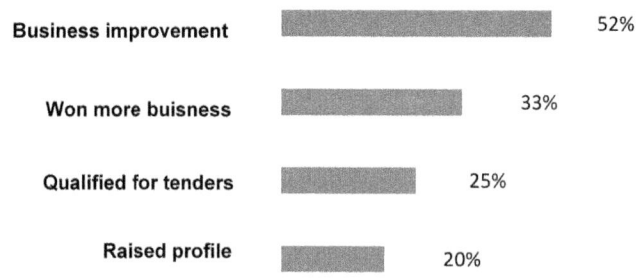

FIGURE 2.12   Benefits of achieving ISO 9001

FIGURE 2.13   Old-fashioned Quality Control!

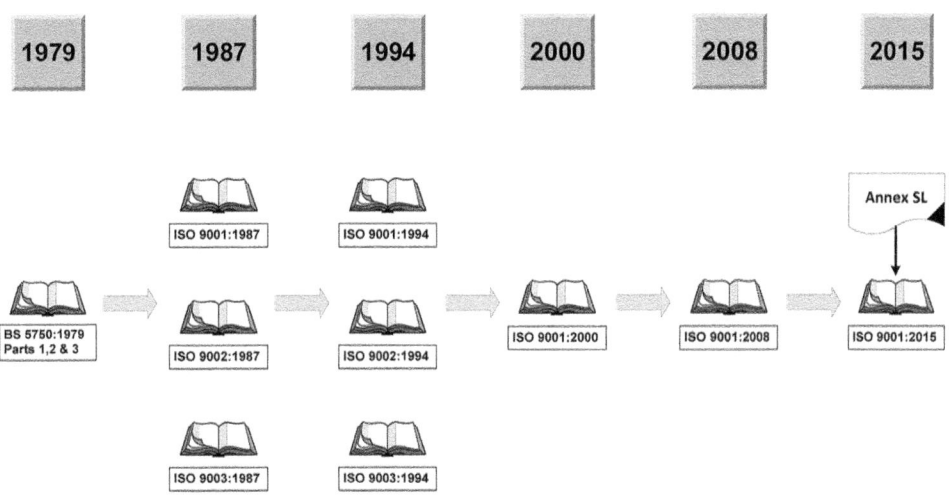

FIGURE 2.14   The history of ISO 9000 so far

So, in a nutshell, ISO 9001:2015 has:

- brought quality and continuous improvement into the heart of every business;
- emphasised the importance of leadership;
- introduced risk and opportunity management;
- introduced a new integrated approach to **Management System Standards**

The new structure detailed in Annex SL (previously known as *ISO Guide 83*) formed the basis for all generic management systems. It has now become mandatory for **all** new and newly revised ISO Management System Standards to abide by this structure, so that in future it will be much easier to implement multiple, integrated management systems. (See Figure 2.14)

AUTHOR'S END NOTE

As you can see from this brief historical overview, the management of quality has increased from small beginnings way back in the thirteenth century to something that now effects virtually all organisations whether they are designers, manufacturers, suppliers, installers or end users. But the next question is, 'What are these standards, and who produces them?'

In Chapter 3, we shall have a look at the interoperability of Management System Standards that we have come to accept as an everyday way of life.

3
WHO PRODUCES QUALITY STANDARDS?

 AUTHOR'S START NOTE

Now that we have seen how quality standards were developed over the last eight centuries or so, the next question is, "Who actually produces these standards?"!

In Chapter 3, you will see that many Standards Bodies are operating in the world today and that, although the International Standards Òrganization (ISO) is by far and away the largest one producing industrial standards, two other very important organisations have been heavily involved in the production of standards for electronic and electrical-related technologies [i.e. the International Electrotechnical Commission (IEC)] and the International Telegraph Union (ITU) for information and communication standardisation], which we shall now have a look at.

As just indicated, three global sister organisations (ISO, IEC and ITU) develop international standards for the world, and, when appropriate, joint committees work together to ensure that international standards fit together seamlessly and complement one another. (See Figure 3.1)

The international standards are, themselves, drawn up by a series of International Technical Committees that have been approved by ISO or IEC member countries, and now many hundreds of different ISO and IEC Standards are available, covering virtually every situation.

Due to this steady growth in international standardisation, ISO and the IEC are now the standards bodies that most countries are affiliated to – via, that is, their own particular National Standards Organization (NSO).

Although these standards were initially published as 'recommendations', they are now globally accepted as international standards in their own right, and the use of the words 'must' and 'shall' (i.e. denoting a mandatory requirement) has become commonplace.

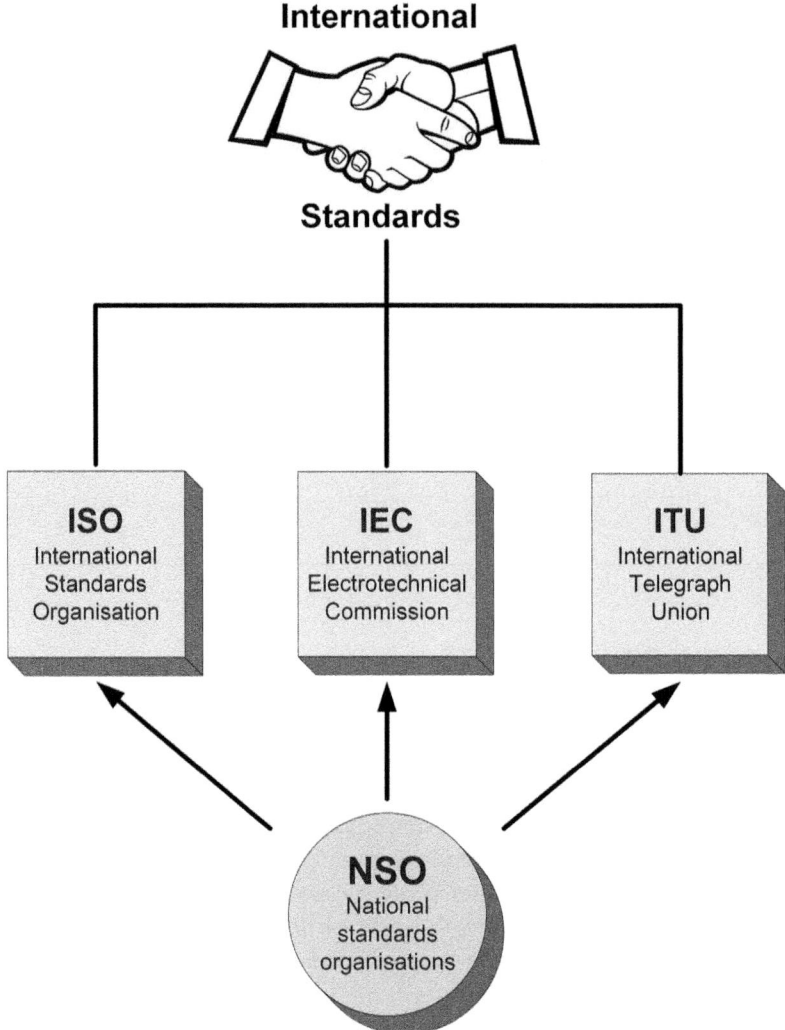

FIGURE 3.1 International standards

3.1 Who and what are the ISO?

In 1946, 25 delegates from 25 countries met at the Institute of Civil Engineers in London and decided to create a new international organisation '*to facilitate the international coordination and unification of industrial standards*'.

As a result, the International Standards Organization (ISO) was established as a United Nations Agency in 1947 and are an independent, non-governmental membership organisation who (at the time of writing this book) is made up of Member Bodies from 162 countries with one standards body representing each member country (e.g. BSI for the United Kingdom and ANSI for the United States). These representatives make up a number of Technical

Bodies (such as ISO/TC 176 for quality management and Quality Assurance) who are responsible for the development of standards. ISO have a Central Secretariat based in Geneva, Switzerland, and are the world's largest producer of voluntary International Standards covering almost all aspects of industry and manufacturing.

 AUTHOR'S HINT

*Because the 'International Organization for Standardization would have different acronyms in different languages [IOS in English, OIN in French (Organisation internationale de normalisation)], the founders decided to give it the short form '**ISO**', which is derived from the Greek isos, meaning equal. Thus, whatever the country, whatever the language, ISO standards are always equally applicable and equally acceptable!*

There are three member categories of ISO. Each enjoys a different level of access and influence over the ISO system, helping ISO to be inclusive while also recognising the different needs and capacity of each national standards body. There are (again at the time of writing this book):

162 full members (or member bodies) who influence ISO standards development and strategy by participating and voting in ISO technical and policy meetings. Full members sell and adopt ISO International Standards nationally.

38 correspondent members who observe the development of ISO standards and strategy by attending ISO technical and policy meetings as observers. Correspondent members can also sell and adopt ISO international standards nationally.

5 subscriber members who keep up to date on ISO's work but cannot participate in it. They do not sell or adopt ISO International Standards nationally.

Since 1947, ISO have published more than 21,500 International Standards covering almost every aspect of technology and business. From food safety to computers, from agriculture to health care, and it is certainly true to say that ISO International Standards impact all of our lives!

3.2 Who and what are the IEC?

Founded in 1906, the IEC (International Electrotechnical Commission) is a not-for-profit, non-governmental organisation responsible for the preparation and publication of international standards for all electrical, electronic and related technologies – collectively known as electrotechnology.

Currently, 60 countries are full members, while another 23 participate in the Affiliate Country Programme (AFS), which, although this is not really a form of membership, it is nevertheless designed to help industrialising countries get involved with the IEC.

IEC enable companies, industries and governments to meet, discuss and develop international standards that are relevant to millions of devices containing electronics and using (or producing) electricity – and that in turn rely on IEC International Standards and Conformity Assessment Systems to perform, fit and work safely together.

The IEC:

- provide a standardised approach to testing and certification;
- allow companies, governments and test labs to verify that a certain product or system conforms to the requirements described in a particular standard;
- help make testing transparent, predictable, comparable from one country to the next and more affordable;
- provide a single set of rules and procedures that prevents unfair advantages for local products in a particular country.

3.3 Who and what are the ITU?

Originally founded in 1865, as the International Telegraph Union, the ITU is the oldest existing international organisation with its headquarters Geneva, Switzerland. The ITU [as a specialised agency of the United Nations (UN)] are responsible for **all** issues that concern information and communication technologies, and they assist undeveloped countries to establish and create telecommunication systems of their own.

The ITU sets and publishes regulations and standards relevant to electronic communication and broadcasting technologies, including radio, television, satellite, telephone and the Internet. Although the recommendations of the ITU are non-binding, most countries adhere to them in the interest of maintaining an effective international electronic communication environment. As well as these ITU regulations, their Committees [i.e. International Telegraph and Telephony Consultative Committee (CCITT) and International Radio Consultative Committee (CCIR)] also publish recommendations. (See Figure 3.2)

3.4 How important is the work of all these committees?

From the consumer's point of view, the importance of international (i.e. ISO and IEC) standardisation is that all major agencies are now committed to recognising these standards. Equipment, modules and components can thus be designed and built so that they will be acceptable to all member countries, and today there is a constant demand for new, revised and updated standards – particularly those with an international relevance. A good example is, of course, ISO 9001, which (as the most generically successful and widely used quality management standard ever devised) has now become the worldwide benchmark for improving business efficiency and competitiveness.

It must not be forgotten, however, that the overall aim of standardisation is not just to produce paperwork that becomes part of a library. The aim is to produce a precise, succinct, readily applied and widely recognised set of principles that are relevant and satisfy the varied needs of business, industry or commerce.

The aim is also that standardisation shouldn't provide exclusive advantage to the products or services of one particular individual supplier and that the application of standards should always be capable of being verified by an independent third-party evaluator (i.e. an auditor).

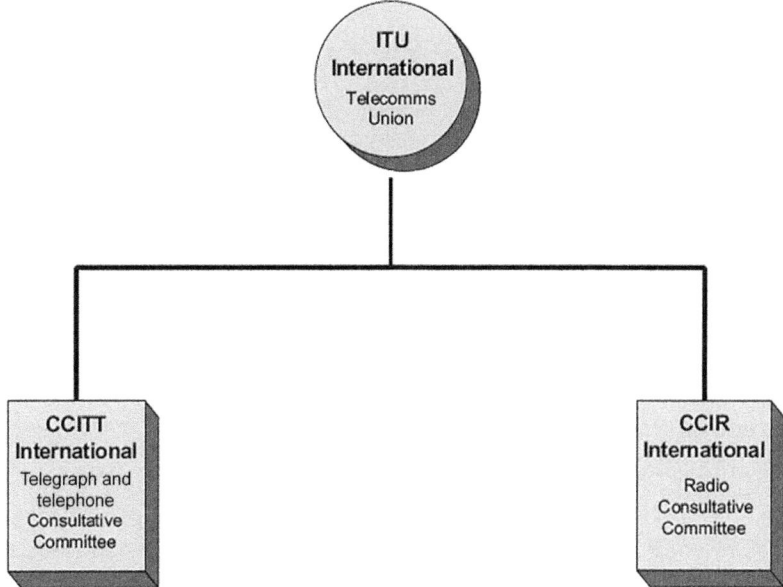

FIGURE 3.2 International Telecommunications Committee

3.5 Military standards

In the military world, the situation is little different. The United Kingdom Ministry of Defence (MOD-UK) use Defence Standards (DEF STANS), the American Division of Defense (DOD) use Military Standards (Mil-Std), the North Atlantic Treaty Organization (NATO) use NATO Allied Quality Assurance Publications (AQAPs), and most other nations have their own particular variations. (See Figure 3.3)

3.6 National standards

A standard is a document that provides requirements, specifications, guidelines or characteristics that can be used consistently to ensure that materials, products, processes and services are fit for their purpose. With literally thousands of standards available worldwide, on every conceivable topic, this can make it difficult to decide which is important to you! (See Figure 3.4)

It has to be said, however, that standards are as international as the markets they serve, and currently the main producers of national Standards in Western Europe are (see Figure 3.5):

- United Kingdom – British Standards Institution (BSI);
- Germany – Deutsch Institut fur Normung e.v. (DIN);
- France – Association Français de Normalisation (AFNOR).

Outside Europe, the most widely used standards come from:

- America – American National Standards Institute (ANSI);
- Canada – Canadian Standards Association (CSA).

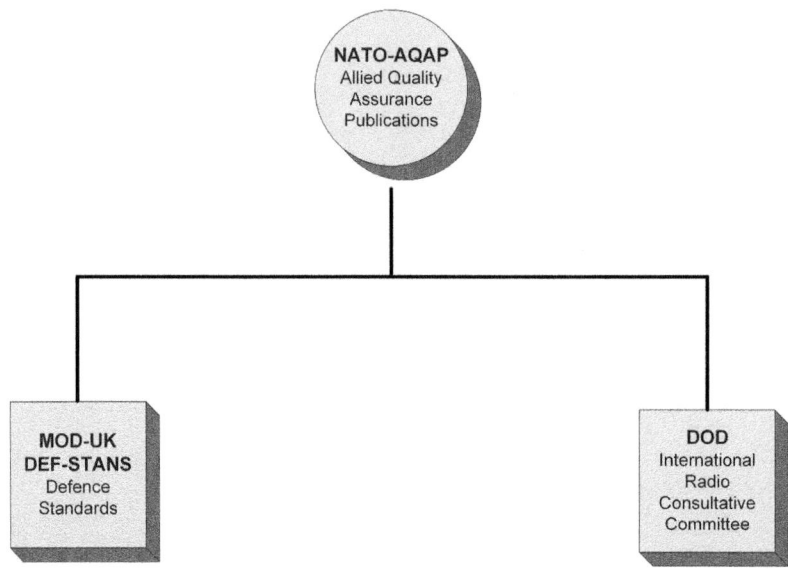

FIGURE 3.3   Military standards

There are others, of course, (like Japan and Saudi Arabia), but Europe and North America are the main Continents.

Nevertheless, although these countries publish what are probably the most used series of standards, virtually every country with an industrial base has its own national organisation producing its own national set of standards. However, national bodies and national stand-ards cannot dictate customer choice. A product that may legally be marketed need not have universal appeal or be internationally acceptable (for example, the three-pin electrical plug used in the UK is totally useless in most other countries!), and this diversity of standards can obviously lead to a lot of confusion, especially with regard to international trade and tenders.

CASE STUDY

If the America government (or an American company) were to invite tenders for a project quoting American National Standards (ANSI) as the minimum criterion, a European organi-sation could find it difficult to submit a proposal, either because it didn't have a copy of the relevant standard, or they wouldn't find it cost-effective to retool their entire works in order to conform to the requirements of that particular American domestic standard.

Indeed, where different national standards persist, they will do so as a reflection of different market preferences and national idiosyncrasies. For industry to survive in this new, 'liberalised' market, therefore, it must have a sound technological base supported by a comprehensive set of internationally approved standards.

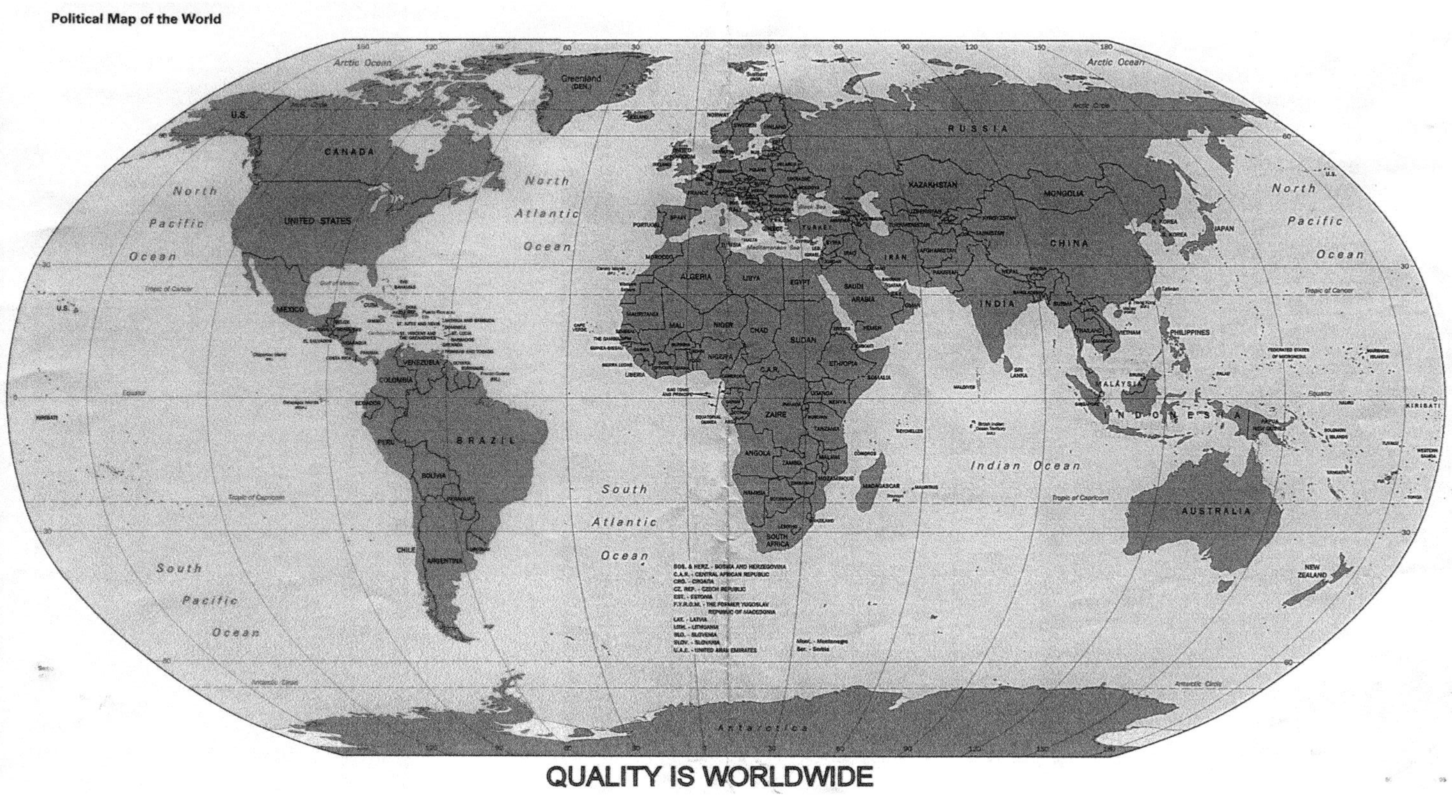

Political Map of the World

QUALITY IS WORLDWIDE

FIGURE 3.4 National Standards

Source: WorldAtlas.com

FIGURE 3.5 Main producers of national standards

Source: WorldAtlas.com

3.6.1 'Quality' has thus become the key word in today's competitive markets

In the UK, the BSI is responsible for the actual production of national standards, and the BSI Committees correspond closely with those of other European and/or International standards organisations. BSI also presents the British viewpoint to the European standards organisations [CEN (Commission European de Normalisation) and CENELEC (European Committee for Electrotechnical Standardisation), as well as ETSI (European Telecommunications Standards Institute)] in the telecommunications field. These organisations seek to develop harmonised European standards that are crucial to the success of the European Single Market. In the broader international arena, it is ISO and the IEC that pursue similar aims for harmonising world standards. Again, BSI is active in ensuring that the views of UK business are represented.

 AUTHOR'S HINT

But it should be remembered that a proposal for a new standard can be made by any country or indeed anybody and will be investigated depending on the support it can attract and, critically, on the ability of the organisation to provide an initial draft within a workable deadline.

In all, there are over 8,000 IEC standards and guides, and since the 1970s, BSI has published most of these as British Standards with a national foreword. Under European agreement, BSI also publishes European Standards (using an EN numbering system) as identical British Standards (e.g. EN 14988–1:2006 for the safety of children's high chairs is published in the UK by BSI as BS EN 14988–1:2006 with a national foreword). (See Figure 3.6)

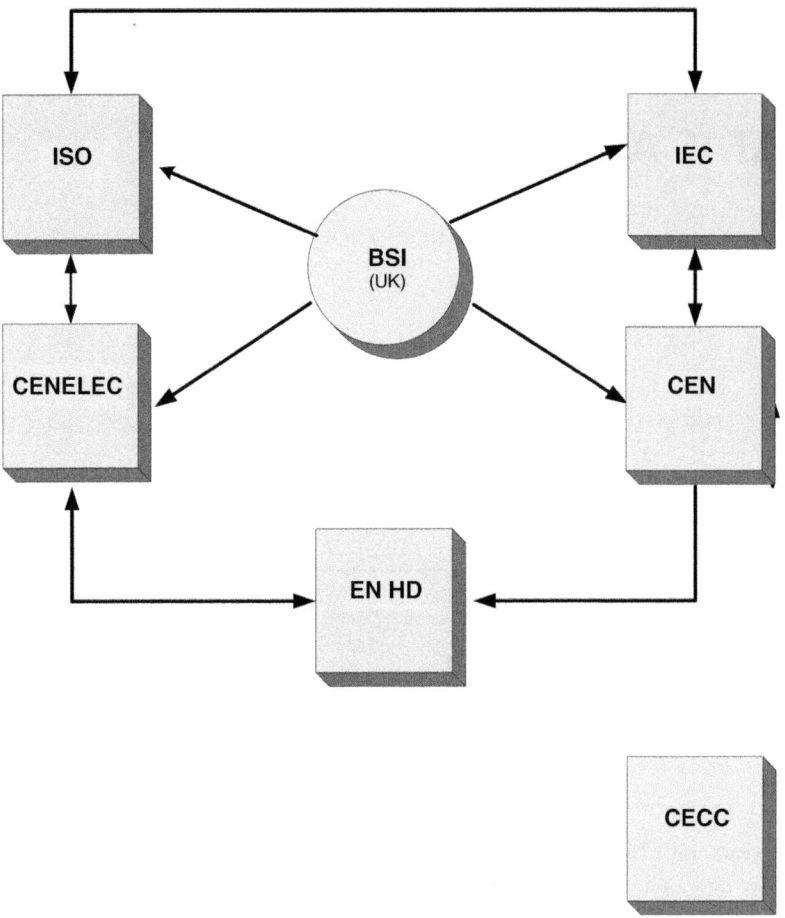

FIGURE 3.6   Interrelationship of the various International Standards Bodies and Committees

 AUTHOR'S END NOTE

Hopefully, these last three Chapters have given you a reasonable overview of what quality management is all about and how the requirement for an organisation to possess a Quality Management System has now become a worldwide normal way of life. Now let's have a look at ISO's Annex SL and the 'beast' we call ISO 9001:2015.

4

WHAT IS ANNEX SL ALL ABOUT?

 AUTHOR'S START NOTE

This chapter provides a full description of the high-level structure that all new and future Management System Standards will have to follow.

Over the years, ISO has published many Management System Standards for topics ranging from quality and environment to information security, business continuity management and records management. Despite sharing common elements, ISO Management System Standards come in many different shapes and structures, which can frequently cause confusion and difficulty at the implementation stage.

But what exactly is this Annex SL thing that everyone is talking about? In short, it's a rule book for standard writers setting out what they must and must not do in the development of any international standard. (See Figure 4.1)

As well as ISO 9001 for Quality Management Systems, ISO also publishes a whole host of other Management System Standards (MSS) (e.g. environmental, occupational health and safety, risk, business continuity, information security, asset management systems etc.). And, of course, many other standards are actually **based** on ISO 9001 (such as ISO/IEC 27001for information security management systems). But the structure and format of each of these standards vary significantly from one another, so it is not surprising, therefore, that these variations continue to cause problems for organisations that need to become certified against multiple schemes.

CASE STUDY

A good example of this was a company that were manufacturing therapeutic medical devices, which, as they concerned patient safety, would have to be assessed against both ISO 9001 (for quality management) and also ISO 13485 for medical devices. They asked for my assistance back in the late 1990s, and this was the first time that I realised how very similar the requirements between the two standards were. So I was able to assist them by combining these requirements into a single Quality Management System that could be audited by a notified body and, in doing so, reduce both time and costs for them.

Thankfully, ISO also realised the potential problems. In an attempt to produce some form of consistency across the standards, they have agreed that in future **all** new (and all revisions to) existing Management System Standards will have to have the same high-level-structure [as detailed in Appendix 3 of ISO/IEC Directives, Part 1 Annex SL (commonly referred to as just Annex SL)] identical core text, as well as common terms and definitions, where suitable, with the overall aim of making them easier to read and understand. This also makes it easier to integrate more than one standard into an overall business management system.

FIGURE 4.1 Is Annex SL going to be of any use to me?

Whilst the high-level structure cannot be changed, sub clauses and discipline-specific text can be added. This commonality requires less maintenance and audit resources, meaning that it can be changed more easily to meet evolving business needs.

So, with the introduction of Annex SL, all of the major clause numbers and titles of **all** ISO Management System Standards will now be identical, such as the introduction, scope and normative references (whose content will be specific to each discipline), terms and definitions (22 terms and definitions have been listed that must be addressed; they cannot be deleted or changed, but each standard can **add** its own additional terms and definitions if required and also add to or modify the notes written against these stated terms and definitions) and operation. ISO have, however, said that, as an option, each standard may have its own bibliography!

In publishing Annex SL (i.e. Appendix 3 of ISO/IEC Directives, Part 1), ISO have provided organisations with an identical structure, text, common terms and definitions for Management System Standards of the future. This will ensure consistency among future and revised MMSs and make their integrated use simpler. It will also make the standards easier to read and more understandable for users.

Following its publication, all technical committees developing Management System Standards **must** now follow its requirements for harmonizing a high-level structure of text, terms and definitions, while leaving the standards developers the flexibility to integrate their specific technical topics and requirements.

4.1 What is the structure of Annex SL?

In accordance with Annex SL, the structure of all current and future quality and Management System Standards **must** now contain ten main clauses instead of the previous eight used by ISO 9001:2008 and other similar management standards, as show in Figure 4.2.

Clause 1: Scope   The scope defines the intended outcomes of the management system. The outcomes are industry-specific and should be aligned with the context of the organisation (see clause 4).

Clause 2: Normative references   Provides details of the reference standards or publications relevant to the particular standard (e.g. for Annex SL, the normative reference is ISO 9000:2015).

Clause 3: Terms and definitions   Details terms and definitions applicable to the management standard in addition to any formal related terms and definitions.

Clause 4: Context of the organisation   Clause 4 is the basic foundation of any management system. It:

- clarifies the needs, expectations and requirements of interested parties and potential clients;
- defines your organisation and its unique context;
- defines the scope of your QMS and its compliance with Annex SL;
- lists the internal and external issues that can impact on its intended outcomes;
- shows how your organisation is structured;
- lists the internal and external issues that can impact on its intended outcomes.

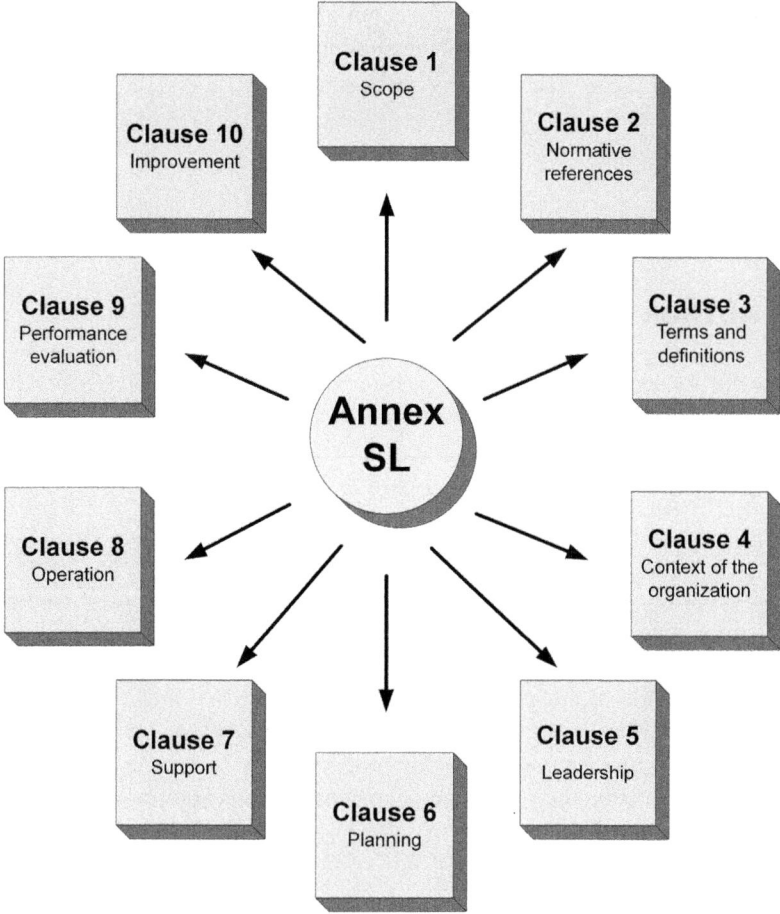

FIGURE 4.2   Management system clauses

Clause 5: Leadership   The new high-level structure places particular emphasis on leadership, as opposed to just management as set out in previous standards. This means top management will now:

- have greater accountability and involvement in the organisation's management system;
- need to:
  - allocate the necessary resources;
  - define roles and responsibilities;
  - focus on quality and customers;
  - ensure the management system achieves its intended outcomes;
  - establish a suitable quality policy;
  - integrate the requirements of the management system into the organisation's Core Business Process.

Top Management is now also responsible for communicating the importance of the management system and heighten employee awareness and involvement.

Clause 6: Planning

Risks and opportunities

AUTHOR'S HINT

This new risk and opportunities approach is a major change to any QMS and replaces preventative action, and this will, in turn, reduce the need for corrective actions later on.

Risk-based thinking is probably **the** most important requirement of Annex SL and means that, once your organisation has highlighted the risks and opportunities in your product or service, you will then need to:

• decide how and when these risks will have to be addressed and, most importantly, by whom;
• define actions to manage risks and address opportunities;
• take into consideration these risks and opportunities when you plan your QMS.

Quality Objectives

These require you to:

• control changes to your Quality Management System;
• develop plans to achieve objectives and evaluate results;
• establish quality objectives for all relevant areas.

Clause 7: Support Having thought about your overall organisational aims and policies, commitment and planning, Annex SL now requires you to consider what infrastructure and manpower is required in order to support your QMS by:

• controlling your organisation's documented information;
• managing the creation, management, revision an use of your organisation's documented information;
• ensuring that you have included all of the documented information that your QMS needs;
• providing the necessary internal and external resources;
• ensuring that people are competent;
• explaining how people can help in the continuance of quality management;

- managing your methods of communicating quality management throughout your organisation;
- providing the infrastructure and appropriate environment that your processes need;
- providing suitable monitoring and measuring resources;
- providing information to assist process operations.

Clause 8: Operation

 Clause 8 contains the lion's share of management system requirements and addresses:

- Overall process management
- In-house and outsourced processes
- Criteria to control these processes
- Ways to manage planned and unintended change

Operational processes will need to be developed to implement and control your operational processes and to clarify how:

- product and service requirements will be specified, managed and reviewed;
- communications with customers will be handled.

Design and development services will need to:

- establish a process to design and develop products and services;
- specify how the design and development process will be controlled;
- plan product and service design and development activities;
- determine product, as well as service design and development inputs;
- check how design and development outputs are produced;
- review and control all design and development changes;
- monitor and control externally provided products and services by:
    - confirming that, external products and services meet requirements;
    - establishing controls for externally provided products and services;
    - discussing your organisation's requirements with external providers;
- manage and control production and service provision activities by:
    - clarifying and complying with all post-delivery requirements;
    - controlling changes for production and service provision;
    - identifying process outputs (and controlling their unique identity);
    - protecting property owned by customers and external providers;
    - preserving outputs during production and service provision;
- implement arrangements to control the release of products and services;
- control nonconforming process outputs, products and services.

Clause 9: Performance evaluation   In accordance with you will now need to establish a process for monitoring, measuring, analysing and evaluating:

- planning and performing management reviews at planned intervals;
- generating management review outputs and retaining results in the format of documented information;
- obtaining customer information;
- monitoring customer satisfaction;
- analysing and evaluating the results of monitoring and measurement activities;
- developing an internal audit program for your organisation that can be used to:

    - examine conformance and performance;
    - audit your QMS at planned intervals;
    - review the suitability, adequacy, and effectiveness of your QMS.

Clause 10: Improvement   It is a well known fact that in an ever changing business world, not everything will always go according to plan. So clause 10 looks at ways to address:

- nonconformities and corrective action;
- strategies for improvement on a continual basis;
- the suitability, adequacy and effectiveness of your QMS.

 AUTHOR'S HINT

ISO management system requirements were, of course, not written for the express purpose of audit and certification! However, the development of an agreed format definitely makes internal, external and third-party auditing far easier for both the auditors and the organisation.

4.2 What are the major changes caused by Annex SL?

The most important changes in the new version of Annex SL are:

- the adoption of the high-level structure for all management system;
- an explicit requirement for risk-based thinking to support and improve the understanding and application of the process approach;
- fewer prescribed requirements;
- greater emphasis on achieving desired outcomes to improve customer satisfaction;
- greater emphasis on leadership engagement;
- help in addressing organisational risks and opportunities;
- improved applicability for services;
- increased emphasis on organisational context;
- less emphasis on documents;
- more user friendly for service and knowledge-based organisations;
- simplified language, common structure and terms;

- supply chain management addressed more effectively;
- the integration and alignment of quality management with the business strategies of an organisation;
- the requirement to define the boundaries of the QMS.

4.3 How have these changes affected existing management standards?

How does ISO 9001:2015 compare with other management standards?

With text and terminology becoming common to all Management System Standards, there have been a number of necessary changes to the content and structure of the new standards. For example:

Continual improvement versus improvement   *'continual improvement'* has been replaced by to just *'improvement'*.

Control of externally provided processes, products and services   *'purchasing'* has been replaced by *'control of externally provided processes, products and services'*.

Control of a nonconforming product   The *'control of nonconforming products'* now includes nonconforming processes as well as outputs and services.

Design and development   The phrase *'design and development'* (planning, review, verification) used in previous editions has now been replaced by *'development of goods and services'*.

Documented information   The term *'documented information'* now replaces *'documented procedure'* and *'records'* in order to align with other international standards, thereby allowing much more freedom for organisations themselves to determine the nature and extent of their document holdings.

Goods and services   In response to feedback received regarding the existing versions of management standards, the view is that many are still too biased towards manufacturing organisations with *'hardware'* products, and so it has been agreed that in future the terminology *'goods and services'* will be used instead of *'product'*.

Internal and external issues   Organisations are now required to identify any internal and external issues that may have an impact on the delivery of their product or service.

Leadership   The title *'Management Responsibility'* has now been replaced by *'Leadership'*.

Process approach   The process approach has now become a mandatory requirement of al management standards.

Products and services   The term *'product'* has been replaced by *'products and services'*.

Quality manager   The role of the *'management representative'* (usually referred to as the quality manager) will no longer exist in current and future standards written in compliance.

Quality Manual   The requirement for an organisation to have a fully documented Quality Manual with (sometimes mandatory) quality procedures and quality records is removed and replaced with the term *'Documented information'*.

Quality management system scope   The scope of the organisation's Quality Management System now needs to take in consideration internal and external issues identified by the context of the organisation.

Requirements   Where requirements were previously implied, the wording of the standard has been amended to make them explicit.

Risks and opportunities   The term '*preventive action*' has now been replaced by '*actions to address risks and opportunities*'.

Terms and definitions   Common terms and definitions for all management systems are now to be found in Annex SL.

4.4 Changed terminology

The clause sequence and some of the terminology have been changed to improve alignment with other Management System Standards as shown in Table 4.1.

TABLE 4.1 Annex SL terminology

Old	New
Continual improvement	Changed to '*Improvement*'
Documentation, quality manual, documented procedures, records	Now referred to as '*Documented information*'
Exclusions	No longer used
Management representative	No longer used
Monitoring and measuring equipment	Changed to '*Monitoring and measuring resources*'
Products	Changed to '*Products and services*'
Preventative action	Changed to '*Actions to address risks and opportunities*'
Purchased product	Changed to '*Externally provided products and services*'
Supplier	Changed to '*External provider*'
Work environment	Changed to '*Environment for the operation of processes*'

4.5 The new clauses in a little more detail

TABLE 4.2 Annex SL clauses

Clause	Change	Details of change and impact
3	Terms and definitions	Common terms and definitions for all management systems are now to be found in ISO 9000:2005.
		However, specific terms and definitions applicable to individual management systems will be found (and explained) in the standard itself.
4	Context of the organisation	Organisations are now required to identify any internal and external issues that may impact their Quality Management System's ability to deliver its intended results. Top Management need to develop a methodology for understanding the needs and expectations of 'interested parties' (i.e. those individuals and/organisations who can be affected by the organisation's decisions or activities.
		Organisations are also required to determine and maintain the knowledge they (and their employees) possess, which is critical in respect of ensuring their products and services conform to requirements. This includes knowledge held not just in documents or on IT systems but also in people's heads.

Clause	Change	Details of change and impact
4.3	Quality management system scope	Greater emphasis has been placed on the need for the organisation's Quality Management System to take in consideration the internal and external issues identified by the context of the organisation.
4.3	Process approach requirement	The process approach is now a mandatory requirement of all management systems.
5	Leadership	The title 'Management Responsibility' has now been replaced by 'Leadership' and in future, top management will be required to be actively involved in **all** aspects of their Quality Management System. The role of the Management Representative (usually referred to as the Quality Manager) now no longer exists, and this activity, instead of operating as an independent system in its own right, has been imbedded into routine business operations.
6.1.1 and 6.1.2	Risks and opportunities	The term *'preventive action'* has now been replaced by *'actions to address risks and opportunities'* and organisations are now required to agree, consider and, where necessary, take action to address any risks or opportunities that may impact (either positively or negatively) on their Quality Management System's ability to deliver its intended outcomes or that could have an effect on customer satisfaction.
7.5	Documented information	This is probably the most contentious change made by Annex SL and viewed by many as a step in the wrong direction! However, after much discussion, it has been decided that the requirement for an organisation to have a fully documented Quality Manual, together with documented (and sometimes mandatory) Quality Procedures and Quality Records, is removed and replaced with the term *'Documented Information'*, which is *'information that the organization will be required to keep, control and maintain'*. How an organisation decides to maintain their *'documented information'* is, however, left open, and, in doing so, ISO believe that this will provide organisations with a far more flexible away of running their business.
8.2	Products and services	The term *'product'* has been replaced by *'products and services'*, which further emphasises that Annex SL is applicable to all organisations whether they are designers, manufacturers, installers and/or end users.
8.4	Control of externally provided processes, products and services	*'Purchasing'* has been replaced by *'control of externally provided processes, products and services'* so as to cover all forms of external provision, whether purchased directly from a supplier, via an associate company or subcontractor or by any other means. Organisations are now required to take a risk-based approach to determine the type and extent of controls appropriate to each external provider and all external provision of products and services.
8.7	Control of nonconforming processes	The *'control of nonconforming product'* now includes nonconforming processes as well as outputs and services.
10	Improvement	ISO have recognised that incremental (continuous) improvement is not the only *improvement* profile as improvement can also arise as a result of periodic breakthroughs, reactive change or reorganisation.

4.6 Are there any other significant changes?

- The wording now emphasises the need to consider the type and complexity of management system required, the needs and expectations of interested parties and associated management processes.
- Top management is now expected to demonstrate leadership and commitment and to engage, direct and support all of their organisation in contributing to the effectiveness of their Quality Management System.
- Much more emphasis has now been placed on planning and how to achieve quality objectives.
- Annex SL recognises the increased availability and use of modern business practices such as electronic systems and outsourcing.
- There is now more emphasis on products and services, the external provision of products and services, and external providers.
- An additional subclause has been introduced to cover the design and development of products and services.
- '*Outsourcing*' is now '*External Provision*'. This supersedes '*Purchasing*' and covers any '*external*' provision where external is outside the scope of the management system. An example is a traditional third-party supplier (or another organisation in the same group or company) if that organisation is not covered by the same scope as the purchasing organisation.
- Annex SL now includes the requirement that the QMSs of all organisations **shall** include a risk assessment process, well as one for a procedural gap analysis assessment

4.6.1 Risk-based thinking

AUTHOR'S HINT

Risk is the possibility of events or activities impeding the achievement of an organisation's strategic and operational objectives. The standard does not tell you what risk methodology you must adopt, and so you are free to decide on your own approach.

Risk-based thinking is probably **the** most important requirement of Annex SL, and the 2015 version of ISO 9001 makes the requirement for risk-based thinking explicit at certain points throughout the standard.

Once your organisation has highlighted the risks and opportunities in your product or service, you will then need to (see Figure 4.3):

- take into consideration these risks and opportunities when you plan your QMS;
- decide how and when these risks will have to be addressed (and, most importantly, by whom);
- define actions to manage risks and address opportunities.

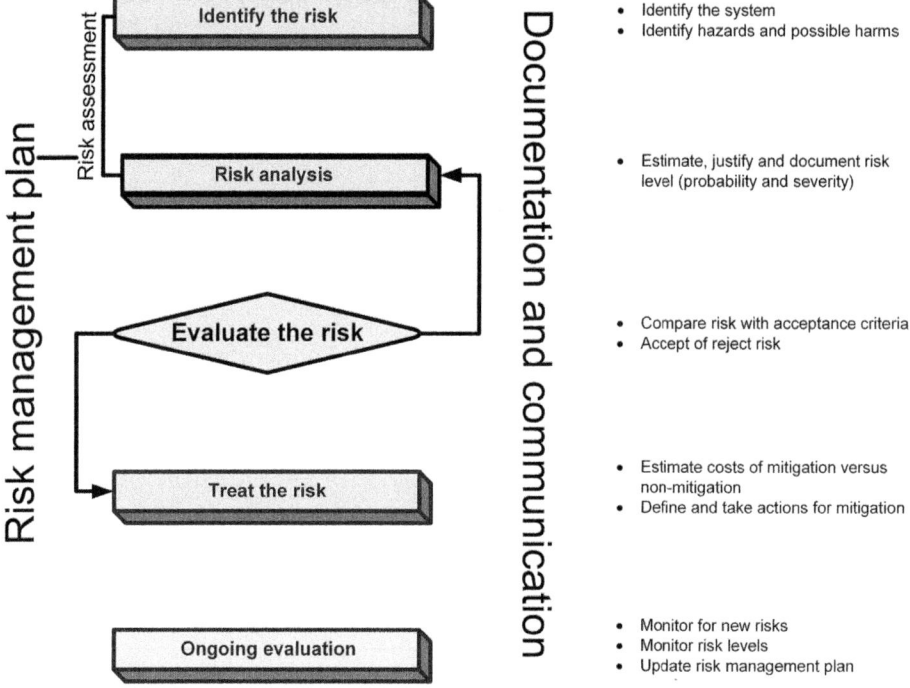

FIGURE 4.3   Risk analysis

All this might seem to be a huge change, but in reality it is something that you have, unknow-ingly, been doing automatically and often subconsciously! Indeed, the concept of risk has always been embedded in all Management System Standards; it is just that Annex SL makes it more explicit and builds it into the whole management system.

Risk is often only thought about in the negative sense but in reality, risk-based thinking can help to identify opportunities for improvement of not only products and services but also your overall Quality Management System. And so there is a very positive side of risk as it can not only improve customer confidence and satisfaction, it can also ensure consistency of qual-ity of goods and services and establish an organisation-wide proactive culture of prevention and improvement.

4.6.1.1 What are the benefits?

- By applying management system controls to risk analysis, you will minimize losses.
- Identify risk methods to find opportunities and therefore improve management systems and organisational resilience.
- Identify and minimize potential losses identified by threats and the use of a risk analysis process.
- Improve management system performance and resilience.
- Improve stakeholder confidence and trust through the use of risk techniques.
- Proactively improve operational efficiency and governance.
- Respond to change effectively and protect your business as you grow.

4.6.1.2 How do you start analysing risks and opportunities?

Risks affecting organisations can have consequences in terms of economic performance and professional reputation, as well as environmental, safety and societal outcomes. Therefore, managing risk effectively helps organisations to perform well in an environment full of uncertainty.

First, you will need to establish a process for identifying the risks and opportunities currently in your organisation. Then:

- analyse and prioritize the risks and opportunities in your organisation (i.e. What is acceptable? What is unacceptable?);
- plan actions to address the risks (i.e. How to avoid or eliminate the risk? How can I mitigate the risk?);
- implement the process or plan;
- check the effectiveness of the actions (i.e. Does it work?);
- learn from experience;
- adopt a process of continual improvement.

4.6.2 Gap analysis

AUTHOR'S HINT

Gap analysis can typically take anywhere from two to five days to perform depending on the size of your organisation, the number of auditors, the state of your current Quality Management System and the experience of your auditors.

Gap refers to the space between 'where you are' (i.e. the present state) and 'where we want to be' (the target state), whilst *gap analysis* involves the comparison of actual performance with potential or desired performance and helps a business understand and quantify the gaps that exist between its ideal future state and its present state.

By analysing these gaps, management can create specific action plans to move the organisation forward towards its goals and close the gaps identified in the gap analysis report. However, a gap analysis does *not* provide the action plan; it provides only the foundation of understanding necessary to create it.

A gap analysis may also be referred to as a 'needs analyses, 'needs assessment' or 'need-gap analyses'.

Gap analysis is more flexible than a SWOT (strengths, weaknesses, opportunities and threats) analysis (which typically follows a four-quadrant pattern) as gap analysis can be more quantitative or conceptual, using either Excel worksheets or flow charts. The analyst therefore has much more freedom in choosing what to focus on.

The basic components of a gap analysis audit is shown in Table 4.3.

TABLE 4.3 The 3 steps of gap analysis

Step 1 State descriptions		Step 2 Bridging the gap		Step 3 Factors and remedies	
Current state	Future state	Gap identification	Gap description	Factors responsible for the gap	Remedies, actions and proposals
ISO 9001:2008	ISO 9001:2015	Yes	Current QMS does not meet the requirements of ISO 9001:2015.	QMS is written in accordance with previous version of ISO 9001.	Quality manager will upgrade the current Quality Manual to comply with the requirements for ISO 9001:2015 and conduct a series of internal audits and training sessions.

4.6.2.1 How to conduct a gap analysis audit

Step 1: State descriptions

Current state – The first step is to conduct a gap analysis to establish specific target objectives by looking at the company's mission statement, strategic goals and improvement objectives. Your focus can be as wide (e.g. affects the whole organisation) or as narrow (e.g. a particular work procedure) as the objective demands. The analysis can be quantitative, qualitative or a bit of both. The key thing is that it has to be specific and factual with an emphasis on identifying weaknesses.

Future State – The future state represents the ideal condition you'd want your organisation to be in. This state can be highly specific (e.g. 'upgrade current QMS to meet the requirements of ISO 9001:2015') or generic ('create a Quality Procedure for Document Information).

Step 2: Bridging the gap

The next step is to identify and describe the gap so as to enable a remedy to be found.

Gap identification – The auditor needs to now record whether a gap exists between the current and future states by inserting a simple 'Yes' or 'No' (a full description of the gap will be made in the next column).

Gap description – The gap description should record all the elements that make up the gap between the current and future state. It can be qualitative ('*Current QMS does not meet the requirements of ISO 9001:2015*') or quantitative ('*need to order and distribute new, updated, copies of QP/6, QP/9 and WI/14*').

 AUTHOR'S HINT

Gap description is only meant (as it says on the tin) as a description and not a remedy!

Step 3: Factors and Remedies

Lastly, after an organisation has compared its target goals against its current state, it can then draw up a comprehensive plan that outlines specific steps to take in order to fill the gap between its current and future states and reach its target objectives.

> **Factors responsible for gap** – The auditor now needs to prepare a list of all the factors responsible for the gap identified in the previous column. This list should be specific, objective and relevant ('*QMS written in accordance with previous version of ISO 9001*').
>
> **Remedies, actions and proposals** – The final step in the gap analysis is to list all the possible remedies for bridging the gap between the current and ideal states. These remedies should directly address the factors listed in the previous column (e.g. '*QMS written in accordance with previous version of ISO 9001*'), and the remedies must be action oriented and specific ('*Quality Manager will upgrade the current Quality Manual to comply with the requirements for ISO 9001:2015 and conduct a series of Internal Audits and Training sessions*').

4.6.2.2 Typical Audit process

Figure 4.4 shows a very simplified procedure for conducting a gap analysis of an organisation's QMS against the requirements of ISO 9001:2015.

4.7 What is the current status of Annex SL revisions?

Over the last decade, there has been a gradual growth in the production of Management System Standards, and (using the ISO 2012 survey as an example) there were a total of 1.5 million certifications globally of which 1.1 million of these were made against ISO 9001. S any revision of ISO 9001 will have global implications based simply on numbers alone.

The year 2015 saw the global adoption of Annex SL and by setting up an identical high-level structure using identical clause titles and sequence of clause titles, text definitions, scope, common references, terms and definitions, organisational structure, leadership and planning support. ISO have ensured at least 30% commonality of text exists among **all** Management System Standards.

ISO described the introduction of Annex SL as '*the most important event since ISO 9001 was first published*', and its adoption has meant implications for **all** those using Management System Standards, be they standard writers, management system implementers, auditors or training providers.

In the past, external audits could become quite disruptive, but the increased commonality of requirements across standards has meant that there is now the potential for a change in the way that third-party assessments can be completed. For example, if an organisation normally has a health and safety audit in January, a quality management audit in May and an environmental management audit in September, they can now combine all of these into one single audit – thus saving time and money!

As stated by ISO Technical Committee No. 176 regarding ISO 9001:2015:

- The revised standard provides a stable, core set of requirements for the next ten years or more.
- Whilst the standard's requirements remain generic, they are now relevant to organisations of all types and sizes operating in any sector.

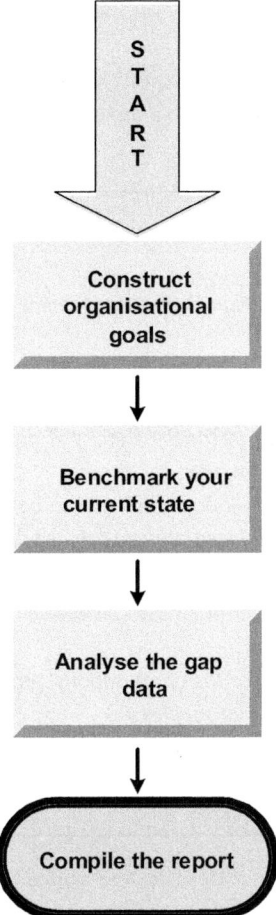

FIGURE 4.4 Gap analysis process

- While maintaining its current focus on effective process management, the standard also reflects the changes in quality management system practices and technology since the last major revision in 2000.
- By applying Annex SL, the revised standard improves compatibility and alignment with other ISO Management System Standards.
- ISO 9001:2015 improves implementation and conformity assessments for first, second and third parties.
- Using simplified language and writing styles, the new updated standard will help all stakeholders to understand and interpret key areas better.

Although ISO emphasise that Annex SL has made its associated management standards to be less of a series of '*requirement standards*' (except for standards like ISO 13485, which has to have some mandatory requirements because of patent safety), Annex SL, nevertheless, by introducing identical core text, has in turn led to 45 'shall' statements – generating

84 requirements with a knock-on effect to ISO 9001:2015, which now has over **130 'shall' requirements!**

The impact of this revision presents a major change for accreditation bodies, certification bodies, training organisations, implementing organisations, procurement organisations, consultants and customers.

CASE STUDY

Organisations may now have to align their management systems with the structure of the revised standard, for example:

- *a Quality Manual may no longer be required but at the very least, the associated processes, procedures and work instructions etc. will probably need to be amended and retained as documented information.*
- *a risk management process will probably need to be developed to determine the level and extent of control for the 'external provision of products and services' if not already in place.*

 This will have implications for the organisations' procurement and outsourcing activities and therefore has implications for suppliers.

Internal auditors will need to become familiar with the revised ISO 9001:2015 standard, and so training may need to be considered.

At first glance, Annex SL appears to make the standard writers lives much easier, but in reality, as organisations begin to understand and appreciate the value of different management systems all speaking a common language, it will be organisations – and in their turn, consumers – who stand to be the true beneficiaries.

So, with the introduction of this new Annex SL, the various ISO Technical Committees will have a lot to do! Having said that, with a harmonized structure, text, terms and definitions, this leaves the standard's developers with a certain amount of flexibility to incorporate their specific technical topics and requirements.

AUTHOR'S END NOTE

Now that you are aware of how standardisation first started and specifically how the various standards have developed over the past couple of hundred years – until we are now at the stage of having a common structure for all Management System Standards as depicted in Annex SL – the next stage is to see how Annex SL can be used by organisations.

As previously indicated, ISO 9001:2015 has been developed by ISO as a common template for all Quality Management System Standards seeking compliance with Annex SL. Many other standards replicate or are broadly based on ISO 9001:2015, but first we need to learn what the principles behind Annex SL are.

5

THE SEVEN PRINCIPLES OF QUALITY MANAGEMENT

 AUTHOR'S START NOTE

As previously shown, ISO 9001 has become the template for all Quality Management System Standards seeking compliance with Annex SL. So many other standards replicate or are broadly based on ISO 9001:2015. It is therefore quite possible that you might have come across some of these 'sons of ISO 9001' that might have had an impact on your organisation. This chapter provides a quick overview of the principles behind Annex SL.

Annex SL's requirements and recommendations for **all** current and future Quality Management Systems and other standards are based on seven quality management principles that are aimed at the continual improvement of an organisation's products and services. (See Figure 5.1) These requirements and recommendations:

- are designed to enable a continual improvement of the business and its overall efficiency;
- enable our organisation to respond to customer needs and expectations in a professional and capable manner;
- reflect best practice.

5.1 Customer focus

PRINCIPLE 1: CUSTOMER FOCUS

The primary focus of quality management is to meet customer requirements and to strive to exceed customer expectations.

(Annex SL)

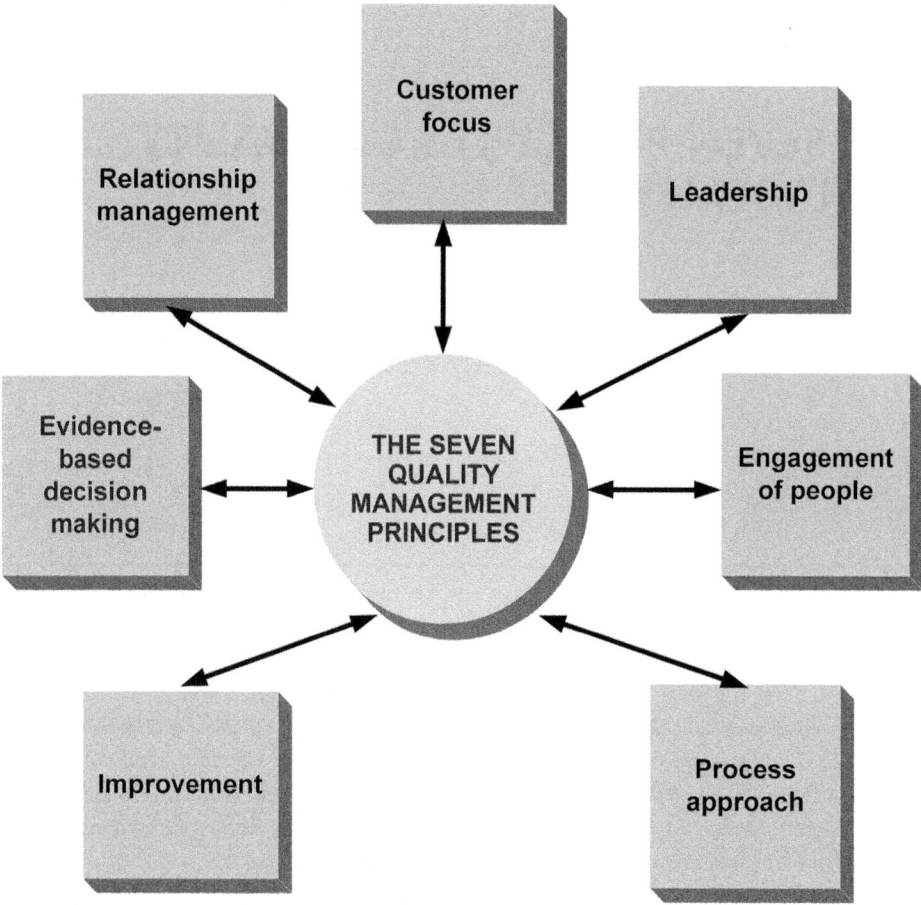

FIGURE 5.1 The seven quality management principles

- Organisations depend on their customers and therefore should understand current and future customers' needs, should meet their requirements and strive to exceed their expectations.

5.1.1 Key benefits

- Better use of the organisation's resources
- Enhanced customer satisfaction
- Flexible and fast response to market opportunities
- Improved customer loyalty
- Increased revenue and market share
- Repeat business

5.2 Leadership

PRINCIPLE 2: LEADERSHIP

Leaders at all levels establish unity of purpose and direction and create conditions in which people are engaged in achieving the quality objectives of the organization.

(Annex SL)

- Leadership is a core skill in today's business world. Without strong leadership, many good businesses fail – and so can management systems.
- Leaders create the environment in which people can become fully involved in achieving the organisation's objectives.
- Without the right support and direction for your organisation, you can't achieve your full potential.

5.2.1 Key benefits

- Better communication levels throughout the organisation
- Better understanding of the reasons for achieving the organisation's goals and objectives
- Evaluation of activities
- Minimising the possibilities for error

5.3 Engagement of people

PRINCIPLE 3: ENGAGEMENT OF PEOPLE

It is essential for the organization that all people are competent, empowered and engaged in delivering value.

(Annex SL)

- 'Employee engagement' should aim at ensuring that all employees are committed to their organisation's goals and values.
- People at all levels are the essence of an organisation, and their full involvement enables their abilities to be used for the organisation's benefit.

5.3.1 Key benefits

- Helping people to be motivated, committed and involved
- Inspiring people to continually improve on their organisation's objectives
- Making people accountable for their own performance
- Stimulating people to always aim for continual improvement

5.4 Process approach

PRINCIPLE 4: PROCESS APPROACH

Consistent and predictable results are achieved more effectively and efficiently when activities are understood and managed as interrelated processes that function as a coherent system.

(Annex SL)

- The logical sequencing of activities helps to efficiently achieve a desired result.
- A desired result is achieved more efficiently when activities and related resources are managed as a process.

5.4.1 Key benefits

- Lower costs and shorter cycle times
- Effective use of resources
- Improved, consistent and predictable results
- Focussed and prioritised opportunities for improvement

5.5 Improvement

PRINCIPLE 5: IMPROVEMENT

Successful organizations have an ongoing focus on improvement.

(Annex SL)

- It is essential for an organisation to maintain current levels of performance and to react to changes in its internal and external conditions in order to create new opportunities.
- The improvement of the organisation's Quality Management System and processes etc. should become a permanent objective of any organisation.

Put simply, it means **getting better all the time**.

5.5.1 Key benefits

- Coordination of all improvement possibilities and activities
- Improving the organisational capability
- Providing the flexibility to react to opportunities quickly

5.6 Evidence-based decision making

PRINCIPLE 6: EVIDENCE-BASED DECISION MAKING

Decisions based on the analysis and evaluation of data and information are more likely to produce desired results.

(Annex SL)

- Decision making based on the analysis of data should always be based on facts and evidence.
- Effective decisions are based on the logical and intuitive analysis of data and information.
- Reliable data gathered via planned measures is the only way this can be achieved.

5.6.1 Key benefits

- Ability to review, challenge and change opinions and decisions

5.7 Relationship management

PRINCIPLE 7: RELATIONSHIP MANAGEMENT

For sustained success, organizations manage their relationships with interested parties, such as suppliers.

(Annex SL)

- The mutual support of an organisation and its suppliers adds value.
- Mutually beneficial relationships between an organisation and its suppliers enhance the ability of both organisations to create value.
- Supplier/customer relationship should always be viewed as an interdependent relationship.

5.7.1 Key benefits

- The ability to react quickly to a changing market and/or customer needs and expectations
- Costs optimised
- Possibilities for creating value for both parties
- Resources used to their best advantage

5.8 Impact of these changes

Organisations may now have to align their existing management system with these management principles. For example (see Figure 5.2):

- The organisation's Quality Manual and its associated processes, procedures and work instructions etc. will probably need to be amended and retained as documented information.

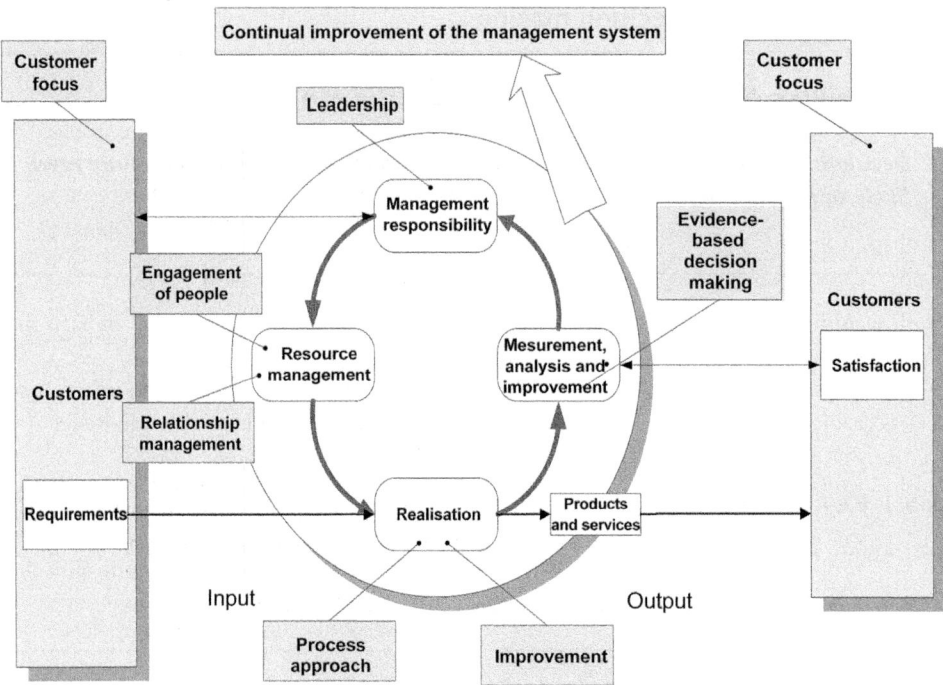

FIGURE 5.2 – A basic management systems process model with its seven management principles

- A risk management process, if not already in place, may need to be developed to determine the level and extent of control for the 'external provision of products and services'.

This will have implications for the organisation's procurement and outsourcing activities and therefore will have implications for suppliers.

- Internal auditors will need to become familiar with the revised standard(s), and so additional training may need to be considered.

6

DETAILED REQUIREMENTS FOR MANAGEMENT SYSTEMS

AUTHOR'S START NOTE

Although the following are definite requirements for an organisation seeking to gain certification to ISO 9001:2015, they need not necessarily apply to all and every Management System Standard (MSS). Many other standards only partially replicate or are broadly based on ISO 9001:2015, and others not only duplicate 9001's requirements but also include some additional obligations (for example, ISO 13485 for medical devices where patient safety is paramount).

As previously mentioned, although not officially referred to as a 'requirements standard', ISO Annex SL (as shown in its main Quality Management Standard – ISO 9001:2015) nevertheless contains 138 '*shalls*' and 2 '*shoulds*'.

'Shall' indicates a requirement, and 'should' indicates a recommendation.

Although the 138 are the main 'shall' requirements applicable to specific clauses within the standard, as most of the clauses have a series of sub-requirements within them (see the following example of clause 4.3), there will, of course be more than one particular aspect to look at.

ISO 9001:2015
Clause 4.3
'Determining the scope
  of the quality management
  system'

*'The organization shall determine the boundaries and applicability of
    the quality management system to establish its scope
When determining this scope, the organization shall consider:
a) the external and internal issues referred to in clause 4.1;
b) the requirements of relevant interested parties referred to in clause 4.2;
c) the products and services of the organization.'*

So, in reality, the 138 'shalls' become a total of **309** as shown and described in Figure 6.1 and Table 6.1.

AUTHOR'S HINT

Not all of these requirements are necessarily applicable to your own particular individual Management System Standard. So if you are seeking compliance to a specific MSS, it would be best to do a bit of background research first. [The British Standards website (https://shop. bsigroup.com/Navigate-by/Standards/) would be a good starting point.]

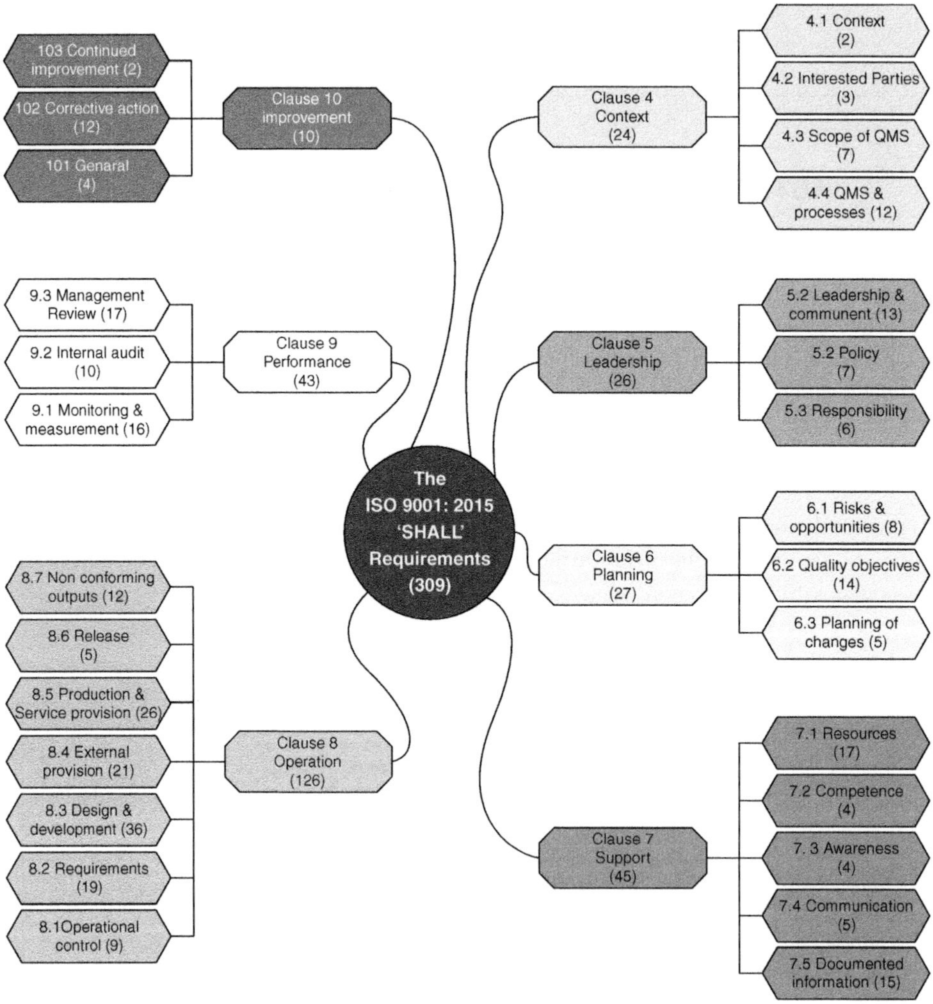

103 Continued improvement (2)

102 Corrective action (12)

101 Genaral (4)

Clause 10 improvement (10)

Clause 4 Context (24)

4.1 Context (2)

4.2 Interested Parties (3)

4.3 Scope of QMS (7)

4.4 QMS & processes (12)

9.3 Management Review (17)

9.2 Internal audit (10)

9.1 Monitoring & measurement (16)

Clause 9 Performance (43)

Clause 5 Leadership (26)

5.2 Leadership & communent (13)

5.2 Policy (7)

5.3 Responsibility (6)

The ISO 9001: 2015 'SHALL' Requirements (309)

Clause 6 Planning (27)

6.1 Risks & opportunities (8)

6.2 Quality objectives (14)

6.3 Planning of changes (5)

8.7 Non conforming outputs (12)

8.6 Release (5)

8.5 Production & Service provision (26)

8.4 External provision (21)

8.3 Design & development (36)

8.2 Requirements (19)

8.1Operational control (9)

Clause 8 Operation (126)

Clause 7 Support (45)

7.1 Resources (17)

7.2 Competence (4)

7. 3 Awareness (4)

7.4 Communication (5)

7.5 Documented information (15)

FIGURE 6.1 The mandatory "shall" requirements for management systems

6.1 Context of the organisation (Annex SL Section 4)

ISO 9001:2015 Management System Requirements

No	Clause	Requirement	Comment
4.1	**Understanding the organisation and its context**		
1	4.1	Determine external and internal issues relevant to the organisation's QMS.	Understand everything that can influence the purpose and strategic direction of the company (corporate culture, innovation, strategic direction, competition, market, compliance obligation).
2	4.1	Monitor and review information about issue.	To determine what one can gain or lose during an activity (factors, conditions)
4.2	**Understanding the needs and expectations of interested parties**		
3	4.2a	Identify the interested parties relevant to the organisation's QMS.	Determine whether your products and services are relevant to their type of business.
4	4.2b	Clarify the requirements of interested parties.	Each need and expectation is unique; aim for a partnership in the long term.
5	4.2	Monitor and review information about interested parties and their requirements.	This *must* be completed before accepting an order.
4.3	**Determining the scope of the Quality Management System**		
6	4.3	Define the scope of the QMS.	Geographic and organisational scope available to interested parties
7	4.3a	Take into account the external and internal issues.	To determine what one can gain or lose during an activity (factors, conditions)
8	4.3b	Take into account the requirements of interested parties.	Determine whether your products and services are relevant to their type of business.
9	4.3c	Take into account the products and services.	Review applicability of all products and services proposed by the company (without exception).
10	4.3	Apply any requirement of the ISO 9001 standard applicable within the scope of the QMS.	The requirements of the standard become internal requirements.
11	4.3	Maintain the scope of the QMS as documented information.	Including details of all products and services covered
12	4.3	Include in the scope of the QMS justification for any requirements that cannot be met.	Every requirement of the ISO 9001 standard that cannot be applied in the company implies a justification.
4.4	**Quality management system and its processes**		
13	4.4.1	Establish, implement, maintain and continually improve a process-based QMS.	Take into consideration the issues (see subclause 4.1) and requirements (see subclause 4.2) when deciding how to apply the QMS.
14	4.4.1	Determine the processes required for the QMS.	Process map

(Continued)

TABLE 6.1 (Continued)

ISO 9001:2015 Management System Requirements

No	Clause	Requirement	Comment
15	4.4.1a	Determine the process inputs and outputs.	Process sheet
16	4.4.1b	Determine the sequence and interaction of processes,	Flow chart
17	4.4.1c	Determine the criteria and methods needed to ensure the effective operation and control of these processes.	Tools of the Quality Manager
18	4.4.1d	Determine and ensure availability of the resources needed for these processes.	Identification of necessary resources
19	4.4.1e	Assign process responsibilities and authorities.	Job description of process owners
20	4.4.1f	Take into account the risks and opportunities for each process.	Plan and implement actions to address these relevant risks and opportunities.
21	4.4.1g	Evaluate processes and, if necessary, modify them so as to ensure that they achieve their intended results.	Identify methods to monitor, measure, check and modify processes.
22	4.4.1h	Determine the improvement opportunities of processes and the QMS.	Internal audit
23	4.4.2	Maintain documented information on process operation.	Process maps
24	4.4.2	Retain documented information on process operation.	The goal is to ensure that processes' results are those planned.

6.2 Leadership (Annex SL Section 5)

No	Clause	Requirement	Comment
5.1 Leadership and commitment			
5.1.1 General			
25	5.1.1a	Assume responsibility for the effectiveness of the QMS.	Top management demonstrates leadership (assumes its responsibility and commitment) by focussing on quality and customers.
26	5.1.1b	Establish a quality policy and quality objectives.	Ensuring that all policies and objectives are compatible with the strategic direction and context of the organisation
27	5.1.1c	Integrate QMS requirements in the internal process requirements.	Establish, implement, maintain and continually improve a process-based QMS.
28	5.1.1d	Raise awareness of the process approach and risk-based approach.	Take into account risks and opportunities.

29	5.1.1e	Provide the necessary resources for the QMS.	Ensuring the support of the QMS
30	5.1.1f	Raise awareness of the importance of an effective and conforming QMS.	Third quality management principle (engagement of people)
31	5.1.1g	Ensure the achievement of intended results of the QMS.	Essential commitment of Top Management
32	5.1.1h	Support the staff contribution to the effectiveness of the QMS.	Ensuring the effectiveness of the QMS
33	5.1.1i	Promote continual improvement.	Take into account the outputs of the analysis, evaluation and management review.
34	5.1.1j	Support the leadership of managers.	Responsibility and authority of managers are backed at all times by top management.

5.1.2 Customer focus

35	5.1.2a	Determine and meet customer, statutory and regulatory requirements.	Top management demonstrates leadership (i.e. assumes its responsibility and commitment) on a permanent basis.
36	5.1.2b	Determine and address the potential risks and opportunities.	Any risk and opportunity that may influence the conformity of products and services and customer satisfaction. Preserving the goal to always provide compliant products and services.
37	5.1.2c	Maintain the objective of better satisfying the customer.	First quality management principle (customer focus)

5.2 Policy
5.2.1 Establishing the quality policy

38	5.2.1a	Establish, implement and maintain a suitable quality policy.	Top management applies a policy adapted to the purpose, strategic direction, culture and business context.
39	5.2.1b	Provide a framework to define, and review the quality objectives.	Establish quality objectives for processes.
40	5.2.1c	Include a commitment to meet the applicable requirements.	Analyse and evaluate inspection data.
41	5.2.1d	Include a commitment to continuously improve the QMS.	Take into account the outputs of the analysis, evaluation and management review.

5.2.2 Communicating the quality policy

42	5.2.2a	Maintain the quality policy as documented information.	Documented information (e.g. quality procedures) to maintain the quality policy
43	5.2.2b	Communicate the quality policy.	So that it is understand and applied
44	5.2.2c	Keep the quality policy available.	The quality policy cannot be a confidential document and must be available to relevant interested parties.

5.3 Organisational roles, responsibilities and authorities

45	5.3	Assign and communicate the responsibilities and authorities.	Top management assigns all relevant roles in the QMS.
46	5.3a	Ensure that that the QMS conforms to the requirements of ISO 9001:2015.	Top management assigns all relevant roles according to the requirements of the standard.
47	5.3b	Ensure that the processes are delivering their intended outputs.	Top management assigns all relevant roles so that processes deliver expected results.

(Continued)

TABLE 6.2 (Continued)

No	Clause	Requirement	Comment
48	5.3c	Report on the performance of the QMS and opportunities for improvement.	Top management assigns all relevant roles so that reporting on the performance of the QMS and improvement opportunities is done.
49	5.3d	Promote customer focus throughout the organisation.	Top management assigns all relevant roles so that customer focus is ensured (first quality management principle).
50	5.3e	Maintain the integrity of the QMS when planned and implemented.	Top management assigns all relevant roles so that implemented changes to the QMS do not affect its integrity.

6.3 Planning (Annex SL Section 6)

No	Clause	Requirement	Comment
6.1 Actions to address risks and opportunities			
51	6.1.1a	Take into account risks and opportunities.	Ensure that the QMS can achieve its expected results.
52	6.1.1b	Take into account opportunities.	In order to increase the desirable effects (positive impact)
53	6.1.1c	Take into account risks.	In order to reduce to prevent or reduce undesirable effects (negative impacts)
54	6.1.1d	Take into account risks and opportunities.	In order to confirm the approach of continual improvement
55	6.1.2a	Plan actions to address risks and opportunities.	Take into account risks in every process.
56	6.1.2b1	Plan how to implement actions.	Define how to integrate actions in the QMS processes.
57	6.1.2b2	Plan how to evaluate actions.	Follow the results of each action.
58	6.1.2	Adapt actions to risks and opportunities.	Compare to the potential impact on the conformity of products and services.
6.2 Quality objectives and planning to achieve them			
59	6.2.1	Establish quality objectives for processes.	Provide a framework to define and review the quality objectives.
60	6.2.1a	Choose quality objectives.	Clarify criteria for setting objectives that are consistent with the quality policy.
61	6.2.1b	Use measurable objectives.	That are realistic.
62	6.2.1c	Consider applicable requirements.	Determine whether your products and services are relevant to their type of business.
63	6.2.1d	Adopt relevant objectives.	In order to ensure the conformity of products and services and improved customer satisfaction
64	6.2.1e	Monitor objectives.	Frequently
65	6.2.1f	Communicate on objectives.	At all levels

No	Clause	Requirement	Comment
66	6.2.1g	Update objectives.	During management review
67	6.2.1	Maintain documented information on the quality objectives.	Documented information (e.g. Quality Procedures)
68	6.2.2a	Plan how to achieve quality objectives	Determine what needs to be done.
69	6.2.2b	Plan necessary resources to achieve quality objectives.	Determine what resources are required.
70	6.2.2c	Plan responsibilities required to achieve quality objectives.	Determine and designate responsibilities.
71	6.2.2d	Plan deadlines in order to achieve quality objectives.	Determine and agree on completion dates.
72	6.2.2e	Plan the way to evaluate results.	In order to achieve quality objectives

6.3 Planning of changes

No	Clause	Requirement	Comment
73	6.3	Plan the need for changes to the QMS.	Establish, implement, maintain and continually improve a process-based QMS.
74	6.3 a	Plan these changes.	Taking into account the purpose of the change and the possible consequences
75	6.3 b	Plan these changes.	Taking into account the maintenance of the integrity of the QMS
76	6.3 c	Plan these changes.	Taking into account the available resources
77	6.3 d	Plan these changes.	Taking into account the assigned responsibilities and authorities

6.4 Support (Annex SL Section 7)

No	Clause	Requirement	Comment
7.1 Resources			
7.1.1 General			
78	7.1.1	Provide the necessary resources.	Ensuring the establishment, implementation, maintenance and continual improvement of the QMS
79	7.1.1a	Take into account existing resources.	Consideration of their capabilities and constraints
80	7.1.1b	Take into account the need for the use of external providers.	In order to provide necessary services not available inside the company
7.1.2 People			
81	7.1.2	Provide suitable people for the effective operation of the QMS and its processes.	Select suitably qualified personnel.
7.1.3 Infrastructure			
82	7.1.3	Provide and maintain the infrastructure necessary to the functioning of processes.	In order to achieve conformity of products and services (e.g. buildings, equipment, transportation, hardware, information technology)

(Continued)

TABLE 6.4 (Continued)

No	Clause	Requirement	Comment
7.1.4 Environment for the operation of processes			
83	7.1.4	Provide and maintain the suitable environment necessary to the functioning of processes.	Providing a combination of human and physical factors in order to achieve conformity of products and services (e.g. corporate culture, work atmosphere, temperature, ergonomics)
7.1.5 Monitoring and measuring resources			
7.1.5.1 General			
84	7.1.5.1	Provide suitable monitoring and measuring resources.	Sufficient to verify the conformity of products and services to requirements
85	7.1.5.1 a	Provide adequate resources to the specific inspections	To inspect and to monitor and measure
86	7.1.5.1 b	Maintain resources.	In order to ensure fitness for their purpose
87	7.1.5.1	Retain documented information on the adequacy of inspection resources.	Documented information (e.g. Quality Procedures) necessary for the effectiveness of these inspections
7.1.5.2 Measurement traceability			
88	7.1.5.2a	Verify or calibrate regularly the measuring equipment.	In order to have confidence in the measurement results (When no such standards exist, retain documented information on the reference used.)
89	7.1.5.2b	Identify the measuring equipment.	In order to monitor the validity of their calibration (or verification)
90	7.1.5.2c	Protect the measuring equipment.	Against activities that may invalidate the results of the measurement (settings or deterioration)
91	7.1.5.2	Conduct corrective action on previous measurement results.	When the verification or calibration of a measuring instrument is not in conformity
7.1.6 Organisational knowledge			
92	7.1.6	Determine the necessary knowledge necessary for the operation of its processes.	In order to control the processes and the conformity of products and services
93	7.1.6	Acquire, maintain and make organisational knowledge available to the extend necessary.	In order to maintain the performance of the QMS
94	7.1.6	Take into account the need for additional knowledge.	When needs and trends have changed
7.2 Competence			
95	7.2a	Determine the necessary competence of person(s) doing work.	Clarify quality competence requirements. Identify people who will have an influence on the quality of performance.

96	7.2b	Ensure that these persons are competent.	Based on appropriate training or experience
97	7.2c	Where applicable, undertake activities to acquire the necessary competence, and evaluate the effectiveness of these activities.	Training, coaching, external providers
98	7.2d	Retain documented information on staff competence.	Maintain documented information (e.g. quality records)

7.3 Awareness

99	7.3a	Ensure personnel are aware of the quality policy.	Including people who carry out work under the company's control
100	7.3b	Ensure personnel are aware of the quality objectives.	Maintain documented information (e.g. quality records)
101	7.3c	Ensure personnel are aware of their contribution to the effectiveness of the QMS.	In order to improve the performance of the QMS
102	7.3d	Ensure personnel are aware of the negative impacts on the effectiveness of the QMS.	Caused if QMS requirements are not met

7.4 Communication

103	7.4a	Define the subjects on which to communicate.	Both internal and external communication
104	7.4b	Define when to communicate.	Respond quickly to claims.
105	7.4c	Define with whom to communicate.	Communication goes both ways.
106	7.4d	Define how to communicate.	Orally, in writing, Internet, video
107	7.4e	Assign who will communicate.	The one who is closest to the subject

7.5 Documented information
7.5.1 General

108	7.5.1a	Include the documented information required by the ISO 9001 standard.	Documented information (e.g. Quality Procedures) to maintain: • scope of the QMS; • process control; • quality policy; • quality objectives; • operational control. Documented information (i.e. Quality Records) to retain: • process performance; • fitness for purpose of inspection resources; • calibration; • staff competence;

(Continued)

TABLE 6.4 (Continued)

No	Clause	Requirement	Comment
			• effectiveness of the QMS;
			• achieving processes as planned, conformity of products and services;
			• results of the review of products' and services' old and new requirements;
			• design and development inputs;
			• design and development expected results, reviews, verifications and validations;
			• design and development outputs;
			• design and development changes;
			• evaluation activities and actions of external providers;
			• product and service characteristics or activities to be performed, results to be achieved;
			• traceability of products and services;
			• situation of the property of a customer;
			• results of the review of changes;
			• release of products and services;
			• treatment of nonconforming products and services;
			• inspection results;
			• audit programme and audit results;
			• management review outputs;
			• nonconformities, actions and results,
109	7.5.1b	Select the documented information deemed necessary to the effectiveness of the QMS.	Retain documented information (e.g. Quality Processes and Procedures) in a secure environment.
7.5.2 Creating and updating			
110	7.5.2a	Create, identify and describe the documented information.	Codification, title, author, subject, product
111	7.5.2b	Choose the format and the media of the documented information.	Language, graphics; paper, electronic
112	7.5.2c	Review and approve the adequacy of the documented information.	Who writes, codifies; who approves
7.5.3 Control of documented information			
113	7.5.3.1a	Control the availability of the documented information.	Where and when required in a form that is suitable for use

No	Clause	Requirement	Comment
114	7.5.3.1b	Control the protection of the documented information.	Loss of confidentiality, loss of integrity, misuse
115	7.5.3.2a	Control the distribution, access and use of the documented information.	Who is in charge, method to use, rule to follow
116	7.5.3.2b	Control the storage of the documented information.	Including preservation, protection and readability
117	7.5.3.2c	Control the changes of the documented information.	Use of updated versions, restricted access to obsolete versions
118	7.5.3.2d	Control the retention time and the removal of the documented information.	Retention period, disposal method
119	7.5.3.2	Control the documented information of external origin.	Unique codification, access, protection
120	7.5.3.2	Protect the documented information.	Who has the right to read; who has the right to change

6.5 Operation (Annex SL Section 8)

No	Clause	Requirement	Comment
8.1 Operational planning and control			
121	8.1a	Plan and determine the requirements for the products and services.	Develop documented information (e.g. Quality Procedure) to maintain a controlled process.
122	8.1b1	Establish the criteria for processes.	Using documented information (e.g. Quality Procedure)
123	8.1b2	Establish the criteria for the acceptance of conforming products and services.	Using documented information (e.g. Quality Procedure)
124	8.1c	Determine necessary resources.	Availability of resources to achieve conformity of products and services
125	8.1d	Control the processes.	Using existing documented information
126	8.1e1	Determine, maintain and retain the documented information on process control.	As detailed in the organisation's QMS
127	8.1e2	Determine, maintain and retain the documented information on product and service conformity.	As detailed in the organisation's QMS
128	8.1	Control planned and unplanned changes.	Analyse the consequences of unplanned changes, actions to limit the effects.
129	8.1	Control the outsourced processes.	As detailed in the organisation's QMS

(Continued)

TABLE 6.5 (Continued)

No	Clause	Requirement	Comment
8.2	**Requirements for products and services**		
8.2.1	**Customer communication**		
130	8.2.1a	Provide information to customers relating to products and services.	As detailed in the organisation's QMS
131	8.2.1b	Control communication with customers.	Related to contracts, orders, changes and consultations
132	8.2.1c	Control communication with customers.	Regarding the perception, opinions, complaints and recommendations
133	8.2.1d	Control communication with customers.	Regarding handling or controlling customer property
134	8.2.1e	Control communication with customers.	Regarding specific requirements for contingency actions
8.2.2	**Determining the requirements related to products and services**		
135	8.2.2a1	Develop specific activities for products and services.	In order to clarify statutory and regulatory requirements
136	8.2.2a2	Define internal requirements.	Related to processes, products and services. And check that the requirements can be met.
137	8.2.2b	Be able to respond to claims.	In a relevant way (with facts)
8.2.3	**Review of requirements related to products and services**		
138	8.2.3.1	Be able to respond to customers.	Regarding requirements of proposed products and services
139	8.2.3.1a	Review explicit customer requirements.	Before order acceptance, including delivery and post-delivery activities requirements
140	8.2.3.1b	Review implicit customer requirements.	Before order acceptance; unformulated requirements but necessary for specified use or use intended by the customer
141	8.2.3.1c	Review internal requirements.	Between requirements of an order and those previously expressed
142	8.2.3.1d	Review statutory and regulatory requirements.	Applicable to the products and services
143	8.2.3.1e	Review gaps.	Between requirements of an order (or contract) and those previously expressed
144	8.2.3.1	Resolve gaps.	Before order acceptance and commitment to provide products and services
145	8.2.3.1	Confirm requirements before accepting an order.	When requirements are not documented
146	8.2.3.2a	Retain the documented information on the results of the reviews of requirements.	As detailed in the organisation's QMS
147	8.2.3.2b	Retain the documented information on any new or changed requirement for the products and services.	As detailed in the organisation's QMS

8.2.4 Changes to requirements for products and services

148	8.2.4	Communicate changes to relevant persons.
		After changing requirements in the documented information

8.3 Design and development of products and services

8.3.1 General

149	8.3.1	Establish, implement and maintain a process of design and development.
		When the product or service requirements have not previously been defined

8.3.2 Design and development planning

150	8.3.2a	Plan the design and development stages.	Taking into account the specificity of design and development activities
151	8.3.2b	Plan the design and development stages.	Taking into account the process requirements and applicable reviews
152	8.3.2c	Plan the design and development stages.	Taking into account the verification and validation activities
153	8.3.2d	Plan the design and development stages.	Taking into account the necessary responsibilities and authorities
154	8.3.2e	Plan the design and development stages.	Taking into account the needs of internal and external resources
155	8.3.2f	Plan the design and development stages.	Taking into account relationship between persons participating in the design and development
156	8.3.2g	Plan the design and development stages.	Taking into account the need for involvement of customers and users
157	8.3.2h	Plan the design and development stages.	Taking into account the requirements for subsequent products and services
158	8.3.2 i	Plan the design and development stages	Taking into account the level of control expected by interested parties
159	8.3.2 j	Plan the design and development stages	Taking into account the documented information meeting design and development requirements.

8.3.3 Design and development inputs

160	8.3.3	Determine essential requirements.	For specific types of products and services from design and development
161	8.3.3a	Determine functional requirements.	Taking into account also the performance requirements
162	8.3.3b	Clarify inputs.	Taking into account the information from similar activities
163	8.3.3c	Clarify inputs.	Taking into account the statutory and regulatory requirements
164	8.3.3d	Clarify inputs.	Taking into account the corporate culture, internal rules of art
165	8.3.3e	Clarify inputs.	Taking into account the potential consequences of product and service failure
166	8.3.3	Check that the input items are complete and unambiguous.	In order to realise suitable design and development process
167	8.3.3	Resolve potential conflicts between inputs.	In order to obtain complete and unambiguous inputs
168	8.3.3	Retain the documented information on design and development inputs.	As detailed in the organisation's QMS

(*Continued*)

TABLE 6.5 (Continued)

No	Clause	Requirement	Comment
8.3.4	**Design and development controls**		
169	8.3.4a	Define clearly the expected results.	Regarding processes, products and services
170	8.3.4.b	Conduct reviews as planned.	Regarding processes, products and services
171	8.3.4.c	Check that outputs meet input requirements.	Using an agreed verification procedure
172	8.3.4.d	Validate products and services.	To ensure that the specified application requirements or those for the intended use are satisfied
173	8.3.4.e	Take actions in response to identified problems.	During reviews, verifications and validations
174	8.3.4.f	Ensure that the documented information is retained.	As detailed in the organisation's QMS
8.3.5	**Design and development outputs**		
175	8.3.5.a	Ensure that outputs meet input requirements.	Using an agreed verification procedure
176	8.3.5b	Ensure that outputs are in line with the subsequent processes.	Regarding the products and services
177	8.3.5c	Ensure that outputs include monitoring and measuring requirements.	Including acceptance criteria
178	8.3.5d	Ensure that outputs are suitable for their intended use.	Proper use or planned by the customer in complete safety
179	8.3.5	Retain the documented information on outputs.	As detailed in the organisation's QMS
8.3.6	**Design and development changes**		
180	8.3.6	Identify, review and control the changes made to inputs and outputs.	To ensure that the changes have no impact on meeting the requirements.
181	8.3.6a	Retain the documented information on changes.	As detailed in the organisation's QMS.
182	8.3.6b	Retain the documented information on results of reviews.	As detailed in the organisation's QMS.
183	8.3.6c	Retain the documented information on who authorised the changes.	As detailed in the organisation's QMS.
184	8.3.6d	Retain the documented information on actions.	In order to prevent negative impacts.
8.4	**Control of externally provided processes, products and services**		
8.4.1	**General**		
185	8.4.1	Ensure that the outputs of external providers meet specified requirements	Externally provided processes, products and services shall be subject to regular auditing
186	8.4.1a	Apply the requirements for the control of products and services from external providers	When the products and services are integrated internally
187	8.4.1b	Apply the requirements for the control of products and services	When the products and services are provided directly to the customers by external providers on behalf of the organisation

188	8.4.1c	Apply the requirements for the control of process done by external providers.	When a decision has been made to outsource the process
189	8.4.1	Establish and implement evaluation and selection criteria of external providers and monitor their performance.	Including regular re-evaluation
190	8.4.1	Retain the documented information on the results of the evaluation and monitoring.	As detailed in the organisation's QMS

8.4.2 Type and extent of control

191	8.4.2	Ensure the level of control of external providers on meeting the requirements.	In order that the provision of external providers do not affect the conformity of products and services delivered to the customer
192	8.4.2a	Ensure that the processes of external providers are controlled.	Any outsourced process is included in the scope of the organisation's QMS.
193	8.4.2b	Define how to control the external provider and its process outputs.	The level of control (or influence) of an external service provider should be suitably applied.
194	8.4.2c1	Take into account the potential impact of the outputs of the external provider.	On meeting the requirements of products and services delivered to the customer and on statutory and regulatory requirements
195	8.4.2c2	Take into account the control of the external provider.	And effectiveness of this control
196	8.4.2d	Define how to control the outputs of externally provided processes.	Verification and other activities necessary to ensure that the provision of external providers does not affect the conformity of products and services delivered to the customer

8.4.3 Information for external providers

197	8.4.3	Check the adequacy of the requirements.	Prior to their being communicated to the external provider
198	8.4.3a	Communicate requirements to the external provider.	Regarding the processes, products and services to be provide
199	8.4.3b1	Communicate requirements to the external provider.	Regarding the approval of products and services
200	8.4.3b2	Communicate requirements to the external provider.	Regarding the approval of methods, processes and equipment
201	8.4.3b3	Communicate requirements to the external provider.	Regarding the approval of the release of products and services
202	8.4.3c	Communicate requirements to the external provider.	Regarding the competence (including required qualifications)
203	8.4.3 d	Communicate requirements to the external provider.	Regarding the relations between the external provider and the company
204	8.4.3 e	Communicate requirements to the external provider.	Regarding the control and monitoring of the external provider's performance
205	8.4.3f	Communicate requirements to the external provider.	Regarding the verification or validation activities that the company or its customer intends to realise at the external provider's premises

8.5 Production and service provision
8.5.1 Control of production and service provision

206	8.5.1	Apply controlled conditions of production and service provision.	Including delivery and post-delivery activities

(Continued)

TABLE 6.5 (Continued)

No	Clause	Requirement	Comment
207	8.5.1a1	Save documented information of specifications of products and services and the expected activities.	As detailed in the organisation's QMS
208	8.5.1a2	Save the documented information of results to be achieved.	As detailed in the organisation's QMS
209	8.5.1.b	Include in the controlled conditions the inspection resources.	As well as the availability and use of suitable monitoring and measuring resources
210	8.5.1.c	Include in the controlled conditions the inspection activities.	To verify that the appropriate stages of the processes' outputs meet the criteria
211	8.5.1.d	Include in the controlled conditions adequate infrastructure and environment.	Ensuring that they are adequate for the operation of the organisation's processes
212	8.5.1.e	Include in the controlled conditions the staff competence.	Including the necessary qualifications
213	8.5.1.f	Include in the controlled conditions the validation of the ability of a process to achieve the expected results.	Only in the case when the outputs cannot be checked post-verification
214	8.5.1.g	Include in the controlled conditions the actions to prevent human error.	As detailed in the organisation's QMS
215	8.5.1.h	Include in the controlled conditions the activities of release, delivery and post-delivery.	As detailed in the organisation's QMS

8.5.2 Identification and traceability

No	Clause	Requirement	Comment
216	8.5.2	Use appropriate means to control the unique identification of process outputs.	In order to ensure the conformity of products and services when needed
217	8.5.2	Inspect processes throughout the production and service provision.	In order to identify the status of process outputs
218	8.5.2	Control the traceability of process outputs.	When traceability is a requirement, the unique identification is used
219	8.5.2	Retain the documented information on traceability.	As detailed in the organisation's QMS

8.5.3 Property belonging to customers or external providers

No	Clause	Requirement	Comment
220	8.5.3	Exercise care with property owned by customer or external provider.	Whilst being used or stored by the organisation
221	8.5.3	Identify, check, protect, monitor and safeguard customer and/or external provider property.	As detailed in the organisation's QMS
222	8.5.3	Notify the customer (or external provider) if their property has been damaged or lost.	As detailed in the organisation's QMS

8.5.4 Preservation

No	Clause	Requirement	Comment
223	8.5.4	Preserve the process outputs throughout production and service provision activities.	Some examples of preservation methods: identification, packaging, handling, storage, transport, protection

8.5.5 Post-delivery activities

224	8.5.5	Meet the requirements for post-delivery activities.	Examples of post-delivery activities: exchange new product, maintenance, recycling, final disposal
225	8.5.5a	Take into account statutory and regulatory requirements.	When determining the extent of post-delivery activities that are required
226	8.5.5b	Take into account negative impacts related to products and services.	These are consequences of potential risks.
227	8.5.5c	Take into account the nature, the intended use and lifetime of products and services.	When the extent of post-delivery activities has been clarified
228	8.5.5d	Take into account the requirements of interested parties.	Particularly with respect to customers
229	8.5.5e	Take into account customer feedback.	Of interested parties, when the extent of post-delivery activities has been clarified

8.5.6 Control of changes

230	8.5.6	Review and control unplanned changes.	to the extent necessary to ensure continuing conformity with requirements
231	8.5.6	Retain the documented information on unplanned changes.	Including the results of reviews, the authorisation of changes and actions implemented

8.6 Release of products and services

232	8.6	Check products and services with activities at appropriate stages.	Document and implement planned arrangements at appropriate stages.
233	8.6	Release products and services after verification of conformity.	Unless written approval (concession) by a competent authority or client
234	8.6	Retain the documented information on the release of products and services.	As detailed in the organisation's QMS
235	8.6a	Include in the documented information evidence of conformity.	The results of inspections compared to the acceptance criteria
236	8.6b	Include in the documented information the traceability of products and services.	Including details of the person having authorised the release of the product or service

8.7 Control of nonconforming outputs

237	8.7.1	Identify and treat nonconforming process, products and services outputs.	Marking and isolation to prevent unintended use or mixing with conforming outputs
238	8.7.1	Carry out corrective actions commensurate to impacts.	Including after delivery
239	8.7.1	Carry out corrective actions on post-delivery activities.	As detailed in the organisation's QMS
240	8.7.1a	Handle nonconforming outputs with corrections.	Repeat work, retouching, repair, recycling

(Continued)

TABLE 6.5 (Continued)

No	Clause	Requirement	Comment
241	8.7.1b	Handle nonconforming outputs by segregation.	Including containment, return or suspension of provision of products and services
242	8.7.1c	Inform the customer	Verbally and in writing
243	8.7.1d	Handle nonconforming outputs by asking authorisation.	To accept under concession)
244	8.7.1	Check conformity after any correction.	After any correction go through the normal flow
245	8.7.2a	Retain the documented information on the description of nonconformities.	As detailed in the organisation's QMS
246	8.7.2b	Retain the documented information on implemented actions.	As detailed in the organisation's QMS
247	8.7.2c	Retain the documented information on approved concessions.	As detailed in the organisation's QMS
248	8.7.2d	Retain the documented information on the person having decided the handling of the nonconformities.	As detailed in the organisation's QMS

6.6 Performance evaluation (Annex SL Section 9)

No	Clause	Requirement	Comment
9.1 Monitoring, measurement, analysis and evaluation			
9.1.1 General			
249	9.1.1a	Determine what is necessary to inspect.	What needs to be monitored and measured
250	9.1.1b	Determine the methods for inspection, analysis and evaluation.	In order to ensure valid results
251	9.1.1c	Determine when to inspect.	At key stages or upon the customer's request
252	9.1.1d	Determine when to analyse and evaluate inspection results.	When the analyses and evaluation brings added value
253	9.1.1	Evaluate the performance and effectiveness of the QMS.	In order to ensure that specified requirements are met
254	9.1.1	Retain the documented information on the inspection results.	As detailed in the organisation's QMS
9.1.2 Customer satisfaction			
255	9.1.2	Regularly monitor customer perception about their level of satisfaction.	As detailed in the organisation's QMS

256	9.1.2	Determine methods for obtaining and using customer information.	Satisfaction surveys, claims, customer returns, recommendations

9.1.3 Analysis and evaluation

257	9.1.3	Analyse and evaluate inspection data.	Establish quality objectives for processes
258	9.1.3a	Use analysis results.	To evaluate how requirements are met
259	9.1.3b	Use analysis results.	To evaluate the level of customer satisfaction
260	9.1.3c	Use analysis results.	To evaluate the performance and effectiveness of the QMS
261	9.1.3d	Use analysis results.	To evaluate the effectiveness of planning
262	9.1.3e	Use analysis results.	To evaluate the effectiveness of actions implemented to address risks and opportunities
263	9.1.3 f	Use analysis results.	To evaluate the performance of external providers
264	9.1.3 g	Use analysis results.	To evaluate the improvement opportunities of the QMS

9.2 Internal audit

265	9.2.1a1	Conduct regularly planned internal audits.	In order to determine whether the QMS meets internal company requirements
266	9.2.1a2	Conduct regularly planned internal audits.	In order to determine whether the QMS meets requirements of the ISO 9001 standard
267	9.2.1b	Conduct regularly planned internal audits.	In order to determine whether the QMS is effectively implemented and maintained
268	9.2.2a	Plan, establish, implement and update an audit programme.	Include the frequency, methods, responsibilities, planning requirements (audit programme) and reporting requirements (audit report)
269	9.2.2a	Take into consideration the programme's essential points during an audit.	Essentials points: • process importance; • changes having an impact on the company; • results of previous audits.
270	9.2.2b	Define the scope and audit criteria.	Limit the area to be audited; use specific and known by the auditee criteria.
271	9.2.2c	Select auditors.	Do not audit your own department.
272	9.2.2d	Communicate audit results to management concerned.	Ensure that all results are adequately covered.
273	9.2.2e	Undertake a correction quickly and corrective actions if necessary.	As detailed in the organisation's QMS
274	9.2.2f	Retain the documented information on the audit programme and the audit reports.	As detailed in the organisation's QMS

(Continued)

TABLE 6.6 (Continued)

No	Clause	Requirement	Comment
9.3 Management review			
9.3.1 General			
275	9.3.1	Review of the organisation's QMS at planned intervals.	In order to confirm that it is still relevant, appropriate and effective
9.3.2 Management review inputs			
276	9.3.2a	Plan and carry out the management review.	Regarding the status of actions of the previous review
277	9.3.2b	Carry out the management review taking into account the changes of external and internal issues for the QMS.	Including strategic direction
278	9.3.2c1	Take into account the information on the performance of the QMS and trends.	Paying particular attention to customer satisfaction reports and feedback
279	9.3.2c2	Take into account the information on the performance of the QMS and trends.	The achievement of quality objectives
280	9.3.2 c 3	Take into account the information on the performance of the QMS and trends.	Process performance and conformity of outputs
281	9.3.2 c 4	Take into account the information on the performance of the QMS and trends.	Nonconformities and corrective actions
282	9.3.2c5	Take into account the information on the performance of the QMS and trends.	Inspection results
283	9.3.2c6	Take into account the information on the performance of the QMS and trends.	Audit results
284	9.3.2 c 7	Take into account the information on the performance of the QMS and trends.	Performance of external providers
285	9.3.2d	Take into account resources	Availability of resources
286	9.3.2e	Take into account the effectiveness of actions.	Implemented to address risks and opportunities
287	9.3.2f	Take into account improvement opportunities.	Continual improvement
9.3.3 Management review outputs			
288	9.3.3a	Include decisions regarding opportunities for continual improvement in the outputs of the management review.	Aim to continually improve the performance of the QMS.
289	9.3.3b	Include decisions regarding eventual changes to the QMS in the outputs of the management review.	Plan the need for changes to the QMS.
290	9.3.3c	Include decisions regarding new resource needs in the outputs of the management review.	Provide the necessary resources.
291	9.3.3	Retain the documented information on outputs of the review of management.	Include the documented information required by the ISO 9001 standard.

6.7 Improvement (Annex SL Section 10)

No	Clause	Requirement	Comment
10.1	**General**		
292	10.1	Find improvement opportunities, and implement necessary actions.	In order to enhance customer satisfaction
293	10.1a	Improve products and services.	Support innovation in order to better meet current requirements and anticipate future requirements.
294	10.1b	Reduce negative impacts.	Implementing corrective actions and global prevention (efficient QMS)
295	10.1c	Improve the results of the QMS.	To achieve the objectives of the QMS regarding performance
10.2	**Nonconformity and corrective action**		
296	10.2.1a1	React to the nonconformity.	In order to reduce costs, including all claims by processing, controlling, correcting
297	10.2.1a2	Take into account consequences.	Think risk-based approach.
298	10.2.1b1	Examine the nonconformity.	And if necessary decide to carry out a corrective action
299	10.2.1b2	Investigate root causes.	So that the nonconformity does not happen again
300	10.2.1b3	Search for similar nonconformities.	As detailed in the organisation's QMS
301	10.2.1c	Implement the necessary corrective actions.	In order to treat the nonconformity
302	10.2.1d	Review the effectiveness of corrective actions.	In order to check whether the action is finalised
303	10.2.1e	Update risks and opportunities.	If necessary
304	10.2.1f	Make changes to the QMS.	If necessary
305	10.2.1	Respond proportionally to nonconformities consequences.	As necessary
306	10.2.2a	Retain documented information on the nature of nonconformities.	As detailed in the organisation's QMS
307	10.2.2a	Retain documented information on results of implemented actions.	As detailed in the organisation's QMS
10.3	**Continual improvement**		
308	10.3	Continually improve suitability, adequacy and effectiveness.	In accordance with the requirements of ISO 9001:2015
309	10.3	Take into account the outputs of the analysis, evaluation and management review.	Ensuring the effectiveness of the QMS and a commitment to continuously improve it

7

THE INTEROPERABILITY OF MANAGEMENT SYSTEM STANDARDS

 AUTHOR'S START NOTE

As previously shown, ISO 9001 has become the template for all Quality Management System Standards seeking compliance with Annex SL. So many other standards replicate or are broadly based on ISO 9001:2015. It is therefore quite possible that you might have come across some of these 'sons of ISO 9001', which might have had an impact on your organisation. I have included the following chapter about the background to the ones that I have come across as of the time of writing this book.

During the last decade, reliance on the ISO 9000 series of quality standards has become a growing trend worldwide, with not just large multinationals seeking registration to ISO 9001 but also an increasing number of small and medium-sized enterprises (SMEs).

Indeed, **small** American companies, although not as quick to jump on the bandwagon as their General Motors–type counterparts, have benefitted from working in compliance with ISO 9001. Definitely (according to a recent McGraw–Hill study), of all those companies registered since 2008, over 65% have been able to recover their ISO 9000 implementation costs in three years or less. Consequently, America has now become one of the world leaders of ISO 9001:2015 SME registered companies.

ISO and ANSI have always worked closely together in producing interpretative standards for both sides of the so-called pond, and previous versions of ISO 9000 standards have been frequently used as the generic template for other industry **Management System Standards**. Currently, although a number of these other national (both American and European) industry management standards are still available, they are all gradually being rewritten (using the same Annex SL structure, format, terminology etc.) around the requirements and recommendations of ISO 9001:2015.

AUTHOR'S HINT

In many cases, it may even be possible for an organisation to adapt an existing management system so that it can establish a QMS that complies with the requirements of ISO 9001:2015. For example, a company designing, producing and installing a medical device, such as a pacemaker for implanting into someone's chest, would normally require registration with both ISO 13485 for medical devices and ISO 9001 for quality management – as it could involve 'patient safety' – and, in doing so, they would probably have two separate (but similar) QMSs. By upgrading both of their existing QMSs to the ISO 9001:2015 format, the organisation would then have only one QMS, making quality management much simpler and (assuming that the organisation was certified to these standards) would require only **one** audit, thereby saving manpower and, most importantly, cash.

At the time of writing, 33 MSSs follow the requirements of Annex SL or are sector specific. A further 26 MSSs are under development.

As I have previously mentioned, management systems will follow Annex SL's structure, as shown in ISO 9001:2015. However, within Annex SL's clauses, a number of subclauses differ according to a particular topic, and an example of this is shown in Table 7.1, where I have compared the ISO standards for Environmental Management Systems (ISO 14001:2015) and Occupational Health and Safety Management Systems (ISO 45001:2018) against ISO 9001:2015 for Quality Management.

 The additions and/or modified wordings are in italics

TABLE 7.1 Differences between Quality, Environmental, Occupational Health and Safety (OH&S) Management Systems

Clause number	ISO 9001:2015 Quality Management	ISO 14001:2015 Environmental Management	ISO 45001:2018 Occupational Health and Safety Management
4	**Context of the organisation**	**Context of the organisation**	**Context of the organisation**
4.1	Understanding the organisation and its context	Understanding the organisation and its context	Understanding the organisation and its context
4.2	Understanding the needs and expectations of interested parties	Understanding the needs and expectations of interested parties	Understanding the needs and expectations of interested parties

(Continued)

TABLE 7.1 (Continued)

Clause number	ISO 9001:2015 Quality Management	ISO 14001:2015 Environmental Management	ISO 45001:2018 Occupational Health and Safety Management
4.3	Determining the scope of the *Quality* Management System	Determining the scope of the *Environment* management system	Determining the scope of the *OH&S* management system
4.4	*Quality* management system *and its processes*	*Environment* management system	*OH&S* management system
5	**Leadership**	**Leadership**	**Leadership *and worker participants***
5.1	Leadership and commitment	Leadership and commitment	Leadership and commitment
	5.1.1 General	–	–
	5.1.2 Customer focus	–	–
5.2	Policy	*Environmental* policy	*OH&S* policy
	5.2.1 Establishing the quality policy	–	–
	5.2.2 Communication quality policy	–	–
5.3	Organisational roles, responsibilities and authorities	Organisational roles, responsibilities and authorities	Organisational roles, responsibilities, *accountabilities* and authorities
5.4	–	–	Participation and consultation
6	**Planning**	**Planning**	**Planning**
6.1	Actions to address risks and opportunities	Actions to address risks and opportunities	Actions to address risks and opportunities
	–	*6.1.1 General*	*6.1.1 General*
	–	*6.1.2 Environmental aspects*	*6.1.2 Hazard identification and assessment of OH&S risks*
	–	*6.1.3 Compliance obligations*	*6.1.3 Determination of applicable legal requirements*
	–	*6.1.4 Planning action*	*6.1.4 Planning to take action*
6.2	*Quality* objectives and planning to achieve them	*Environmental* objectives and planning to achieve them	*OH&S* objectives and planning to achieve them
6.3	*Planning of changes*	–	–
7	**Support**	**Support**	**Support**
7.1	Resources	Resources	Resources
	7.1.1 General	–	–
	7.1.2 People	–	–
	7.1.3 Infrastructure	–	–
	7.1.4 Environment for the operation of processes	–	–
	7.1.5 Monitoring and measuring resources	–	–

Clause number	ISO 9001:2015 Quality Management	ISO 14001:2015 Environmental Management	ISO 45001:2018 Occupational Health and Safety Management
	7.1.6 Organisational knowledge	–	–
7.2	Competence	Competence	Competence
7.3	Awareness	Awareness	Awareness
7.4	Communication	Communication	Information and communication
	–	*7.4.1 General*	–
	–	*7.4.2 Internal communication*	–
	–	*7.4.3 External communication*	–
7.5	Documented information	Documented information	Documented information
	7.5.1 General	7.5.1 General	7.5.1 General
	7.5.2 Creating and updating	7.5.2 Creating and updating	7.5.2 Creating and updating
	7.5.3 Control of documented information	7.5.3 Control of documented information	7.5.3 Control of documented information
8	**Operation**	**Operation**	**Operation**
8.1	Operational planning and control	Operational planning and control	Operational planning and control
	–	–	*8.1.1 General*
	–	–	*8.1.2 Hierarchy of controls*
8.2	*Requirements for products and services*	*Emergency preparedness and response*	*Management of change*
	8.2.1 Customer communication	–	–
	8.2.2 Determining of requirements for products and services	–	–
	8.2.3 Review of requirements for products and services	–	–
	8.2.4 Changes to the requirements for products and services	–	–
8.3	*Design and development of products and services*	–	*Outsourcing*
	8.3.1 General	–	–
	8.3.2 Design and development planning	–	–
	8.3.3 Design and development inputs	–	–
	8.3.4 Design and development controls	–	–
	8.3.5 Design and development outputs	–	–
	8.3.6 Design and development changes		–
8.4	*Control of externally provided processes, products and services*	–	*Procurement*
	8.4.1 General	–	–

(Continued)

TABLE 7.1 (Continued)

Clause number	ISO 9001:2015 Quality Management	ISO 14001:2015 Environmental Management	ISO 45001:2018 Occupational Health and Safety Management
	8.4.2 Type and extent of control	–	–
	8.4.3 Information for external providers	–	–
8.5	Production and service provision	–	Contractors
	8.5.1 Control of production and service provision	–	–
	8.5.2 Identification and traceability	–	–
	8.5.3 Property belonging to customers or external providers	–	–
	8.5.4 Preservation	–	–
	8.5.5 Post-delivery activities	–	–
	8.5.6 Control of changes	–	–
8.6	Release of products and services	–	Emergency preparedness and response
8.7	Control of nonconforming outputs	–	–
9	**Performance evaluation**	**Performance evaluation**	**Performance evaluation**
9.1	Monitoring, measurement, analysis and evaluation	Monitoring, measurement, analysis and evaluation	Monitoring, measurement, analysis and evaluation
	9.1.1 General	9.1.1 General	9.1.1 General
	9.1.2 Customer satisfaction	9.1.2 Evaluation of compliance	9.1.2 Evaluation of compliance with legal requirements and other requirements
	9.1.3 Analysis and evaluation	–	–
9.2	Internal audit	Internal audit	Internal audit
		9.2.1 General	9.2.1 Internal audit objectives
		9.2.2 Internal audit program	9.2.2 Internal audit process
9.3	Management review	Management review	Management review
	9.3.1 General	–	–
	9.3.2 Management review inputs	–	–
	9.3.3 Management review outputs	–	–
10	**Improvement**	**Improvement**	**Improvement**
10.1	General	General	Incident, nonconformity and corrective action
10.2	Nonconformity and corrective action	Nonconformity and corrective action	Continual improvement
	–	–	10.2.1 Continual improvement objectives
	–	–	10.2.1 Continual improvement process
10.3	Continual improvement	Continual improvement	–

7.1 MSSs that conform to (are based on or provide guidance to) the requirements of Annex SL

 AUTHOR'S HINT

All the requirements of ISO 9001:2015 are generic and are intended to be applicable to any organisation, regardless of its type or size or the products and services it provides.

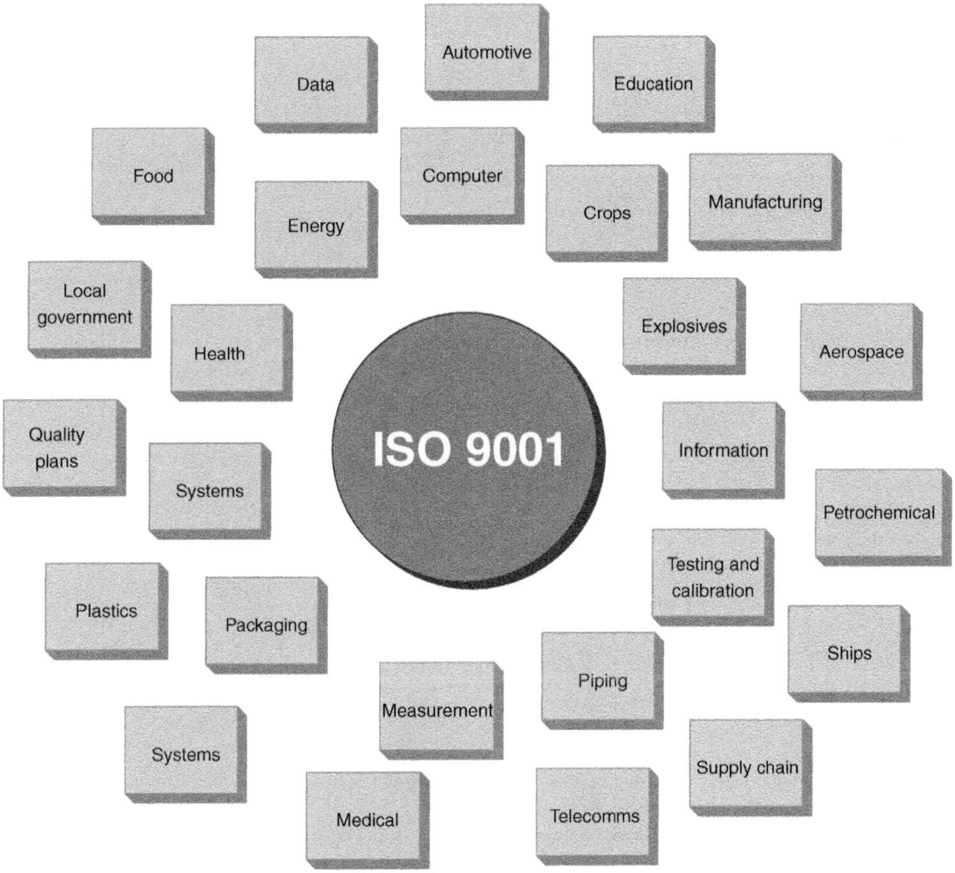

FIGURE 7.1 The size of the ever growing ISO 9001:2015 family

TABLE 7.2 MSSs that are based on Annex SLs

ISO 21401:2018	Accommodation facilities –sustainability management system
ISO 21101:2014	Adventure tourism –safety management systems
ISO 37001:2016	Anti-bribery management systems
ISO 55001:2014	Asset management
ISO/TR 27918:2018	CCS process (capture, transportation, or storage) – life cycle risk management
ISO 44001:2017	Collaborative business relationship management
ISO/IEC 17021–3:2017	Conformity assessment – competence requirements for auditing and certification of Quality Management Systems
ISO 21001:2018	Educational organisations – management systems for educational organisations
ISO 50001:2018	Energy management systems
ISO 14001:2015	Environmental management systems
ISO 20121:2012	Event sustainability management systems
ISO 41001:2018	Facility management systems
ISO 22000:2018	Food safety management systems – requirements for any organisation in the food chain
ISO/IEC 17025:2017	General requirements for the competence of testing and calibration laboratories
ISO 30301:2011	Information and documentation –management systems for records
ISO/IEC 19770–1:2017	Information technology – IT asset management
ISO/IEC TS 33073:2017	Information technology –process capability assessment model for quality management
ISO/IEC 40180:2017	Information technology –quality for learning, education and training – fundamentals and reference framework
ISO/IEC 27552:2018	Information technology – Security techniques – Enhancement to ISO/IEC 27001 for privacy management
ISO/IEC 27001:2013	Information technology – information security management systems
ISO/IEC 20000-1:2018	Information technology – service management system requirements
ISO 18788:2015	Management system for private security operations
ISO 10012:2003	Measurement management systems –requirements for measurement processes and measuring equipment
ISO/TR 80002–2:2017	Medical device software –validation of software for medical device quality system
ISO 13485:2016	Medical devices – Quality Management Systems –requirements for regulatory purposes

As patient safety is involved, virtually **all** of the requirements of ISO 13485 are mandatory!

ISO 19443:2018	Nuclear energy Quality Management Systems –specific requirements for the application of ISO 9001:2015 by organisations in the supply chain of the nuclear energy sector supplying products and services important to nuclear safety (ITNS)
ISO 45001:2018	Occupational health and safety management systems
ISO 15378:2017	Primary packaging materials for medicinal products –particular requirements for the application of ISO 9001:2015, with reference to good manufacturing practice (GMP)
ISO 10006:2017	Quality management –guidelines for quality management in projects
ISO 9001:2015	Quality Management Systems
ISO 22163:2017	Railway applications –business management system requirements for rail organisations
ISO 39001:2012	Road traffic safety (RTS) management systems
ISO 37101:2016	Sustainable development in communities –management system

7.2 MSSs currently under development to comply with Annex SL

TABLE 7.3 MSSs currently under development to comply with Annex SL

ISO/TS 8000–150:2011	Data quality – Part 150: Master data: Quality management framework
ISO 21401:2018	Accommodation facilities – sustainability management system
AS/EN/JIS 9100: 2009	Aerospace –internationally recognised quality system standard specific to the aerospace industry based on ISO 9001
ISO/TS 16949:2009	Automotive Quality Management Systems – particular requirements for the application of ISO 9001:2008 for automotive production and relevant service part organisations
ISO 22006:2009	Crop production Quality Management Systems – guidelines for the application of ISO 9001:2008 to crop production
ISO 10002:2014	Customer satisfaction – guidelines for complaints handling in organisations
ISO/IEC 80079-34:2011	Explosive atmospheres – Part 34: Application of quality systems for equipment manufacture
ISO 14298:2013	Graphic technology – graphic technology – management of security printing processes
ISO 19011:2011	Guidelines for auditing management systems
ISO 30401	Human resource management – knowledge management systems
ISO 16000-40	Indoor air – Part 40: Indoor air Quality Management System
ISO 35001	Laboratory biorisk management system
ISO 18091:2014	Local government Quality Management Systems – guidelines for the application of ISO 9001:2008 in local government
ISO 16106:2006	Packaging – transport packages for dangerous goods –dangerous goods packagings, intermediate bulk containers (IBCs) and large packagings – guidelines for the application of ISO 9001
ISO 29001:2010	Petroleum, petrochemical and natural gas industries – sector-specific Quality Management Systems – requirements for product and service supply organisations
ISO 10005:2005	Quality management – guidelines for quality plans
ISO 17582:2014	Quality management systems – particular requirements for the application of ISO 9001:2008 for electoral organisations at all levels of government
ISO 39001:2012	Road traffic safety (RTS) management systems
ISO 30000:2009	Ships and marine technology – ship recycling management systems – specifications for management systems for safe and environmentally sound ship recycling facilities
ISO 22301:2012	Societal security – business continuity management systems
ISO/IEC 90003:2014	Software engineering – guidelines for the application of ISO 9001:2008 to computer software
ISO 27025:2010	Space systems – quality assurance requirement for program management
ISO 28000:2007	Supply chain management – specification for security management systems
ISO TR 90005:2008	Systems engineering – guidelines for the application of ISO 9001 to system life cycle processes
TL 9000	Telecommunication – quality management standard based on ISO 9001
ISO 24526	Water efficiency management systems – requirements with guidance for use

AUTHOR'S END NOTE

Although this book has provided you with only a very brief overview of what Annex SL and ISO 9001:2015 is all about, it should nevertheless be sufficient to enable you to understand the advantages of producing your own Quality Management System for your organisation – if you really want to.

The following chapter looks at what is required for compliance with the current edition of the General Data Protection Requirements (GDPR) in more detail

8

THE IMPORTANCE OF DATA PROTECTION

Samantha Alford

AUTHOR'S START NOTE

The General Data Protection Regulation (GDPR) is the latest European Union Regulation on data protection and privacy for individuals and came into effect on 25 May 2018. Like many pieces of legislation, GDPR can appear extremely complex at first glance, but it is based on the simple concept that every individual has a right to privacy and a right to decide what happens to their personal data.

The risks of getting data protection wrong are worrying for the people concerned, and the fines for noncompliance that can be imposed on a business or organisation can be quite large. Therefore, whether the undertaking is large or small, it is essential to take GDPR seriously.

Much already has been written on the subject of GDPR both in books and online, but a lot of this information is focussed on large enterprises that process highly sensitive information about large numbers of people. These organisations are likely to have their own in-house GDPR processes and procedures and in many cases their own data protection officer (DPO) and team to keep them compliant.

The GDPR, however, isn't just for large organisations! It is intended to cover **all** types of organisations regardless of their size, and small businesses and individuals will normally have to rely on obtaining help and guidance from government sources, websites and books on the subject – which at times can be confusing.

The intention of Chapter 8 is to provide a simple explanation of the most relevant aspects of GDPR to the business owner – what the regulation says and how to comply with it.

This chapter is aimed at helping you to:

- identify how GDPR applies to your particular organisation;
- understand your organisation's role in relation to personal data;
- analyse what data the organisation holds and how the organisation uses it;
- plan the necessary processes and procedures in order to meet the requirements of the GDPR;
- plan how to deal with staff training and manage any breaches.

8.1 What is meant by the General Data Protection Regulation (GDPR)?

The GDPR in effect consolidates all the previous data privacy laws from across Europe. At the same time, it protects the privacy of individuals (be they EU/EFTA/EEA citizens, persons living or working in the EU or those whose personal data is processed by an entity based in the EU).

GDPR defines *'personal data'* as *'any information relating to an identified or identifiable data subject'*: in other words, any information that is clearly about a particular living person and who could be directly or indirectly identified through this data. Personal data can include names, contact details, CCTV, photographs, car registrations as well as dates of birth, credit card details and the like. Even if the amount of data an organisation holds is very small, they must still ensure that the organisation complies with GDPR.

Personal data can be held in paper files, on a phone or in a computer database. Irrespective of how it is held, **all** data held on file is covered by the legislation.

CASE STUDY

If you keep someone's name and contact details in or on any form of database and you use this for business within the EU, then the GDPR applies to you.

The only time that GDPR does not apply is if the processing is carried out for purely personal or in-house activities or for law enforcement or national security reasons.

8.2 How to obtain more information about GDPR?

The GDPR established the European Data Protection Board (EDPB) as an independent European body, based in Brussels, who are responsible for ensuring the uniformity of data protection rules throughout the European Union and for promoting cooperation among the EU's national data protection authorities (DPAs).

The EDPB is composed of data protection authorities from 32 EU/EFTA countries whose national details can be found on the EDPB's website at https://edpb.europa.eu/about-edpb/board/members_en. In addition to the contact details of the various countries, the EDPB's website also provides general guidance (including guidelines, recommendations and best practice) to clarify GDPR law and also downloadable (.pdf) copies of EDPB Plenary Sessions that are held to discuss, amend and finalise various important aspects of the GDPR.

For example, at the 5th Plenary Session held in December 2018, one of the Agenda items was to discuss the convergence between the Japanese legal framework and the European one. Although not expecting the Japanese legal framework to replicate European data protection, the aim of this discussion was to obtain an adequate level of data protection for individuals in the Japanese framework.

8.2.1 How to obtain GDPR information specific to the UK

Within the UK, the Information Commissioners Office (ICO) are the supervising authority. (See Figure 8.1 and Table 8.1) They publish a vast array of information on their website (https://ico.org.uk) and are available for advice and guidance by phone and email.

FIGURE 8.1   Information Commissioners Office

TABLE 8.1 Contact details of UK's Information Commissioners Office

Country	National Data Protection Authority	Contact details	Website
United Kingdom	Information Commissioner's Office	Water Lane, Wycliffe House Wilmslow Cheshire SK9 5AF Tel. +44 1625 545 745 email: international. team@ico.org.uk	https://ico.org.uk

The ICO also host online questionnaires (https://ico.org.uk/for-organisations/ resources-and-support/data-protection-self-assessment) which businesses can use to find out if they comply with the GDPR legislation.

8.2.2 What is its relationship to the UK's Data Protection Act 1998?

The good news is that if your business followed previous data protection laws (such as the UK's 1998 Data Protection Act that was updated to incorporate GDPR in May 2018), then you will already be well on the way to being compliant under GDPR, as many of the new rules and themes build on these previous laws. There is therefore normally no need to completely change what is already being done.

8.3 The seven GDPR privacy principles

Over the past few years, companies have been collecting and processing ever increasing amounts of data about their customers, employees and users. As personal data becomes more valuable, governments around the world have gradually made laws requiring that this data collection should be limited in favour of individuals' fundamental right to privacy. The European Union's GDPR ensures that companies can no longer choose how to use individual's personal data, and the control of this personal data is returned to the data subjects.

As described in Figure 8.2, the GDPR contains seven data protection principles that you must comply with when collecting, processing and managing the personal information data for all European citizens.

Organisations that breach the regulations risk fines of up to €20 million or 4% of global turnover and bans from processing such data in the future!

8.3.1 Lawfulness, fairness and transparency

> *Personal data shall be processed lawfully, fairly and in a transparent manner in relation to the data subject (lawfulness, fairness, transparency).*
>
> [article 5, clause 1(a)]

To meet this requirement, you must:

- identify a lawful basis for collecting and using personal data;
- ensure that you do not do anything with personal data that is unlawful;
- use (or process) personal data only so that is not unduly detrimental, unexpected or misleading to the individuals concerned;
- be clear, open and honest with the individuals concerning how you will use their personal data.

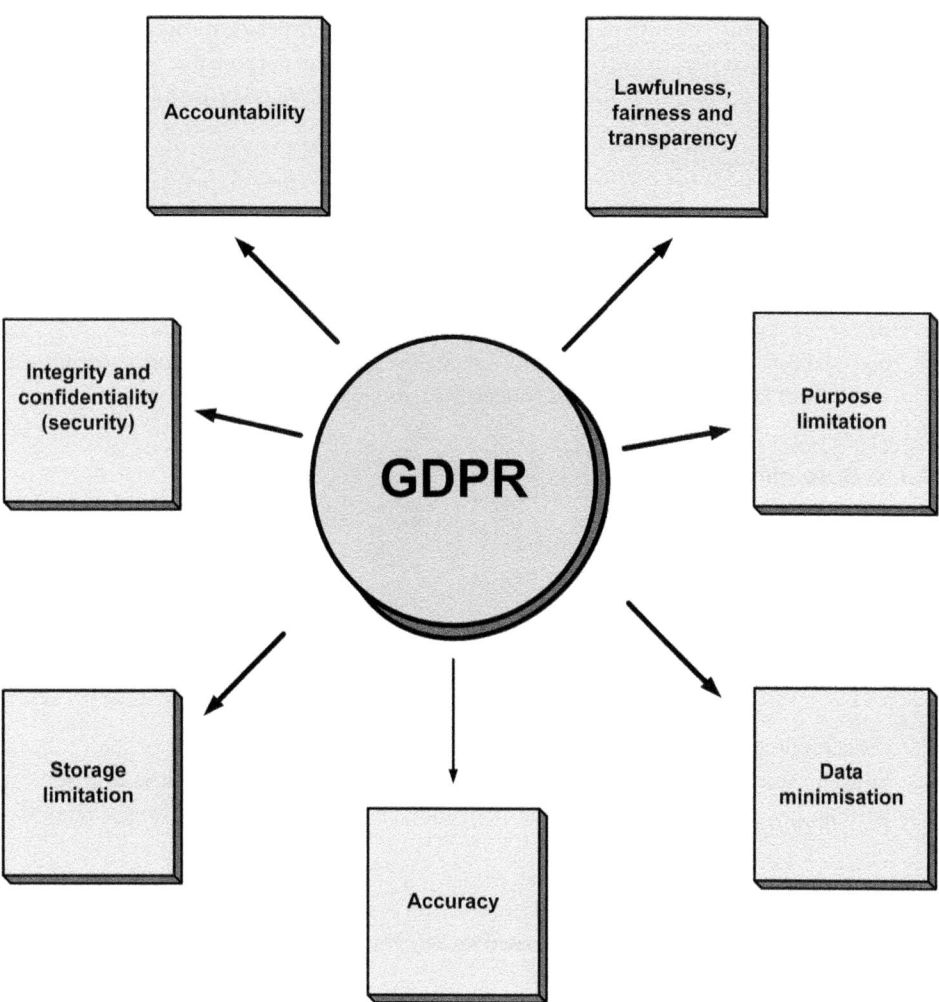

FIGURE 8.2 Seven principles of the GDPR

Organisations should incorporate accessible and straightforward privacy policies to meet the rights of the individuals.

8.3.2 Purpose limitation

Personal data can only be obtained for specified, explicit and legitimate purposes.
[article 5, clause 1(b)]

In practice, this means that you must:

- be clear from the outset why you are collecting personal data and what you intend to do with it;

- inform individuals about your purpose for collecting their personal data;
- ensure that if you plan to use or disclose personal data for any purpose that is additional to or different from the originally specified purpose, that the new use is fair, lawful and transparent.

And you must ensure that:

- data can be used only for a specific processing purpose that the subject has been made aware of;
- processing personal data is permissible only if and to the extent that it is compliant with the original purpose for which data was collected;
- personal data can be collected **only** for specified, explicit, agreed and legitimate purposes;
- you do not keep personal data for longer than you need it.

8.3.3 Data minimisation

Personal data shall be adequate, relevant and limited to what is necessary in relation to the purposes for which they are processed.

[article 5, clause 1(c)]

This requires that you:

- collect only personal data you actually need for the specified purposes;
- limit the amount of personal data that is necessary for a particular business function;
- periodically review the data that you hold and delete anything you no longer require.

8.3.4 Accuracy

Personal data shall be accurate and where necessary kept up to date.

[article 5, clause 1(d)]

You must:

- ensure that the source and status of personal data are clear;
- ensure that all personal data is accurate and kept up to date;
- delete anything that is incorrect, misleading or no longer required.

8.3.5 Storage limitation

Personal data must be kept in a form which permits identification of data subjects for no longer than necessary.
[article 5, clause 1(e)].

In essence, this means:

- you do not keep personal data for longer than you need it (unless it is required for public archiving, scientific or historical research or for statistical purposes);

- data no longer required is securely removed or deleted;
- a regular review process should be in place together with a database cleansing process.

8.3.6 Integrity and confidentiality (security)

Personal data shall be processed in a manner that ensures appropriate security of the personal data including protection against unlawful processing or accidental loss, destruction or damage.

[article 5, clause 1(f)]

This requires you to ensure that:

- all personal data is protected against unauthorised access (e.g. through the use of appropriate organisational and technical measures such as encryption or password protection);
- the confidentiality and integrity of the personal data are maintained;
- measures are taken to protect against unlawful processing, accidental loss as well as the destruction or damage of personal data.

 AUTHOR'S HINT

Fines for serious data breaches can be up to 4% of annual global turnover or €20 million, whichever is higher. In the first major UK fine under the GDPR legislation in July 2019 the UK ICO fined British Airways £183 Million - in September 2018 hackers diverted about 500,000 customers from the BA site to a fraudulent one and harvested customer details including names, email addresses and credit card details.

8.3.7 Accountability

The controller shall be responsible for, and be able to demonstrate compliance with paragraph 1 ('accountability').

[article 5(2)]

To ensure compliance with this principal:

- a data protection officer should be appointed where required;
- data protection policies need to be implemented;
- technical and organisational measures should be in place to meet the requirements of accountability;
- written contracts should be in place with organisations that process personal data on your behalf;
- appropriate security measures should be implemented;
- personal data breaches should be reported and recorded;
- data protection impact assessments should be used where appropriate.

8.4 Key issues

Organisations must be able to demonstrate to the governing bodies that they have taken all necessary steps to minimise the risk that their data subjects face. To ensure compliance, organisations must be sure that every step within the GDPR strategy is auditable and can be compiled as evidence quickly and efficiently.

 AUTHOR'S HINT

For example, the GDPR requires organisations to respond to requests from individuals regarding what data is currently held about them, and the organisation must be able to promptly retrieve that data and share it with the subject, if desired.

Organisations need not only to have a process in place to manage these requests but also to have a full audit trail to prove that they took the proper actions.

The GDPR applies to personal information relating to an 'identifiable person'. It covers **all** companies and organisations that process the personal data of individuals in the EU regardless of where the company is located. GDPR also applies to organisations processing the personal data of individuals outside the EU, thus making the GDPR one of the most significant data protection laws in the world.

GDPR insists that companies use clear language to notify individuals about what data they hold and how they use it. Should this personal data be compromised, then the individual must be informed within 72 hours of the data breach occurring.

In order to meet the requirements of the GDPR, all businesses will need to reshape their methods for collecting, using and storing an individual's personal information. Individuals have a right to know how their information is used when it is shared, with whom it is shared as well as how and when it will be disposed of or deleted.

Individuals have improved rights to learn how their data is going to be used and processed. In some cases, they can request that their data is erased or made more accurate. Individuals also have the right to obtain a copy of the personal data that organisations collect about them (via subject access request).

8.4.1 Legal basis

For any personal data processed, the organisation must be able to specify that it has been lawfully processed in accordance with and as specified by GDPR. These grounds are:

- individuals' consent;
- contract with the individual;
- complying with an existing obligation;
- it is necessary for a task in public interest or authority;
- it is necessary in the legitimate interest of an organisation or third party.

The controller is accountable under GDPR for compliance with these principles, and they should be able to demonstrate their compliance with the regulation. Any personal data that an organisation or stores and uses has to have been freely given by that person and can be used only subject to the data subject's wishes

8.4.2 Data protection officer

One of the requirements of the GDPR is for organisations to consider whether they need to appoint their own data protection officer (DPO) to oversee and advise on the best means of protecting personal data (obtained internally or externally) from misuse.

Not every organisation is required to appoint a DPO, but it is a **mandatory requirement** for all organisations, large or small, to ensure compliance with GDPR's obligations regarding the security of personal information – **if**:

- they are a public authority (or public body) with a legal mandate to govern or administrate any part or aspect of public life;
- their core activities involve large-scale data processing operations that require regular and systematic monitoring of data subjects; or
- they complete large-scale processing of special categories of sensitive data (such as personal information on health, religion, race or sexual orientation) and/or personal data relating to criminal convictions and offences.

 Small and medium-sized enterprises (SMEs) are **not** exempt from the DPO requirement if any or all of the preceding situations apply to them.

The DPO reports directly to top management and must be given all resources necessary to carry out the required functions and their job is to inform and advise all personnel within an organisation of its data protection obligations and to:

- act as point of contact with the supervisory authority on all data protection issues;

Note: Within the UK, this will be the Information Commissioner's Office (ICO).

- act as the point of contact with other supervisory authorities, EU residents and their internal teams;
- advise on whether a Data Protection Impact Assessment (DPIA – a process to help identify and minimise the data protection risks of a particular project) is necessary, how to conduct one and the expected outcomes and then inform and advise the organisation and its employees of their data protection obligations under the terms of the GDPR;
- identify and evaluate the company's data processing activities;
- monitor the organisation's compliance with the GDPR and ensure that its internal data protection policies and procedures comply with the regulation (including the assignment of responsibilities);
- raise awareness and train all staff involved;

- serve as the contact point for data subjects on privacy matters, including data subject access requests (SAR – a written request made by or on behalf of an individual for the information that he or she is entitled to ask for).

Note: A number of ISO 17024:2012 GDPR conformity assessment training courses are currently available for DPOs, which can provide them with all the specialist knowledge and skills needed to deliver GDPR compliance.

8.4.3 Email marketing

Email marketing is more strictly controlled under GDPR. As an email marketer, you need to collect *freely given, specific, informed and unambiguous consent* (article 32).

To achieve compliance, you have to implement new procedures and practices, such as:

- new consumer opt-in permission rules;
- proof of consent storing systems; and
- a method through which consumers can ask for their personal information to be removed,

This will require you to:

- complete a thorough audit of your current database;
- be aware of your contacts and how you acquired them.

 AUTHOR'S HINT

*The GDPR is raising many questions among employers, not least whether a work email address should be regarded as personal data. The short answer is, '**Yes**, it is?'*

*In contrast, generic business email addresses (e.g. enquiry@ or info@) are **not** personal data.*

8.4.3.1 Can I still send email marketing campaigns to my existing contact list?

GDPR doesn't apply *only* to the data collected after its effective date (e.g. 25 May 25 2018) but to *all* data gathered before or after, and so, if you have changed your purposes, then by law you require new consent from your clients. If you are still processing the data for the same purpose as before and you previously had consent, then it is best practice to obtain new opt-in permission from all existing clients and members on your contact list(s). At the very least, you should provide clients with the option to unsubscribe from the list each time an email is sent.

8.4.4 Security of data

Security of data is at the very centre of GDPR as it protects all your external email communications so that data – whether it is a company's data, personal data or partner data – remains confidential at all times.

A multi-layered security solution that has confidentiality as its core aim should use virtual security appliances such as firewalls, intrusion detection systems to identity/access management systems, encryption and password protection.

A little deception is always good, though, so routing traffic to virtual honeypots will help fool and expose 'bad actors'.

8.4.5 Securing the network itself

In today's IT environment, it is not sufficient to just encrypt user data; metadata information can also be used by enemies to map out the network and plan attacks even without access to the encrypted application layer.

You should therefore secure the actual network itself by encrypting at the lowest layer possible on the network to ensure that *all* data is undecipherable to a hacker who taps into the fibre strand.

8.4.6 Fines/penalties

One in four organisations will experience a data breach, and so recognising that data breaches can occur and managing your business in such a way to reduce risks as far as possible are key to a successful GDPR strategy.

There are considerable fines for getting data protection wrong, as shown in the recent examples of data breach fines in the UK in Table 8.2.

8.4.7 Personal data

According to the law, *personal data* means any information relating to an individual (for example, an identification number such as one's social security number) that can be used to identify that individual, directly or indirectly, and that is held by a third-party organisation. With our current dependence on the Internet to gather information, once you have handed your data over, it can be then be mined or resold, ending up in large databases of personal data. (See Figure 8.3)

Examples of the main users of our personal data are, of course, as follows:

* Google and Facebook (which dominate the digital advertising market) use your data to allow marketers better targeting options as they have access to every advertisement you ever clicked on.
* Loyalty Cards also work in a similar manner because your personal records help businesses collect data on you and your spending habits;

TABLE 8.2 UK ICO fines imposed for data breaches June–October 2018

Date	Organisation	Reason for fine	Amount
Jul 2019	UK Marriott Hotels	Failure to protect personal data (approximately 339 million guest records)	£99 Million
Jul 2019	Netherlands Haga Hospital	Failure to put measures in place to protect patients' information (staff members illicitly accessed a TV star's records)	€460,000
Jun 2019	Italy La Liga	Using a football league app to combat piracy by collecting audio and location data	€250,000
Apr 2019	Poland Bisnode (a Swedish Company)	Failure to tell 6 million data subjects that it had their data (which had been 'scraped' from the internet). The company thought it was too expensive to inform data subjects	€220,000
Mar 2019	Denmark Taxa 4x35	Failure to delete customer's telephone numbers (approx. 8,873,333 customers)	€180,000
Jan 2019	France Google	Failure to be transparent about data use. No legal basis to personalise adverts	€50 Million
Jan 2019	UK Uber	Paying hackers but not informing the victims whose personal details had been stolen (approx. 2.7 million UK customers)	£385,000
Nov 2018	UK CPS	Loosing unencrypted DVDs of police interviews	£325,000
Jan 2019	Germany Undisclosed Org	Allowing health-related data to be seen	€80,000

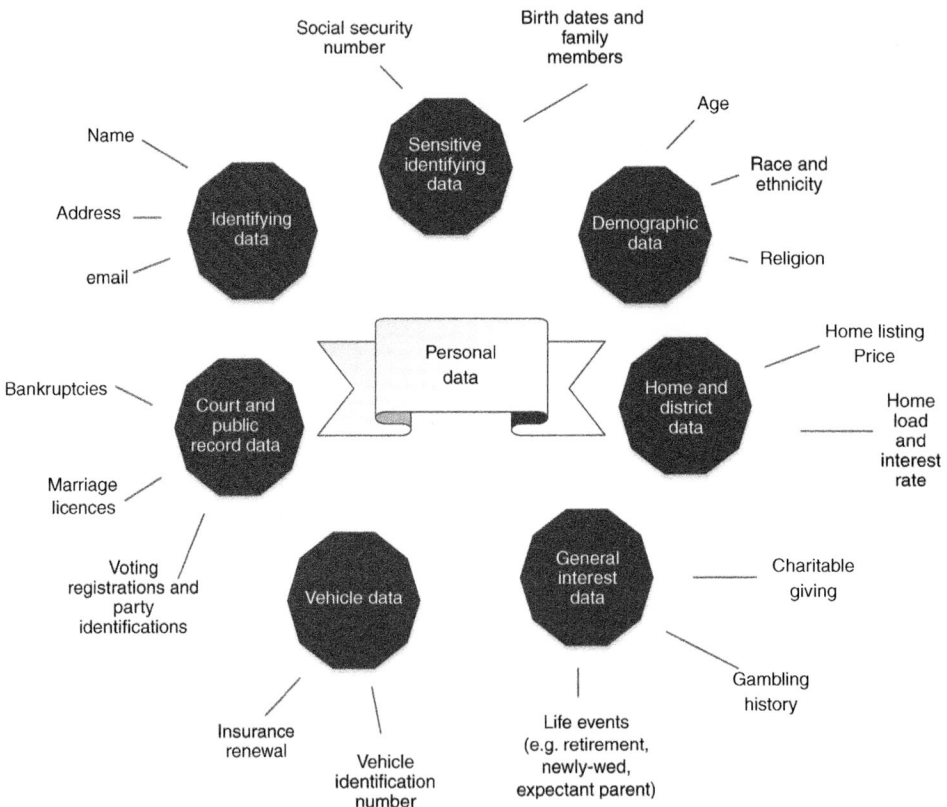

FIGURE 8.3 How much is your personal data worth?

- eBay has become the world's online marketplace; a place for buyers and sellers to come together and to buy or sell almost anything – and in doing so, interexchange your own personal data!
- Mobile phone companies use data (such as geolocation) from your mobile phones, and this can also be resold by your telecommunications company to other groups.

Under the terms of the GDPR, you do, however, have the right to find out whether an organisation is using or storing your personal data, and you can exercise this right of access by asking (either verbally or via correspondence) for a copy of the data. This is commonly known as making a *subject access request*.

It is advisable to keep a thorough record of any such verbal or written requests, as well as any responses, for future reference if required!

8.4.8 Cookies

The use of cookies and similar technologies that download a small file of letters and numbers onto your computer when you visit a website have now become commonplace. These are particularly important to online retailers as they remember your preferences, record what you have put into your shopping basket and count the number of people looking at a website.

Using such technologies is **not**, however, prohibited by the regulations, which **do** require that people are told about cookies and given the choice as to which of their online activities are monitored in this way.

8.4.9 Privacy impact assessment

Where a type of processing (in particular, using new state-of-the-art technologies) is likely to result in a high risk to the rights and freedoms of natural persons, the data protection officer must, prior to the processing, carry out an impact assessment of the processing operation on the protection of personal data.

8.5 How to meet the requirements of the GDPR

In order to meet the requirements of the GDPR, you will need to ensure that you have an agreed that the process and procedures are in place to enable you to:

- increase awareness within the organisation and make sure all parties understand their roles;
- analyse what personal data the organisation holds and who the subjects are;
- simplify the language around personal data and write a draft privacy notice;
- draw up a simple diagram of how/where the organisation holds data and whom it is shared with;
- turn this simple data map diagram into a data audit, answering these questions:
  - What information is held?
  - What is its source?

- Why was it collected (legal basis)?
- How long is it kept?
- Whom it is shared with?
- When is it to be deleted, and how will that happens?

- complete a simple risk analysis of the systems the organisation uses (concentrating on physical, procedural and software security);
- consider who will fulfil the organisation's data protection officer's role;
- put in place regular data protection training for all staff;
- review and update personal data practices and auditing procedures on a regular basis.

8.5.1 Identifying how GDPR applies to the organisation

In order to identify how GDPR will apply to your particular company or business, you first have to work out how big and complex the task is. Table 8.3 presents the three basic questions to ask.

To help organisations better understand the requirements of the GDPR, the UK's Information Commissioner's Office has produced a package of tools and resources that is available on their website (https://ico.org.uk/for-organisations/business).

TABLE 8.3 Determining the organisations requirements for GDPR

	Question	Action	
		If answer is NO	*If answer is YES*
1	*Does your organisation collect, use, store or do anything else with the personal information of employees, customers or both?*	No further action is required.	You will have to take into consideration the requirements of the GDPR for the retention of such information.
2	*Does your organisation comply with the previous data protection laws?*	You will need to produce a data protection process that meets the requirements of the GDPR.	You will need to upgrade your data protection process to meet the requirements of the GDPR.
3	*Does the organisation work with sensitive personal information (e.g. health, religious or philosophical beliefs) or special categories of data (e.g. trade union membership, genetic or biometric data)?*	No further action is required.	You will have to have in place an auditable GDPR data process.

8.5.2 Is the organisation a controller or a processor?

Once an organisation has begun to consider how far the regulations apply to their business, the next step is to work out whether they process personal data as a *'controller'* or *'processor'* (in some cases, organisations may be both a controller and a processor).

A *controller* is a person or organisation who (alone or jointly) determines the purposes for which data is processed and the way it is processed.

The *data processor* can be any person who processes the data on behalf of the data controller.

8.5.2.1 Data controller

The controller has overall responsibility for the data and for making sure that the organisation has a GDPR-compliant contract with their processor, specifying (in particular):

- the legal obligations of the processor;
- the legal basis for collecting data;
- which individuals they need to collect data about;
- what items of personal data to collect;
- the method of collecting data;
- how long to retain the data; and
- maintaining records of personal data and processing activities.

8.5.2.2 Data processor

Data processors make the following decisions:

- How to store the personal data
- Which IT systems or other methods to use for collecting and retaining personal data
- The detail of the security surrounding the personal data
- The means used to transfer the personal data from one organisation to another
- The means used to retrieve personal data about certain individuals
- The method for ensuring a retention schedule is adhered to
- The means used to delete or dispose of the data

8.5.3 Analysing what data is held and how it is used

Personal data includes any information relating to an individual who could be identified, directly or indirectly by that data such as by reference to a person by name, identification number, online user, location and other factors specific to the physical, physiological, genetic, mental, economic, cultural or social identity of that person.

The data collected by an organisation can range from the simplest (such as names, email addresses or telephone numbers) to the more complicated specialist categories of information (such as medical and/or financial information).

8.5.4 Drawing up a GDPR compliance data map

A simple data map diagram is a high-level mechanism to look at the systems the organisation uses to process personal information. It should also capture whom the organisation shares information with and who is responsible for it. (See Figure 8.4)

***This is a typical
checklist for GDPR compliance***

Awareness and communication.
Ensure your employee understand GDPR and communicate with service and staff about why you are collecting the data.

Analysis of personal data.
Analyse a list of all sensitive data you store and process

Review procedures.
Have a suitable privacy policy in place and review it regularly

Customer consent.
Ensure your customers consent to you processing their data

Access rights.
List what access rights should be granted and how changes should be handled

Data breaches.
Implement procedures for handling data breeches

Impact assessments.
Carry out data protection impact assessments

Data protection officers.
Determine whether you need a data protection officer (DPO)

FIGURE 8.4   Checklist for GDPR compliance

8.5.5 Privacy notices

 AUTHOR'S HINT

Data privacy is the branch of information security dealing with the proper handling of data concerning consent, notice, sensitivity and regulatory concerns.

The term *'privacy notice'* is used to describe the way an organisation looks after an individual's privacy. It can be provided in a range of ways, such as:

Via signage   for example, an information poster in a public area;

Electronically   in text messages, on websites, in emails or in mobile apps;

In writing   through print media, print adverts, contact or medical forms, such as financial applications or job application forms;

At meetings   either face to face or on the telephone (but make sure the organisation documents these 'discussions'!).

The privacy notice should contain:

- the organisation's name;
- whom it relates to;
- the date it was printed and when it is next due for renewal;
- a description of why the organisation needs to collect and use personal information;
- information on how the organisation collects personal information;
- details of any information obtained on a consent basis;
- details of how the organisation will store this information;
- details of how the organisation collect this information;
- details of who the organisation share information with (and why it is shared);
- details of how individuals can request access to their personal data;
- the individuals' rights in respect of the data. The organisation should provide details about the person in the organisation to contact in order to discuss anything in the organisation's privacy notice (name, number, email).

Note: To ensure documentation that the data subject has read and understood the organisation's privacy notice, the organisation can prepare a *declaration* for individuals to complete.

8.5.6 The data audit

Once an organisation knows which elements of personal information it processes and whether it is a controller or processor, the next step is to complete a data audit. To some organisations, this can be quite a daunting task as it is quite a significant undertaking; however, provided you have an adequate quality procedure in place, you shouldn't have too much trouble.

8.5.7 Data protection training

Different organisations approach the issue of staff training in their own ways. How they do depends on the complexity of the business and on the number of individuals involved, but basically there are three options to choose from:

External courses A simple Internet search using the term 'GDPR Training' provides a wide selection of offerings for organisations to choose from. These vary in price and complexity and can be both classroom and Internet based.

Seminars and briefings The ICOs have a number of films on their YouTube channels and/or their Vimeo channels which showing you all about data protection and freedom of information. Some of these training videos also have accompanying scripts and viewer notes.

Local training Where the organisation has a large number of staff to train, then it may wish to train them in-house, using in-house or external trainers.

8.5.8 How to keep data safe

All staff within the organisation should be made aware of the personal data that the organisation holds and the systems it is held on. Selecting those who hold access to this information will depend on their role. Some steps that organisations could take to ensure that staff keep data safe would be to apply the following guidance by way of a data safety policy:

- Password-protect portable memory devices containing personal data and keep them safe.
- Be mindful of possible vulnerability when using off site wi-fi to log in to emails etc.
- Be conscious of what is on the screen when others can see it.
- Keep personal data only for the minimum amount of time necessary.
- Do not share personal data with others unless authorised to do so.
- Delete/shred or securely dispose of personal data that is no longer required.
- Report a data breach.
- Complete a simple risk analysis of the systems the organisation uses, concentrating on physical, procedural and software security.

8.5.8.1 What is a personal data breach?

A personal data breach is a breach of security and can be either accidental or deliberate. A personal data breach is an occasion when:

- personal data is lost, destroyed, corrupted or disclosed;
- someone accesses personal data or passes it on without proper authorisation;
- personal data is made unavailable, for example, when it has been encrypted by ransomware or accidentally lost or destroyed.

 All staff should know how to respond to a data breach.

8.5.8.2 Reporting a data breach

Under the terms of the GDPR, organisations have a duty to report personal data breaches to their Supervisory Authority within 72 hours of becoming aware of the breach. They are also obliged to inform the individuals concerned without undue delay if it is likely that there is a high risk of the breach adversely affecting their rights and freedoms.

8.5.9 Sharing information electronically

Under GDPR, organisations may **not** share personal data without a lawful reason. This includes another person's email address or phone number.

CASE STUDY

In June 2018, the Gloucestershire Police were fined £80,000 by the UK ICO after it sent out a bulk email that identified victims of non-recent child abuse. The force was investigating allegations of abuse relating to multiple victims when in December 2016, an officer sent an update on the case to 56 recipients by email. The email addresses were entered in the 'To' field, and all concerned were able to see the names of the other potential victims.

To comply with GDPR, organisations should make sure that when they create a process or system, they *design in* privacy considerations to ensure that personal data is stored and shared only when it is needed. This means:

- making sure emails are sent to the correct recipients;
- encrypting any critical personal information when sending it by email;
- protecting the email addresses of the people receiving the information to by using the BCC field, a MailChimp-style application or by sending individual emails.

Do not use *opt-outs/automatic opt-ins* as preticked **opt-in** boxes are banned under the GDPR! The regulations also require organisations to provide information about how personal data will be stored/deleted/used. It is useful to have a check box to confirm that users understand and acknowledge these details.

Take precautions with personal information, and check the email trail so that the information is shared only with the intended recipient rather than with a mail list.

 Be wary of the Reply to all button, and use it only if everyone needs to see your comments.

8.5.10 An individual's right to access records under GDPR

Under GDPR, there are three ways in which individuals can access the data that an organisation holds:

Subject access request   which must be answered by the organisation within 1 month of receipt. This can be used if individuals want to know what personal data an organisation holds about them to check it for accuracy.

Freedom of information request   which must be responded to within 20 working days. This request is used when individuals or organisations are conducting research and wish to obtain specific information from a public body about their business.

Request to access a specific type of record   e.g. medical/educational records. The time-line for this is in line with industry guidelines. Requests to access specific records may be used when individuals want to see their medical/school records.

8.5.11 Subject access request

Individuals have the right to receive a copy of any personal data and other supplementary information that an organisation has on them

Subject access requests can be made either verbally or in written form as long as they are from the subject (or the person with parental responsibility if the subject is under 13). The organisation has one month to reply and should provide the information free of charge (unless there are special reasons for a charge). It is essential to verify that the person requesting it is entitled to the information. The one-month deadline may be increased in special circumstances.

The individual is entitled to:

- confirmation that the organisation is processing their personal data (i.e. data from which they can be identified either directly or from the use of a combination of information in the data);

- a copy of their personal data;
- any other supplementary information. The information should be contained in the organisation's privacy notice, which could be attached to the response. The information that the subject requires is:

  - the organisation's purpose for processing;
  - the categories of data the organisation processes;
  - who the organisation shares the data with or discloses it to;
  - how long the organisation stores the data or how the organisation determines how long to store it;
  - confirmation that individuals have a right to request rectification, erasure or restriction or to object to such processing (depending on the organisation's legal basis for processing);
  - confirmation that they have a right to complain to their ICO or another supervisory authority;
  - information about the data source (if it is not themselves);
  - information on any automated decision making (including profiling);
  - details of the safeguards the organisation provides if the organisation transfers personal data to a third country or international organisation.

An individual is **not**, however, entitled to information relating to other people (unless they are acting on behalf of someone), and it is the organisation's responsibility to remove or omit data on other people. It is also up to the organisation to establish whether the information requested falls within the definition of personal data.

8.5.12 Freedom of information requests

For a request to be valid under the Freedom of Information Act, it must be in writing, but requesters do not have to mention the Act or direct their request to a designated member of staff. So while it is good practice to provide the contact details of your freedom of information officer, it is not essential that he or she is used as the contact. Public organisations may **not** ignore or refuse a request simply because it is incorrectly addressed. **Any** letter or email to a public authority asking for information is recognised as a **formal request** for recorded information under the Act.

Under GDPR, responses may not contain any personal information.

8.5.13 Requests to see specific records

Guidance on requests to access a specific types of record e.g. educational or medical records are still being developed with respect to GDPR.

8.5.14 Retaining and deleting data

One of the key tenants of GDPR is the minimisation of data. This means that organisations can no longer keep records for prolonged periods unless they have good reasons to do so. The ICO offer the following advice on data retention:

- Do not keep personal data for longer than it is needed.
- Think about – and be able to justify – how long to keep personal data. This will depend on the purposes for holding the data.
- Develop a policy setting standard retention periods wherever possible in order to comply with documentation requirements.
- Periodically review the data held, and erase or anonymise it when it is no longer needed.
- Carefully consider any challenges to the organisation's retention of data. Individuals have a right to erasure if the data is no longer needed.
- Personal data may be kept longer if it is for public interest archiving, for scientific or historical research or for statistical purposes.

8.5.15 Do you need to register (notify) under the Data Protection Act?

Within the UK, the Data Protection Act **requires all data controllers who are processing personal information to register with the ICO**, unless they are exempt.

There is no need, however, to register if you handle personal data only for core business purposes of staff administration, advertising/marketing and PR, and accounts and record keeping.

ANNEX A

Articles of the GDPR (at a glance)

As previously explained, the GDPR contains seven data protection principles that you must comply with when collecting, processing and managing the personal information data concerning all European citizens. These data protection principles are then covered by a virtual library of documents, explaining how they can be achieved in real life via 11 general practice GDPR Articles. (See Figure 8.5)

The 11 articles (or clauses of the GDPR) are then subdivided as shown in the Table 8.4.

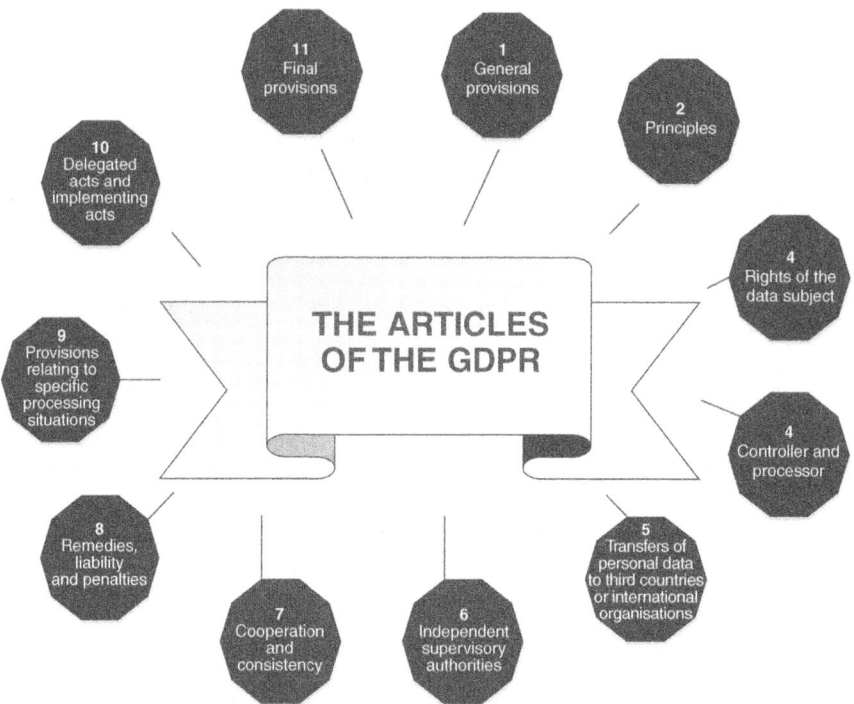

FIGURE 8.5 Chapters of the GDPR

TABLE 8.4 *The 99 Articles of GDPR*

Chapter number	Chapter title	Description	Articles in the chapter
1	**General Provisions**	This chapter consists of four articles that discuss the aim of the regulation, the scope of the regulation (where it applies and whom it applies to) and essential definitions.	1. Subject matter and objectives 2. Material scope 3. Territorial scope 4. Definitions
2	**Principles**	This chapter consists of seven articles that outline the rules for processing and protecting personal data.	5. Principles relating to processing of personal data 6. Lawfulness of processing 7. Conditions for consent 8. Conditions applicable to child's consent in relation to information society services 9. Processing of special categories of personal data 10. Processing of personal data relating to criminal convictions and offences 11. Processing that does not require identification
3	**Rights of the Data Subject**	This chapter consists of 12 articles discusses the rights of the data subject, including the right to be forgotten, right to rectification and right to restriction of processing.	12. Transparent information, communication and modalities for the exercise of the rights of the data subject 13. Information to be provided where personal data are collected from the data subject 14. Information to be provided where personal data have not been obtained from the data subject 15. Right of access by the data subject 16. Right to rectification 17. Right to erasure (commonly referred to as the *right to be forgotten*) 18. Right to restriction of processing 19. Notification obligation regarding rectification or erasure of personal data or restriction of processing 20. Right to data portability 21. Right to object 22. Automated individual decision making, including profiling 23. Restrictions

(Continued)

TABLE 8.4 (Continued)

Chapter number	Chapter title	Description	Articles in the chapter
4	**Controller and Processor**	This chapter consists of 20 articles that cover the general obligations and necessary security measures of data controllers and processors, as well as data protection impact assessment, the role of the data protection officer, codes of conduct and certifications.	24. Responsibility of the controller 25. Data protection by design and by default 26. Joint controllers 27. Representatives of controllers or processors not established in the Union 28. Processor 29. Processing under the authority of the controller or processor 30. Records of processing activities 31. Cooperation with the supervisory authority 32. Security of processing 33. Notification of a personal data breach to the supervisory authority 34. Communication of a personal data breach to the data subject 35. Data protection impact assessment 36. Prior consultation 37. Designation of the data protection officer 38. Position of the data protection officer 39. Tasks of the data protection officer 40. Codes of conduct 41. Monitoring of approved codes of conduct 42. Certification 43. Certification bodies
5	**Transfers of Personal Data to Third Countries or International Organisations**	This chapter consists of 7 articles that provide the rules for transferring personal data that is undergoing or will undergo processing outside of the Union.	44. General principle for transfers 45. Transfers on the basis of an adequacy decision 46. Transfers subject to appropriate safeguards 47. Binding corporate rules 48. Transfers or disclosures not authorised by Union law 49. Derogations for specific situations 50. International cooperation for the protection of personal data

6	Independent Supervisory Authorities +.	This chapter consists of 9 articles requiring that each member state have a competent supervisory authority with certain tasks and powers.	51. Supervisory authority 52. Independence 53. General conditions for the members of the supervisory authority 54. Rules on the establishment of the supervisory authority 55. Competence 56. Competence of the lead supervisory authority 57. Tasks 58. Powers 59. Activity reports
7	Cooperation and Consistency	This chapter consists of 17 articles that outline how supervisory authorities will cooperate with one another and ways they can remain consistent when applying this regulation and that define the European Data Protection Board and its purpose.	60. Cooperation within the lead supervisory authority 61. Mutual assistance 62. Joint operations of supervisory authorities 63. Consistency mechanism 64. Opinion of the Board 65. Dispute resolution by the Board 66. Urgency procedure 67. Exchange of information 68. European Data Protection Board 69. Independence 70. Tasks of the Board 71. Reports 72. Procedure 73. Chair 74. Tasks of the Chair 75. Secretariat 76. Confidentiality
8	Remedies, Liability and Penalties	This chapter consists of eight Articles that cover the rights of data subjects to judicial remedies and the penalties for controllers and processors.	77. Right to lodge a complaint with a supervisory authority 78. Right to an effective judicial remedy against a supervisory authority 79. Right to an effective judicial remedy against a controller or processor 80. Representation of data subjects 81. Suspension of proceedings 82. Right to compensation and liability 83. General conditions for imposing administrative fines 84. Penalties

(Continued)

TABLE 8.4 (Continued)

Chapter number	Chapter title	Description	Articles in the chapter
9	**Provisions Relating to Specific Processing Situations**	This chapter consists of seven articles that cover some exceptions to the regulation and enables Member States to create their own specific rules.	85. Processing and freedom of expression and information 86. Processing and public access to official documents 87. Processing of the national identification number 88. Processing in the context of employment 89. Safeguards and derogations relating to processing for archiving purposes in the public interest, scientific or historical research purposes or statistical purposes 90. Obligations of secrecy 91. Existing data protection rules of churches and religious associations
10	**Delegated Acts and Implementing Acts**	This chapter covers the rights of the Commission and consists of two articles.	92. Exercise of the delegation 93. Committee procedure
11	**Final Provisions**	This chapter consists of six articles explaining the relationship with this regulation to past directives and agreements on the same subject matter.	94. Repeal of Directive 95/46/EC 95. Relationship with Directive 2002/58/EC 96. Relationship with previously concluded agreements 97. Commission reports 98. Review of other Union legal acts on data protection 99. Entry into force and application

AUTHOR'S END NOTE

Chapter 8 was meant to provide only a quick overview of the requirements for the protection of personal data as covered by the GDPR.

However, if you need a more in-depth book about these regulations, I have no hesitation in recommending Samantha Alford's current book entitled "GDPR-A Game of Snakes and Ladders" published by Routlledge.

9

WHAT ABOUT AUDITING YOUR QUALITY MANAGEMENT SYSTEM?

 AUTHOR'S START NOTE

The increased drive towards quality-led production now means that today's major purchasers are not just expecting quality; they are also demanding proof that a company is capable of supplying quality products and/or quality services!

The provision of this proof normally takes the form of an independent third-party evaluation and eventual certification, and this is possibly the single most important requirement for any organisation, whether they provide products or services.

Chapter 9 covers the often overlooked topic of self-assessment and methods for completing management reviews, internal, external as well as third-party audits and evaluations.

One of the mandatory requirements of ISO 9001:2015 (Section 9.2) is that:

> *The organization shall conduct internal audits at planned intervals to provide information on whether the quality management system:*
>
> a) *conforms to*
>
> - *the organization's own requirements for its quality management system;*
> - *the requirements of ISO 9001:2015*
>
> b) *is effectively implemented and maintained.*

9.1 Purpose of an audit

The primary purpose of an audit is to enable an organisation to evaluate its process management systems, determine deficiencies and generate cost-effective and efficient solutions. An audit is performed to check practice against procedure and to thoroughly document any differences. It is used to measure an organisation's ability to do what it says it is going to do.

For example, suppose you state in a process that staff must wear hard hats to perform a particularly dangerous job, and a safety auditor visits a site only to discover they are not wearing any form of headgear. Then your process is not being followed, and the auditor will ensure, by issuing a non-conformance, that hard hats are worn in the future. (See Figure 9.1)

This is a very typical example of how an auditor can maintain discipline within a workforce and ensures that your management system is being adhered to. The auditor may also have saved someone's life, not to mention the costs of an accident claim.

Auditing generally follows a linear process, starting with establishing the criteria against which you are auditing and leading to a report concluding whether the criteria are being met. Should the audit find problems with the performance of a process, then you will implement corrective action aimed at preventing reoccurrence. A simple process map of the internal audit procedure is shown in Figure 9.2.

Remember, auditing is not a witch-hunt aimed at finding a fault and then blaming someone for it. When things go wrong, it is usually the fault of the process, not the person performing it.

9.2 Types of audit

Several types of audit can be completed under the general umbrella of 'audits measuring conformance with ISO 9001:2015', such as:

Quality system audits	– an overall measurement of an organisation's capability to meet the requirements of ISO 9001:2015
Management audits	– confirmation that an organisation's strategic plan reflects their business objectives and continues to meet their clients' requirements
Process audits	– checks that focus specifically on a single process to verify whether an organisation is capable of delivering the outputs expected of them
Procedural audits	– verification that documented practices are sufficient to ensure the implementation of approved policies and are capable of controlling the organisation's operations
System audits	– checks to ensure that a business management system is sufficiently comprehensive to control all of the activities within that business (Generally, this type of audit would look for gaps in the management system that may result in their not achieving their business objectives.)
Products and services audits	– verification that an organisation's plans and proposals for supplying products and services fully meets specified requirements

FIGURE 9.1   Auditing is good for you!

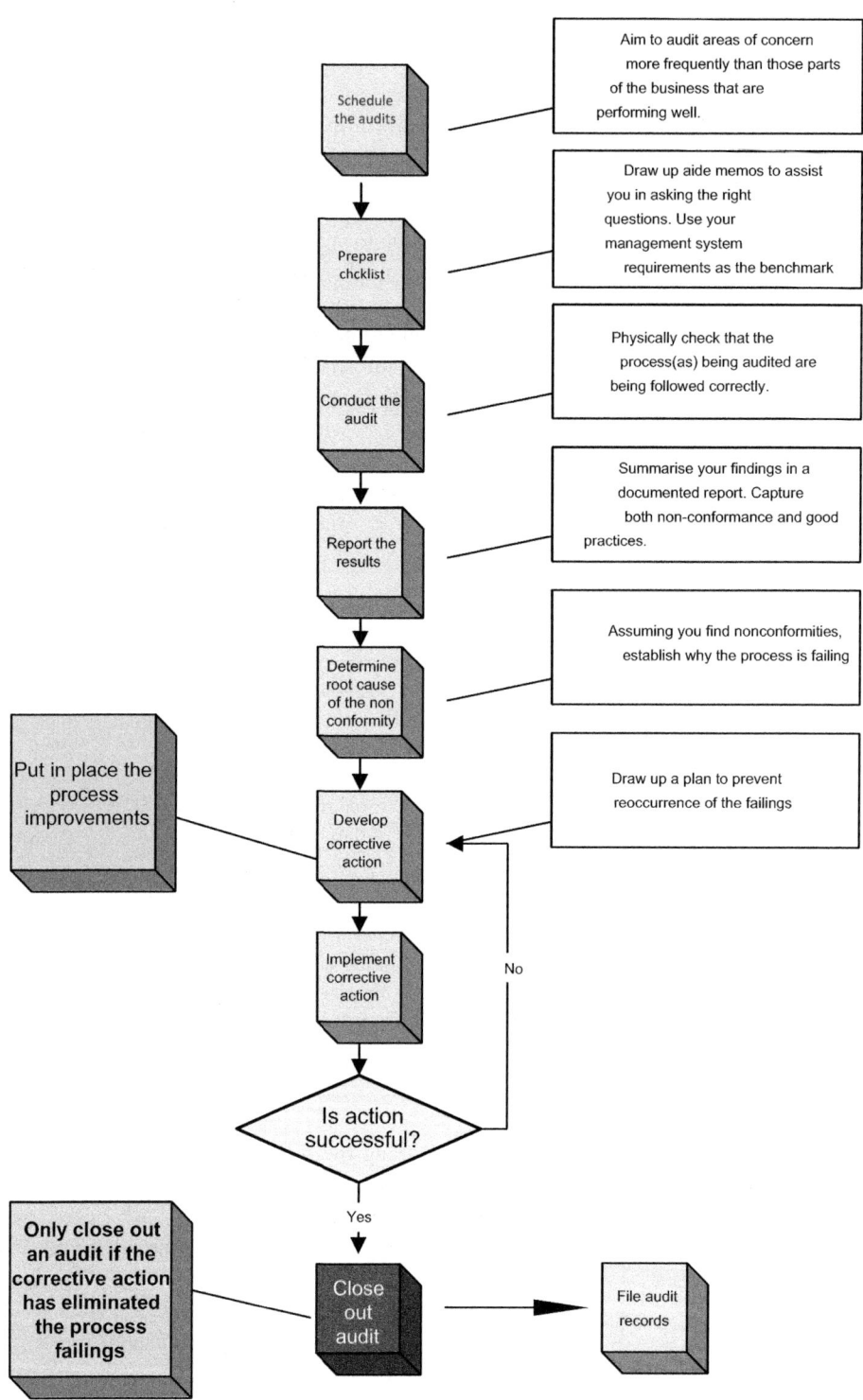

FIGURE 9.2 A generic audit process

9.3 Audit categories

You may come across three generic categories of audit (see Figure 9.3):

First party   Also known as internal auditing, where (as the name suggests) members of an organisation look inwards at their own processes. This is the least effective form of auditing, as generally the auditors will find it difficult to criticise their own work. To minimise this, it is desirable to get staff to audit one another's processes, thereby instilling a degree of independence.

Second party   These are audits carried out by your customers to satisfy themselves you are capable of doing a job and are generally referred to as vendor audits.

Third party   Personnel who are *neither* staff working within your business *nor* your customers carry out this type of audit. So who are they? Generally these are employees of accredited certification bodies. These are notified bodies that audit your business and, if found to be compliant, certify you to ISO 9001.

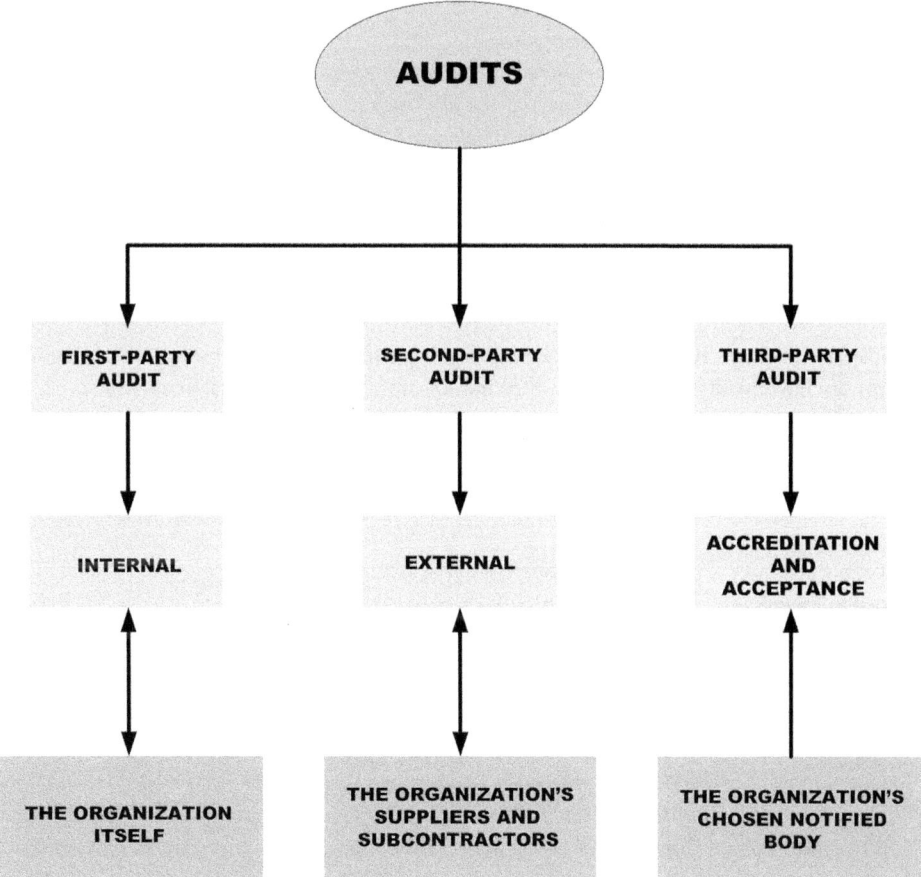

FIGURE 9.3   Types of audit

In addition to the three categories of audit, other types of audit can be used to measure conformance to ISO 9001:2015, such as:

System audits   carried out to ensure a business management system is sufficiently comprehensive to control all of the activities within that business. Generally, this type of audit would look for gaps in the management system that may result in not achieving their business objectives.

Process audits   focus specifically on single processes to verify whether they are capable of delivering the outputs expected of them.

Management audits   checks carried out to see whether an organisation's strategic plan reflects their business objectives, and, more specifically, they have met the requirements of the intended market.

 AUTHOR'S HINT

These are just a few different audit types.

*If you would like to see some more examples of these audits plus a whole host of audit checklists and typical auditing forms and the like, may I suggest (and **no**, I haven't got my 'marketing hat' on, it is just that I want to help you!) that you get a copy of one of the other books that I have written in this ISO 9001 series, namely, ISO 9001:2015 Audit Procedures'.*

9.4 Auditing multiple Management System Standards

In today's corporate environment, organisations tend to combine a number of management systems, such as quality, environment, health and safety, information security and so on. As a result, many organisations now want to harmonize these systems and, where possible, combine the auditing process for each of these. Obviously, this is possible now that we have Annex SL as the benchmark for all Management System Standards!

CASE STUDY

In 2001, I was approached by a company who had just developed a TENS machine (or, to give it its correct name, a Transcutaneous Electric Nerve Simulation machine), which is designed to help relieve and reduce pain by emitting a mild electrical current that allows your muscles to relax and endorphins (the body's natural painkillers) to be released.

In order to get it on the market, they needed not only certification for Quality (i.e. ISO 9001:2000) but also for Medical Devices (i.e. ISO 13485:2001). They had sought advice from various consultants, who all said that they would have to have two separate Quality

Management Systems, which would require two different certification companies to audit their company and their product.

Having just researched ISO 9001:2001 for a book, I was pretty well up on what a QMS should consist of, and, looking through the text of ISO 13485:2001, I realised that there were distinct similarities (e.g. the requirements for Document Control, Management Reviews and Audits etc.). The only real difference was anything that concerned patient safety – which was obviously a mandatory requirement.

With this in mind, I compiled a QMS for them that covered the requirements of both of these standards and then had a certification company evaluate their product. This third-party audit was successful, and the company was duly certified as meeting the requirements of both standards, thus saving them the cost (and time) of having to have two separate audits.

I adopted the same method for other companies requiring cortication for not only Quality but (for example) Environmental (i.e. ISO 14001) and Health & Safety (i.e. the old BS OHSAS 18001, now updated to ISO 45001) Management Standards. With the introduction of Annex SL and its ISO 9001:2015 template, it is now, of course, possible to combine virtually every management requirement into one common Quality Management System. Well done, ISO!

ISO 19011:2011 (Guidelines for Auditing Management Systems) is an excellent standard that provides the fundamental knowledge needed for auditing management systems and has been expanded to reflect modern thinking and the intricacies of auditing multiple Management System Standards.

It has been designed to help organisations optimize and facilitate the integration of their management systems and, by introducing a single audit programme, streamline the audit processes whilst reducing the duplication of effort and disruption of multiple units being audited.

This single document provides the critical tools to help you make the right decisions when planning, conducting and evaluating audits. It allows users to:

- gain a clear explanation of the principles of management systems auditing;
- learn how to conduct and assess internal or external audits;
- obtain guidance on the management of audit programmes;
- reduce paperwork and the need to brief multiple audit teams;
- self-declare in a recognisable way;
- streamline the audit management process, from objectives to analysis.

The standard provides top management with the crucial tools that they will need to carry out successful audits and achieve the objectives of their organisation by minimizing disruption to commercial activities.

10

WHAT TO DO ONCE THE QMS IS ESTABLISHED

Many of today's contracts (particularly those for the military or government – but also for many large businesses) now **insist** that applicants hold a current up to date Management System Standard (MSS) compliance certificate before they will even be considered for the job – whatever the deliverable, product or service.

Indeed, in many tender documents, this is the first question that has to be answered, and to a small business (who has probably never envisaged going outside its own particular market), this can cause a lot of anguish.

If the organisation has a well documented, properly audited, management-led Quality Management System (QMS) in place that is subject to continuous improvement and is always seeking customer satisfaction, then the road to gaining ISO 9001:2015 (or other associated MSS) and then certification need not be too onerous. But the obvious questions, though, that a small business is going to ask are, *'How much is it going to cost to implement and operate?'* and *'Is it going to be worth having the ISO Certificate hanging on the managing director's wall?'*

Obviously, each business is different, and the cost of ISO registration will vary depending on the size and complexity of your organisation and on whether you already have some elements of a QMS in place. Consequently, no book could possibly answer this question with any accuracy; however, in Table 8.4, I have shown typical budgetary costs for obtaining ISO 9001:2015 Certification which will, I hope, be beneficial to you.

But naturally the first question that has to be answered is **do** you actually **need** to become an ISO-registered company? Or would simply '*working in compliance with ISO . . .*' be sufficient? Only your top management will know the answer to that one!

10.1 What are the benefits of achieving certification to ISO and ISO MSS?

The benefit of gaining MSS certification by an accredited certification body is that:

- it shows commitment to quality, customers and a willingness to work towards improving efficiency;
- it demonstrates the organisation has in existence of an effective QMS that satisfies the rigours of an independent, external audit;
- it enhances company image in the eyes of customers, employees and shareholders alike;
- it also gives a competitive edge to an organisation's marketing.

An organisation can also decide to seek certification because it:

- is a contractual or regulatory requirement;
- is necessary to meet customer preferences;
- falls within the context of a risk management programme;
- helps motivate staff by setting a clear goal for the development of its management system.

But the whole aim of companies becoming accredited to one of ISO's Management System Standards is to ensure that their products and services are safe, reliable, of good quality but, most importantly, satisfy their customers' requirements.

For businesses, the standards are strategic tools that reduce costs by reducing waste and errors) whilst at the same time increasing productivity. Accreditation helps companies not only to gain access new markets but also, in doing so, to become more professional as an organisation and improve their client relationships – as shown by the results of the recent (i.e. in 2018) ISO 9001:2015 study of mixed businesses shown in Figure 10.1.

More than 80% of organisations confirmed that they had become more competitive and had won more business as a result of becoming ISO 9001:2015 certified, and in the last decade, certification to ISO 9001 has grown into a worldwide business requirement. Indeed, at the time of writing this book, over 1 million companies and organisations in over 170 countries are certified to ISO 9001 – 10% of whom are from the UK alone!

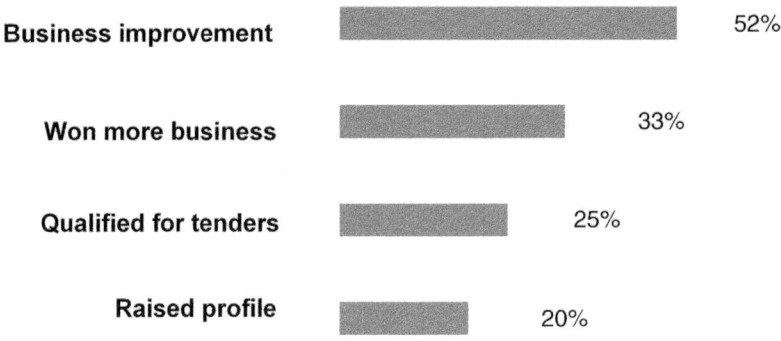

FIGURE 10.1 Benefits of achieving ISO 9001

10.2 What is the difference between being a certified, accredited and/or registered organisation?

Certification is the provision by an independent body of written assurance (a certificate) that the deliverable (product, service or system in question) meets specific requirements.

Registration 'Certification' is very often referred to as 'registration' in North America – but it is one and the same thing.

Accreditation This is the formal recognition by an independent Accreditation Body (e.g. in the UK and UKAS, and in the USA, ANSI), that a Certification Body has been formally approved as being capable of carrying out the certification of an organisation's QMS. Accreditation is *not* obligatory, but it adds another level of confidence, as 'accredited' means the Certification Body has been independently checked to make sure it operates according to international standards.

As ISO 9001:2015 and other MSSs are so-called process standards, when a company says that it is certified or compliant, it is *not* actually saying that its products and/or services **fully meet** the requirements of a particular MSS. So be careful!

10.2.1 But can't I just work 'in compliance' with a particular standard?

If your organisation simply needs to prove that it only has to work in compliance with the requirements of an ISO MSS, then all that is required is to possess an auditable and complete set of documents and records showing how they maintain total quality in the design, build, and operation & maintenance (DBOM) of their products and services.

10.2.2 OK, so how do I become a registered organisation then?

Assuming that you definitely decided that you want to be certified, then you will need to:

• purchase a copy of ISO 9001:2015 (or the particular MSS you need);
• identify which requirements of the standard are applicable to your type of organisation;

- agree on your organisational quality objectives, quality policy and quality plans;
- produce a fully documented QMS (consisting of a Quality Manual plus its associated Quality Processes and Procedures and Work Instructions) that is fully compliant with the requirements of that particular MSS;
- implement these processes and procedures throughout your organisation;
- complete a series of internal audits to ensure that these processes and procedures are suitable and adhered to.

Once all the requirements of the MSS have been met within your organisation and any non-compliances that were identified during your internal audit have been rectified, it is time for an external audit by a third-party certification body. (See Figure 10.2)

Certificates are awarded by accredited Certification Bodies (also known as Registrars) who have met the requirements of an Accreditation Body such as UKAS or ANSI.

Be warned, however, that not *all* companies who profess being able to award ISO 9001:2015 certificates are accredited!

The cost of certification can vary significantly as Certification Bodies have different pricing structures. Some will charge for each and every visit, assessment and follow-up surveillance inspections. Others may be happy to just settle for a one-off fixed payment to take you through the certification process, followed by an annual renewal fee.

When considering a suitable Certification Body, you are strongly advised to obtain a number of quotes to establish the best offer.

10.3 What would the budgetary costs be for doing all this?

The cost for an organisation seeking Registration in the UK would (at the time of publication) be in the region of the figures shown in Table 10.1.

10.4 How long will it take to become certified?

With the right preparation and a good understanding of what is required for certification, most organisations can expect to achieve certification within six to nine months depending on their size and complexity – but I cannot overemphasise the importance of having the **complete backing** of top management, and it is absolutely vital that you have someone (either internal or perhaps, in the case of a micro business, an external consultant) who has experience with implementing QMSs and who knows what will be required in order to gain accreditation.

10.5 What is the certification process?

The chosen certification body will thoroughly review your quality processes and procedures and the like to see that your organisation's management programme is measurable and achievable.

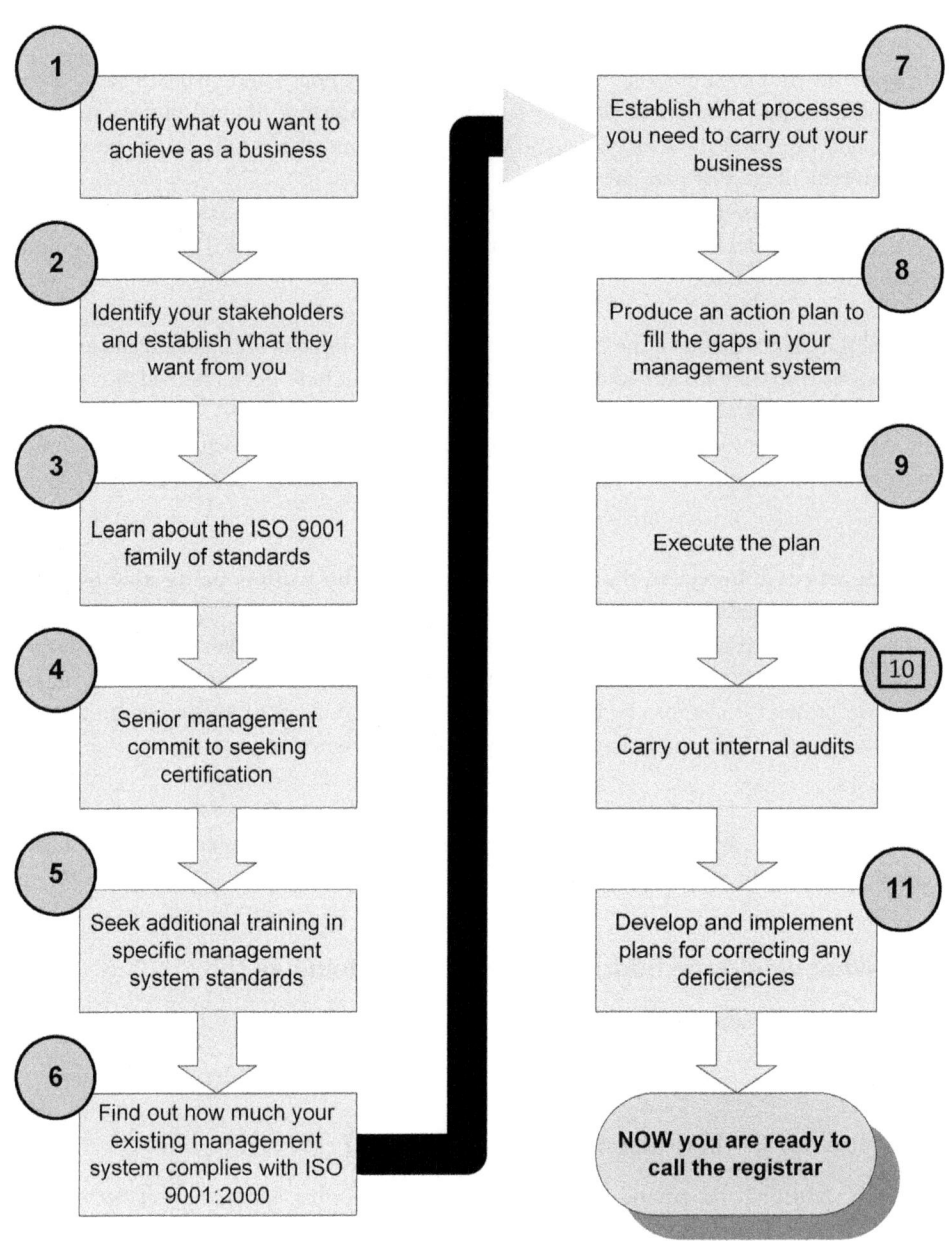

FIGURE 10.2   Getting the QMS up and running

TABLE 10.1 Possible budgetary costs for obtaining ISO 9001:2015 certification

Enterprise Category	headcount	First stage	Second stage	Yearly
		third-party audit	third-party audit	assessments
Medium-sized	< 250	£750	£2,500	£1,500
Small	< 50	£750	£1,500	£750 – £1,500
Micro	< 10	£350	£700	£500

For a small business, this could consist either of a desktop study or of a one-day visit to your organisation's premises. For a large organisation, a site visit would probably be required – dependent on your product or service. The certification body may also send you a few simple questionnaires to complete. (See Figure 10.3)

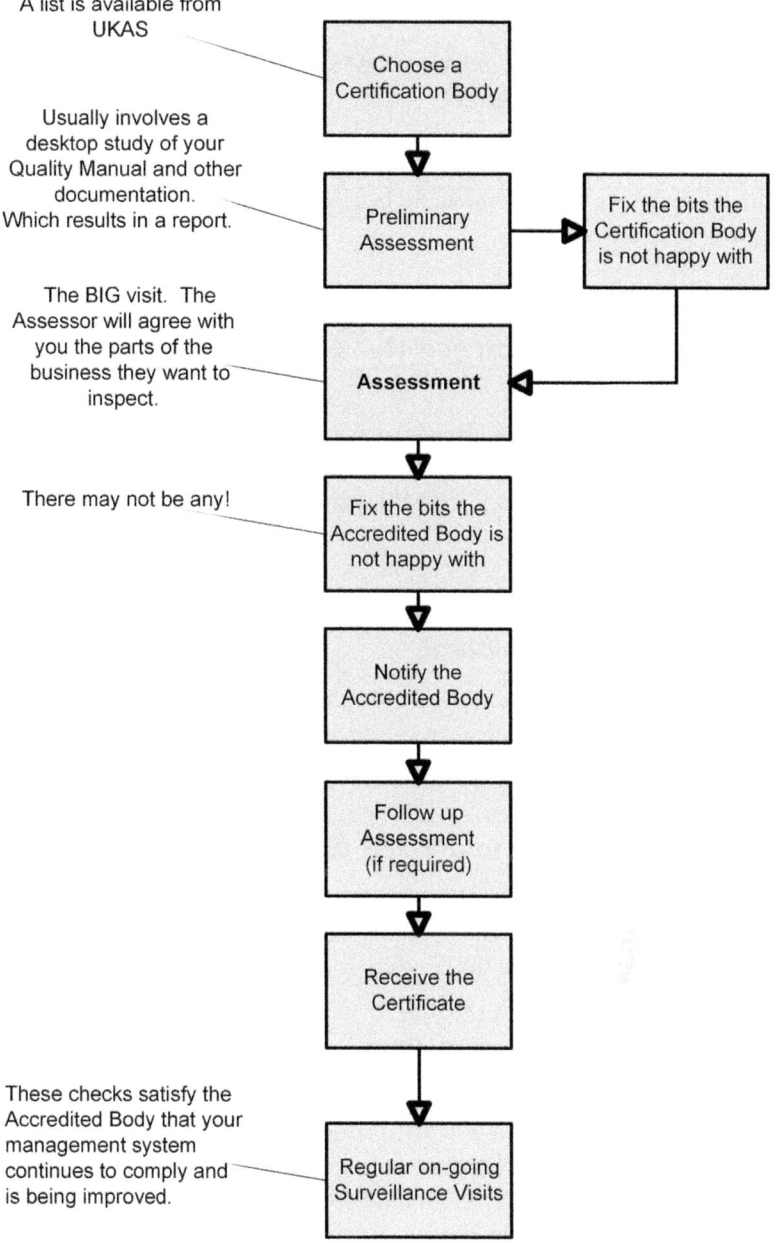

FIGURE 10.3   A typical route to certification

Assuming that this Stage 1 audit is successful, then this will be followed (at a later date) by a full, on-site audit to ensure that working practices observe all of your policies, procedures and stated objectives and that appropriate records are maintained.

If this Stage 2 audit is successful, then the certification body will issue you with a certificate of registration to ISO 9001 (or your particular chosen Management System Standard). This will then be followed by annual (or in some cases, depending on the size and complexity of your organisation, biannual) surveillance visits to ensure that the system continues to work.

10.6 How do I upgrade my existing QMS registration to meet ISO 9001:2015's requirements?

The following are some of the more basic questions that most organisations have to contend with.

10.6.1 Does my organisation have to scrap its existing processes and procedures and start again?

NO.

Most organisations that have implemented the previous ISO 9001:*2008* standard (or a similar MSS) will find that their existing systems already meet *many* requirements of the new standard. So you can keep these in place with slight modifications in order to fully comply with the updated ISO 9001:*2015*.

10.6.2 Does my organisation need to re-certify immediately now that ISO 9001:2015 is published?

The new standard was published on September 15, 2015, which means that the ISO 9001:2008 standard becomes obsolete on September 14, 2018. As a result, *all* ISO 9001:2008 certifications issued after that date now bear an expiry date of September 14, 2018.

10.6.3 Will all our staff have to complete transition training?

Generally speaking, you will be expected to provide some form of transition training for your staff that, as a minimum, should include familiarisation training of the new standard's requirements, as well as an assessment of the new standard's impact on the various processes and personnel.

10.6.4 What about our internal auditors – will they have to complete transitional training?

As your organisation is responsible for determining what competencies are required for its internal auditors, as well as the methods to be used to achieve those competencies, you will have to decide on the extent to which transition training will be needed. In all probability, a seasoned team of internal auditors could complete a period of self-study and quickly become proficient in the ramifications of auditing your ISO 9001:2015-compliant QMS.

10.6.5 What steps can we take right now?

It is recommended that you take the steps shown in Figure 10.4 in your transition to ISO 9001:2015:

- Conduct a Gap Analysis review to identify the gaps that need to be addressed.
- Develop your implementation plan, which should also include assigned responsibilities.
- Update all of your QMS documents (i.e. Quality Manual, Quality Procedures etc.) to reflect any new or revised Quality Processes.
- Complete any transition training that is required.
- Complete a full system internal audit, followed by a management review.
- Complete any corrective actions that require following the internal audit – and then re-audit).
- Coordinate the ISO 9001:2015 transition arrangements with your registrar.

10.6.6 How do I upgrade my existing ISO 9001:2008 registration to meet ISO 9001:2015's requirements?

10.6.6.1 First: select a registrar

Assuming that you were already registered to an existing Management System Standard, then you will already have your own registrar who is working closely with you and who can help you in the process of upgrading your registration to meet Annex SL's requirements.

If this is not the case (and bearing in mind that you will be starting a relationship that will last at least three years – most likely longer), then one of the first things you will need to do is to talk to a selection of registrars who will come to your location and discuss the registration process, costs, time frames and other matters. You will then need to make a careful decision so as to lay the groundwork for a smooth and lasting relationship.

It is best to talk to at least **three** different registrars – and don't always choose the cheapest!

10.6.6.2 Next: internal preparation

Strong leadership (i.e. by top management) has now become a major '*must*' for all organisations as they are required to:

- demonstrate a thorough understanding of their business environment and how it impacts on their organisational strategy;
- demonstrate alignment between system objectives and their organisation's strategic direction;
- ensure that they have identified all the significant risks that can have an impact on system objectives (e.g. customer satisfaction);
- ensure that clear responsibilities and authorities have been defined for all of the organisation's processes;

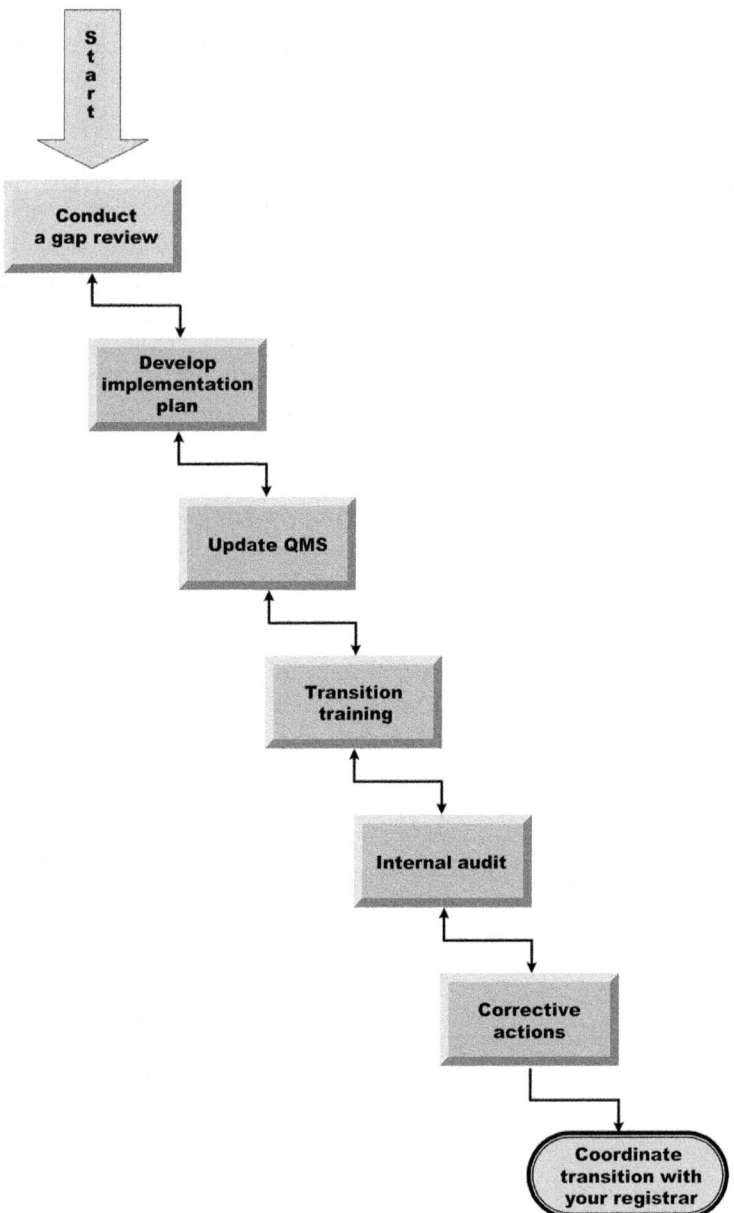

FIGURE 10.4 Initial steps towards transition

- ensure that the organisation's internal communication channels are effective;
- oversee the process for managing change and development within the organisation so as to ensure that the effectiveness of the system is maintained during improvement and other organisational changes;
- review existing processes and perform a gap analysis.

10.6.7 How can all this be achieved?

As previously mentioned, before you can really make a start in your transition process, you will need to compare your current MSSs to the requirements of the Annex SL/ISO 9001:2015 standard using a gap analysis following the well known PDCA (plan-do-check-act) route. See Figure 10.5.

With ISO 9001:2015 now being the accepted generic Management System Standard for quality, you will find it much easier to incorporate your organisation's QMS into your Core Business Processes and get more involvement from top management, as indicated in Figure 10.6.

As ISO 9001:2015 has been written in accordance with Annex SL, the new high-el structure of this standard can be applied to the plan-do-check-act cycle, which may be applied to all processes and to the QMS as a whole.

Clause 4: Context of the organisation

This is a new clause that establishes the framework of your QMS. Firstly, you will need to determine external and internal issues that are relevant to your organisation's purpose,

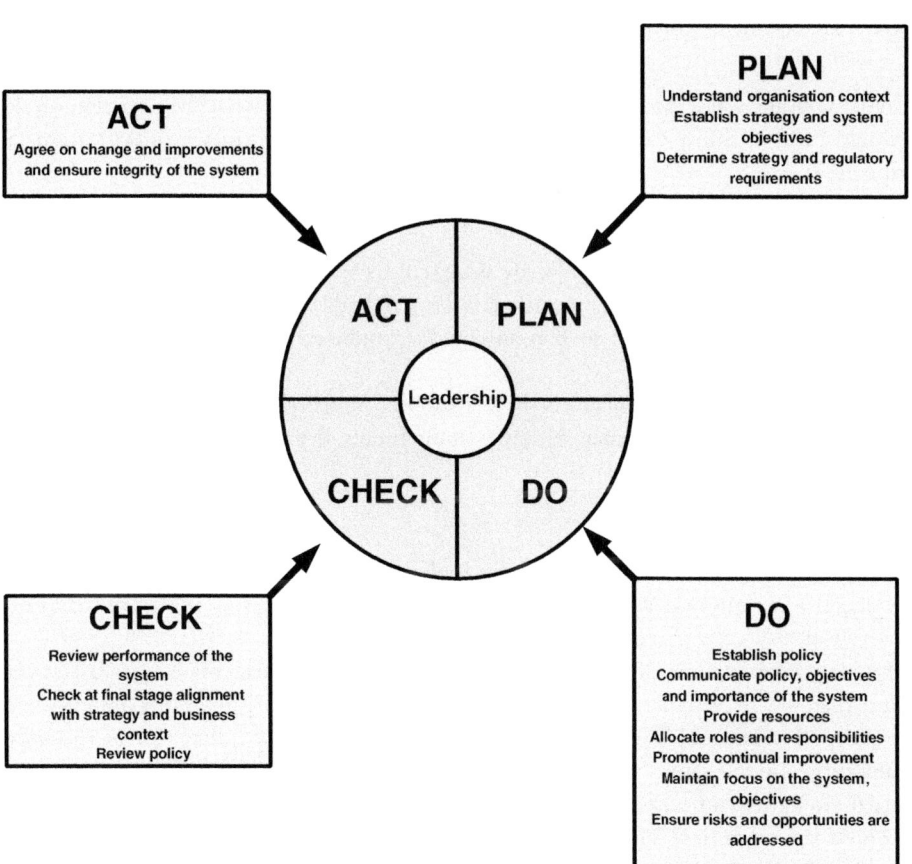

FIGURE 10.5 How organisations should prepare for their change to ISO 9001:2015

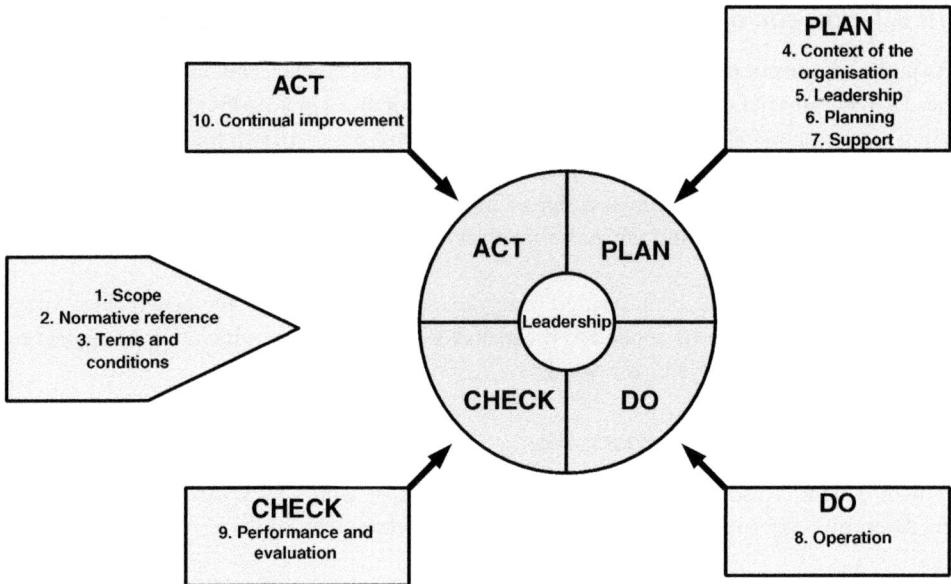

FIGURE 10.6 Guide to ISO 9001–2015 using the PDCA route

i.e. what relevant issues, both inside and out, have an impact on what the organisation does or would affect its ability to achieve the intended outcome(s) of its management system. (See Figure 10.7)

It should be noted that the term 'issue' covers not only problems that would have been the subject of preventive action in previous standards but also important topics for the management system to address, such as any market assurance and governance goals that the organisation might set.

The final requirement in clause 4 is to establish, implement, maintain and continually improve your QMS in accordance with the requirements of the standard.

Clause 5: Leadership

This clause *firmly* places the requirement for leadership on top management's shoulders, who now need to demonstrate leadership and commitment by leading (not unsurprisingly!) from the very top.

Top management now have greater involvement in the management system and must ensure that the requirements of it are integrated into your organisation's processes and that the policy and objectives are compatible with the strategic direction of the whole organisation. In the same context, they need be completely aware of the organisation's internal strengths and weaknesses and how these could impact on the ability to deliver their products or services. This will strengthen the concept of business process management, including the need to allocate specific responsibilities for processes and to demonstrate an understanding of the key risks associated with each process and the approach taken to manage, reduce or transfer risk.

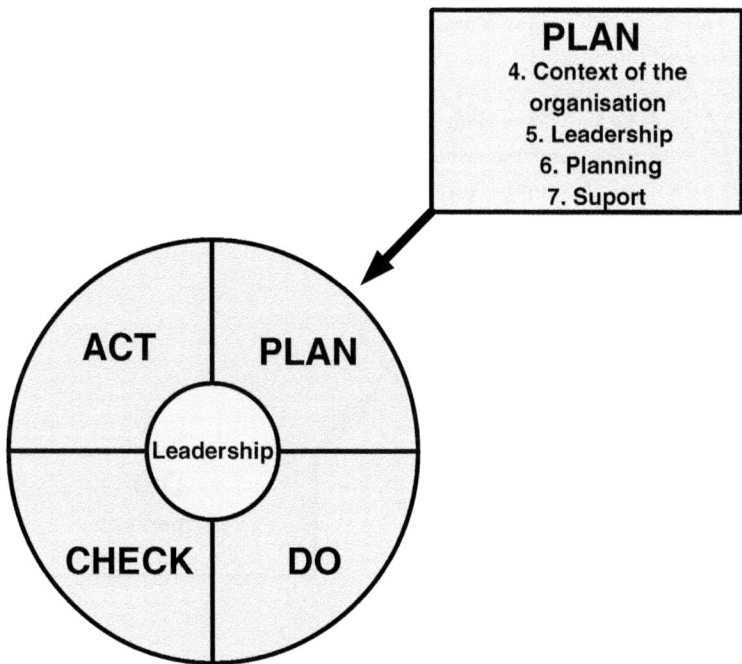

FIGURE 10.7 Establishing strategy and system objectives

Finally, the clause places requirements on top management to assign QMS-relevant responsibilities and authorities for the QMS whilst still remaining accountable for the effectiveness of the whole system.

Clause 6: Planning

This clause works with clauses 4.1 and 4.2 to complete the new way of dealing with preventive actions. The first part of this clause concerns risk assessment, whilst the second part is concerned with risk treatment. Your organisation will need to plan actions to address both risks and opportunities, how to integrate and implement the actions into your organisation's management system processes and how to evaluate the effectiveness of these actions.

Clause 7: Support

This clause requires your organisation to determine and provide the necessary resources to establish, implement, maintain and continually improve your QMS. The clause also includes requirements for competence, awareness and communication. The final part of this clause concerns the requirements for 'documented information' (the new term, which replaces the references in the 2008 standard to 'documents' and 'records').

Clause 8: Operation

This clause deals with the execution of the plans and processes that enable your organisation to meet customer requirements and design products and services. (See Figure 10.8)

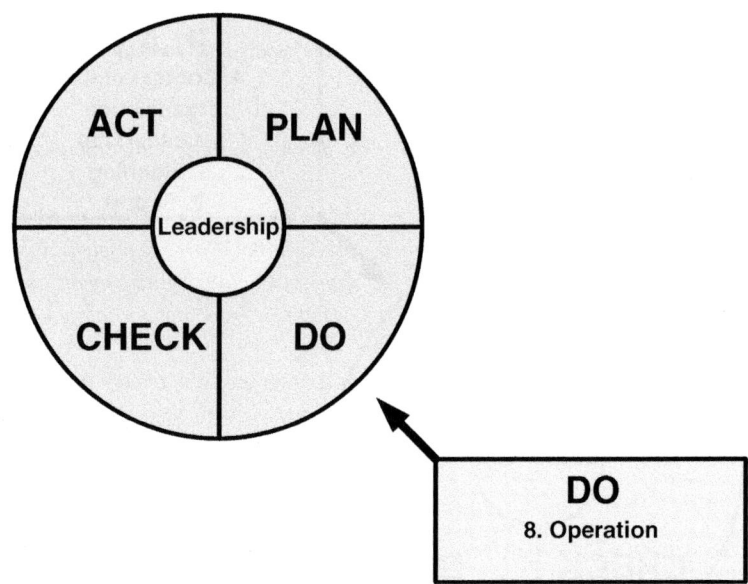

FIGURE 10.8 Establishing the organisation's policy

Note: Claus 8 includes much of what was previously referred to in clause 7 ('*Product Realisation*') of the 2008 version.

Clause 9: Performance evaluation

Performance evaluation covers many of the areas previously featured in clause 8 ('*Measurement, Analysis and Improvement*') of the 2008 version, but you will now need to consider what needs to be measured, what methods are employed, when data should be analysed and reported on, and at what intervals. (See Figure 10.9)

Internal audits and management reviews must also be conducted at planned intervals in order to ensure the continuing suitability, adequacy and effectiveness of your QMS.

Clause 10: Improvement

Due to the new way of handling preventive actions, there are no actual preventive action requirements in this clause. (See Figure 10.10) However, there are some new corrective action requirements. The first is to react to nonconformities and take action, as applicable, to control and correct the nonconformity and deal with any consequences that these might have caused. The second is to determine whether similar nonconformities exist or could potentially occur – and deal with them accordingly.

The requirement for continual improvement, therefore, has been extended to cover the suitability and adequacy of the QMS as well as its effectiveness, but it no longer specifies how an organisation achieves this.

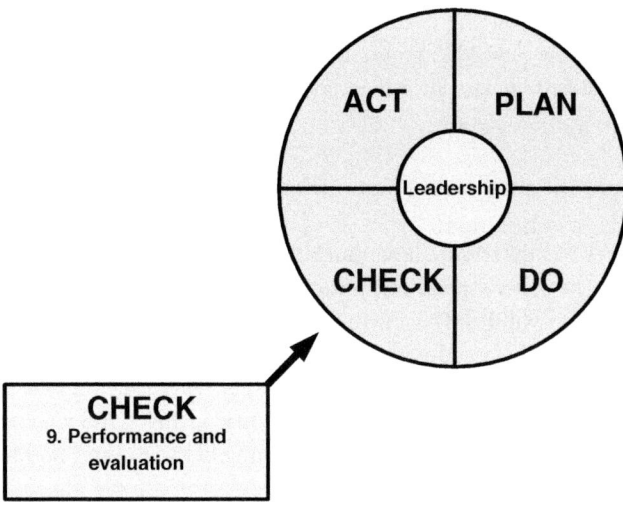

FIGURE 10.9   Reviewing the performance of the system

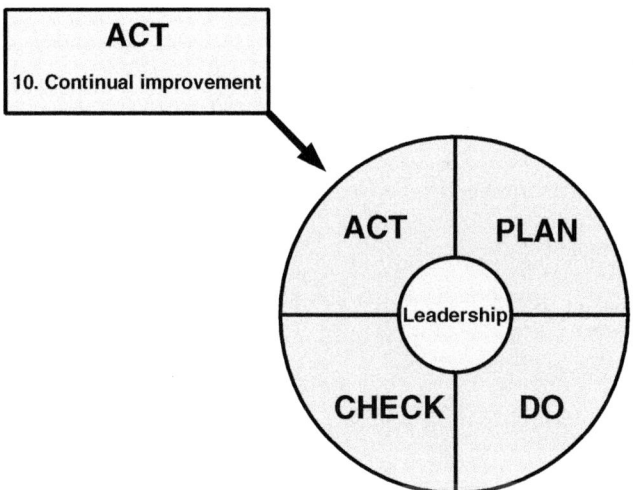

FIGURE 10.10   Reviewing and ensuring the integrity of the system

10.6.8 How long will it take to become certified to ISO 9001:2015?

Getting ready for registration involves building your QMS so that it fully meets the new standard, documenting that system and implementing it throughout your organisation.

The time that it takes a company to complete these tasks depends on several factors:

- Do you have a creditable QMS or parts of a system already in place?
- How much time needs to be allowed for the development of your organisation's QMS?
- What tools or assistance will you have to use, and are these currently available?

As you plan your project, you will need to think about those questions. You can measure your current QMS against the new MSS requirements by identifying what parts of the Annex SL/ISO 9001:2015 Standard you are already in compliance with.

This will provide a very useful information for planning a timeline for your transition project.

You will also need to determine how much time will be spent on this project by internal personnel. Will they be able to spend one hour a week on the project? Five hours a week? Or even 1 day a week? You will need to answer these questions so that you are fully aware what internal resources are available and whether outside assistance will be required.

So how long will it take? Well, the straight answer is, '*How long is a piece of string*' as it will depend very much on the commitment of your top management and your employees. However, realistically speaking, the timeline can be anything between three and nine months. For your assistance, Table 10.2 shows an example schedule for completing this task in in nine months.

TABLE 10.2 Sample nine-month plan

Task or task group	Apr	May	Jun	Jul	Aug	Sep	Oct	Nov	Dec
Gap analysis	X								
First steering team meeting: assign team members	X								
Train team members	X								
Control of documented information: meet weekly	X	X	X	X					
Control of quality records: meet weekly		X	X						
Management responsibility: meet weekly	X	X	X	X					
Competence, awareness and training: meet weekly		X	X						
Infrastructure: meet weekly		X	X						
Planning of product realization processes: meet weekly	X	X	X	X	X				
Customer-related processes: meet weekly:		X	X	X					
Design and development: meet weekly	X	X	X	X	X				
Purchasing: meet weekly		X	X	X					
Control of production and service provision: meet weekly	X	X	X	X					
Identification and traceability: meet weekly					X	X	X		
Customer property: meet weekly					X	X	X		

Task or task group	Apr	May	Jun	Jul	Aug	Sep	Oct	Nov	Dec
Preservation of product: meet weekly					X	X	X		
Control of measuring and monitoring devices: meet weekly	X	X	X	X					
Monitoring, measuring and analysis of customer satisfaction: meet weekly:					X	X	X		
Internal audits: meet weekly					X	X	X		
Monitoring, measuring and analysis of product and realization processes: meet weekly					X	X	X		
Control of nonconforming product: meet weekly					X	X	X		
Corrective action and preventive action: meet weekly					X	X			
Start internal audits							X		
Hold management review							X	X	
Train all employees					X				
Finalise management system tests as each team completes their part of the management system by registration audit							X		

10.7 Conclusion

The publication of Annex SL's template (i.e. ISO 9001:2015) in September 2015 signalled the start of a three-year transition period during which those organisations wishing to move to the new version of the standard had to make changes to their existing QMSs.

The amount of work involved will very much depend on each organisation's starting point. Those who have embraced both the substance and the spirit of the 2008 version of ISO 9001 will have respectively less work compared to those who are simply meeting the base requirements at present. Irrespective of the starting position, the migration process should begin now.

Top management need to understand their new obligations and must be prepared to show leadership in managing their organisation's QMS. They should start by familiarising themselves with the revised requirements as described in this book and should then prepare plans to modify their existing QMSs as necessary.

ISO's records show that there was a significant dip in 9001 registrations immediately following the last major revision of the standard in the year 2000. While it is unclear exactly why this was the case, at least some of the reduction has been attributed to **organisations leaving it too late to align their systems to the 2000 requirements, and, as a consequence, their certificates were withdrawn!**

For organisations that rely on their management system certification to demonstrate their competency as a supplier, the loss of such certification will invariably have a direct impact on profitability.

10.7.1 What are the costs involved in an organisation obtaining registration to this standard?

The one area that an organisation (particularly a small business) will want to know is how much it is going to cost to implement and operate a QMS compliant with ISO 9001:2015 – and is it going to be worth all the trouble and cost?!

Obviously, each business is different, and the cost of ISO 9001 registration will vary depending on the size and complexity of your organisation and on whether you already have some elements of a QMS in place.

Consequently, no book could answer this question with any accuracy; however, the following examples may, I hope, be beneficial to you.

The first question to be answered, however, is whether you actually need to become an ISO 9001-registered company, or would simply 'working in compliance with ISO 9001:2015' be sufficient?!

Quite often the answer to this question is 'yes' because, in order to tender for a particular project, service or deliverable, a mandatory requirement is often that your company **is** ISO 9001:2015 registered.

So the next questions that the managing director asks of the finance manager are, '*How much will it cost?*' and '*Who can we get to do it?*'

There is no general rule to the amount that it will cost a particular organisation to become ISO 9001:2015 registered as it will depend very much on the size of the company, its type of product, its client range and a whole host of other questions. At the time of writing this book (December 2015), however, the budgetary cost for an organisation seeking registration in the UK would be in the region of that shown in Table 10.3.

10.7.2 But, as a small business do I need to be certified and/or registered to a particular MSS?

It is widely acknowledged that proper quality management improves business, which often has a positive effect on investment, market share, sales growth, sales margins, competitive advantage and avoidance of litigation. Being able to provide proof of conformity to an MSS such as ISO 9001:2015 has therefore almost become a prerequisite of business today.

To obtain ISO 9001:2015 certification and registration, your QMS must meet all of the requirements of the standard. To do this, you will have to undergo an audit (i.e. a

TABLE 10.3 Possible budgetary costs for obtaining ISO 9001:2015 certification

Enterprise Category headcount		First-stage Third-party audit	Second-stage Third-party audit	Yearly assessments
Medium-sized	< 250	£750	£2500	£1500
Small	< 50	£750	£1500	£750 – £1500
Micro	< 10	£350	£700	£500

detailed test and examination) to establish whether the management system your organisation uses complies with (and meets) **all** of the requirements of ISO 9001. This audit **cannot** be done internally. It has to be completed by a properly accredited certifier or registrar.

If successful, you get a certificate (which will please your managing director as it can go in pride of place on his office wall!), and you can then advertise (on marketing material, letterheads and so on) the fact that you are a fully certified and registered quality organisation.

 AUTHOR'S HINT

A word of warning, however. You must ask yourself, *'Is certification itself important to the marketing plans of our company?'* If not, then do not rush to certification because even without it, your company can still utilise the ISO 9000 model as a benchmark to assess the adequacy of your quality programmes. In any case, you can always advertise the fact that your organisation possesses an auditable management system that is fully compliant with ISO 9001:2015.

10.7.3 Who can certify an organisation?

A number of companies (i.e. notified bodies and/or registrars) are available to carry out ISO 9001:2015 certification (e.g. TÜC, BSI, SGS, Yardley etc.), and which one you eventually choose really depends on which country you are situated in and where your organisation's main market is going to be. Organisations are therefore recommended to review quotes and get feedback from at least two or three organisations to assess their experience and suitability to fit with their specific organisational needs.

10.7.4 What is required for certification?

The first and foremost requirement is a fully documented, auditable QMS that is totally supported by top management and one that is implemented throughout the organisation.

The QMS should consist of:

- **Quality Manual** (or some other file containing all of your documented information) – describing how an organisation meets the requirements of ISO 9001:2015 (objectives, goals, roles, organisation and responsibilities etc.);
- **Processes** – describing the end-to-end activities involved in project management;
- **Quality Procedures** – describing the method by which the processes are managed;
- **Work Instructions** – describing how individual tasks and activities are carried out.

AUTHOR'S END NOTE

Quality Management Systems: A Practical Guide to Standards Implementation is meant only as a sort of quick reference to this standard of quality.

However, if you need a more in-depth book, then my main book in the current ISO 9001:2015 series (i.e. ISO 9001:2015 for Small Businesses) is the book for you.

ISO 9001:2015 for Small Businesses (sixth edition) is accompanied by a fully customisable copy of the Quality Management System files presented in the book. To save you having to copy or retype all of the documentation, 'unlocked', fully accessible, non-PDF soft copies of all of these files are available – at no additional charge – directly from the publisher.

ANNEX 1

Abbreviations and acronyms

Abbreviation	Definition
AFNOR	Association Français de Normalisation (French Institute for Standardisation)
ANSI	American National Standards Institute
Annex SL	A universal high-level structure, identical core text, and common terms and definitions for all Management System Standards
AQAP	NATO Allied Quality Assurance Publications
ACSI	American Customer Satisfaction Index
BS	British Standard
BSI	British Standards Institution
CAD	Computer–Aided Design
CCIR	International Radio Consultative Committee
CCITT	International Telegraph and Telephony Consultative Committee
CECC	CENELEC Electronic Components Committee
CEN	Commission European de Normalisation Electrotechnique
CENELEC	Comité Européen de Normalisation Électrotechnique (i.e. the European Committee for Electrotechnical Standardization)
CMI	British Chartered Management Institute
COS	Corporation of Open Systems
CP	Core Business Process
CQI	Chartered Quality Institute
CSA	Canadian Standards Association
DBOM	Design, Build, and Operation and Maintenance
DEF STANS	Defence Standards
DIN	Deutsch Institut für Normung e.v (German Institute for Standardisation)
DOA	Dictionary of Abbreviations
DOD	Department of Defense (US)
DPA	Data Protection Authority
DPIA	Data Protection Impact Assessment

(Continued)

Abbreviation	Definition
DPO	Data Protection Officer
DTI	Department of Trade and Industry
EDPB	European Data Protection Board
EEA	European Economic Area
EFTA	European Free Trade Association
ETSI	European Telecommunications Standards Institute
EMS	Environmental Management System
EN	European Norm
EQFM	European Foundation for Quality Management
ES	European Standard
EU	European Union
FOCUS	A selected group of experts who gather people's opinions, ideas, and beliefs on a certain topic or product.
FR	Failure Rate
FTA	Fault Tree Analysis
GDPR	General Data Protection Regulation
ICO	Information Commissioners Office
IEC	International Electrotechnical Commission
ILU	Integrated Logistic Unit
IMS	Integrated Management System
IRCA	International Register of Certified Auditors
ISO	International Organization for Standardization
IT	Information Technology
ITU	International Telecommunications Union
LAN	Local Area Network
LUR	Light Usable Regulations
MDD	Medical Devices Directive
MDR	Medical Devices Regulation
Mil-Stds	Military Standards
MOD-UK	United Kingdom Ministry of Defence
MSS	Management System Standards
MTBF	Mean Time Between Failures
NAFAAD	North American Field Advanced Audit Division
NATO	North Atlantic Treaty Organization
NSO	National Standards Organization
OHS	Occupational Health & Safety
OHSAS	Occupational Health & Safety Assessment Series
OSI	Open Systems Interconnection
PDCA	Plan-Do-Check-Act
PF	Probability Function

Abbreviation	Definition
QA	Quality Assurance
QC	Quality Control
QM	Quality Manual
QMS	Quality Management System
QP	Quality Procedure
RAMS	Reliability, Availability, Maintainability and Safety
RMP	Risk Management Programme
SEVEN	Nickname for HQ USAF programs usually connected with surveys
SME	Small and Medium-sized Enterprises
SMMB	Small, Medium and Micro Enterprises
SWOP	Strengths, Weaknesses, Opportunities and Threats
SP	Supporting Process
TC	Technical Committee
TQM	Total Quality Management
TS	Technical Specifications
UK	United Kingdom
UKAS	United Kingdom Accreditation Service
UN	United Nations
USA	United States of America
WAMH	Workplace Applied Medical Health
WAUILF	Workplace Applied Uniform Indicated Low Frequency (application)
WI	Work Instruction
YFR	Yearly Forecast Rationale

ANNEX 2

Reference standards for Quality Management Systems

Number	Title
BS 4778	*Quality vocabulary – Availability, reliability and maintainability terms. Guide to concepts and related definitions*
ISO 9000	*Quality management systems – Fundamentals and vocabulary*
ISO 9001	*Quality management systems – Requirements*
ISO 9004	*Managing for the sustained success of an organization – A quality management approach*
ISO 10001	*Quality management – Customer satisfaction – Guidelines for codes of conduct for organizations*
ISO 10002	*Quality management – Customer satisfaction – Guidelines for complaints handling in organizations*
ISO 10003	*Quality management – Customer satisfaction – Guidelines for dispute resolution external to organizations*
ISO 10004	*Quality management – Customer satisfaction – Guidelines for monitoring and measuring*
ISO 10005	*Quality management – guidelines for quality plans*
ISO 10006	*Quality management systems – Guidelines for quality management in projects*
ISO 10007	*Quality management systems – Guidelines for configuration management*
ISO 10008	*Quality management – Customer satisfaction – Guidelines for business-to-consumer electronic commerce transactions*
ISO 10018	*Quality management – Guidelines on people involvement and competence*
ISO 14001	*Environmental management systems – Requirements with guidance for use*
ISO 19011	*Guidelines for quality and/or environmental management systems auditing*
ISO 45001	*Occupational health and safety management systems – Requirements with guidance for use*

Complete copies of these standards are available from ISO member countries in their own languages. The British version (e.g. BS **EN** ISO 19011) can be obtained, by post, from Customer Services, BSI Standards, 389 Chiswick High Road, London W4 4AL.

Note: Extracts from British Standards are reproduced in this book with the kind permission of the British Standards Institute.

ANNEX 3

Glossary of terms used in Quality Management System Standards

Acceptable Quality Level A measure of the number of failures that a production process is allowed. Usually expressed as a percentage.

Accreditation Certification, by a duly recognised body, of facilities, capability, objectivity, competence and integrity of an agency, service or operational group or individual to provide the specific service/s or operation/s as needed.

Assemblies Several pieces of equipment assembled by a manufacturer to constitute an integrated and functional whole.

Audit Systematic, independent and documented process for obtaining evidence and evaluating it objectively to determine the extent to which audit criteria are fulfilled.

Audit Team One or more auditors conducting an audit, one of whom is appointed as leader.

Certification The procedure and action by a duly authorised body of determining, verifying and attesting in writing to the qualifications of personnel, processes, procedures, or items in accordance with applicable requirements.

Certification Body An impartial body, governmental or non-governmental, possessing the necessary competence and reliability to operate a certification system, in which the interests of all parties concerned with the functioning of the system are represented.

Chief Inspector An individual who is responsible for the manufacturer's Quality Management System.

Company Term used primarily to refer to a business first party, the purpose of which is to supply a product or service.

Compliance An affirmative indication or judgement that a product or service has met the requirements of the relevant specifications, contract or regulation. Also the state of meeting the requirements.

Conformance An affirmative indication or judgement that a product or service has met the requirements of the relevant specifications, contract or regulation. Also the state of meeting the requirements.

Contract   Agreed requirements between a supplier and customer transmitted by any means.

Customer   The ultimate consumer, user, client, beneficiary or second party.

Customer Satisfaction   Customer's opinion of the degree to which a transaction has met the customer's needs and expectations.

Defect   Non-fulfilment of a requirement related to an intended or specified use.

Design and Development   Set of processes that transforms requirements into specified characteristics and into the specification of the product realisation process.

Distributor   Organisation that is contractually authorised by one or more manufacturers to store, repack and sell completely finished components from these manufacturers.

Document   Information and its support medium.

Documented Information   Information that the organisation will be required to keep, control and maintain.

Environment   All of the external physical conditions that may influence the performance of a product or service.

Equipment   Machines, apparatus, fixed or mobile devices, control components and instrumentation thereof and detection or prevention systems that, separately or jointly, are intended for the generation, transfer, storage, measurement, control and conversion of energy for the processing of material and that are capable of causing an explosion through their own potential sources of ignition.

In-Process Inspection   Inspection carried out at various stages during processing.

International Organization for Standardisation (ISO)   Comprises the national standards bodies of 163 member countries whose aim is to coordinate the international harmonisation of national standards.

Item   A part, a component, equipment, subsystem or system or defined quantity of material or service that can be individually considered and separately examined or tested.

Maintenance   The combination of technical and administrative actions that are taken to retain or restore an item to a state in which it can perform its stated function.

Management   Coordinated activities to direct and control an organisation.

Management System   The establishment of policies and objectives to achieve ISO 9001:2015 objectives.

Manufacturer   An organisation that carries out or controls such stages in the manufacture of components or assemblies.

Material   Generic term covering equipment, stores, supplies and spares that form the subject of a contract.

Nonconformity   Nonfulfillment of a requirement.

Organisation   A single person or a group of people who achieve their objectives by using their own functions, responsibilities, authorities and relationships. It can be a company, corporation, enterprise, firm, partnership, charity, association or institution either privately or publicly owned. It can also be an operating unit that is part of a larger entity.

Organisational Structure   Orderly arrangement of responsibilities, authorities and relationships between people.

Procedure   The way to perform an activity or process.

Product   Result of a process that does not include activities performed at the interface between the supplier (provider) and the customer.

Note: There are four agreed generic product categories:

*   hardware (e.g. engine mechanical part);
*   software (e.g. computer program);
*   services (e.g. transport);
*   processed materials (e.g. lubricant).

Hardware and processed materials are generally tangible products, while software or services are generally intangible.

Most products comprise elements belonging to different generic product categories. Whether the product is then called hardware, processed material, software or service depends on the dominant element.

Project   Unique process, consisting of a set of coordinated and controlled activities with start and finish dates, undertaken to achieve an objective conforming to specific requirements, including the constraints of time, costs and resources.

Quality   The totality of features and characteristics of a product or service that bear upon its ability to satisfy stated or implied needs.

Quality Assurance   The assembly of all planned and systematic actions necessary to provide adequate confidence that a product, process, or service will satisfy given quality requirements.

Quality Characteristic   Essential characteristics of a product, process or system derived from a requirement.

Quality Control   The operational techniques and activities that are used to fulfil requirements for quality.

Quality Loop   Conceptual model of interacting activities that influence the quality of a product or service in the various stages ranging from the identification of needs to the assessment of whether these needs have been satisfied.

Quality Management   Aspect of the overall management function that determines and implements the quality policy.

Quality Management System   System to establish a quality policy and quality objectives.

Quality Management System Review   A formal evaluation by top management of the status and adequacy of the Quality Management System in relation to quality policy and new objectives resulting from changing circumstances.

Quality Manager   A person who is nominated by top management to be responsible for the organisation's Quality Management System (also sometimes referred to as the chief inspector).

Quality Manual   Document specifying the Quality Management System of an organisation and setting out the quality policies, systems and practices of an organisation.

Quality Plan   Document specifying the Quality Management System elements and the resources to be applied in a specific case.

Quality Policy   The overall quality intentions and direction of an organisation as regards quality, as formally expressed by top management.

Quality Procedure   A description of the method by which quality system activities are managed.

Quality Process   A system that uses resources to transform inputs into outputs.

Quality System   The organisational structure, responsibilities, procedures, processes and resources for implementing quality management.

Requirement   Need or expectation that is stated, customarily implied or obligatory.

Review   Activity undertaken to ensure the suitability, adequacy, effectiveness and efficiency of the subject matter to achieve established objectives.

Service   Result of a process that includes at least one activity carried out at the interface between the supplier (provider) and the customer. Example of service:

- Activity performed on a customer-supplied tangible product (e.g. the repair of a car) or intangible product such as the preparation of a tax return
- Delivery of a tangible product (e.g. in the transportation industry)
- Delivery of an intangible product (e.g. the delivery of knowledge) or the creation of ambience for the customer (e.g. in the hospitality industry)

Shall   Auxiliary verb indicating that a certain course of action is mandatory.

Should   Auxiliary verb indicating that a certain course of action is preferred but not necessarily required.

Supplier   The organisation that provides a product to the customer. In a contractual situation, the supplier may be called the contractor; may be, for example, the producer, distributor, importer, assembler or service organisation; and may be either external or internal to the organisation.

Top Management   Person or group of people who direct and control an organisation at the highest level.

Work Instruction   A description of how a specific task is carried out.

ANNEX 4

Books by the same author

Title	Extracts from book reviews	ISBN
ISO 9001:2015 for *Small Businesses* **(Sixth Edition)**	The new edition of this top-selling quality management book now includes: Relevant examples that put the concepts and requirements of the standard into a real-life context. Down-to-earth explanations to help you determine what you need to work in compliance with and/or achieve certification to ISO 9001:2015. An example of a complete, generic, Quality Management System consisting of a Quality Manual plus a whole host of Quality Processes, Quality Procedures and Work Instructions. Access to a free software copy of this generic QMS files (available from the author) to give you a starting point from which to develop your own documentation.	Routledge ISBN 13: 978–1138025837
ISO 9001:2015 *Audit Procedures* **(Fourth Edition)**	Fully revised, updated and expanded, this 4th edition provides access to methods for auditing an organisation's Quality Management System against the requirements of ISO 9001:2015. Although primarily aimed at showing how auditors from small businesses can complete management reviews and internal, external and third-party quality audits, this book will prove invaluable to professional auditors. Containing an overview of the changes made by the 2015 edition of ISO 9001 and how these will affect how audits need to be completed in future, the book also includes access to free copies of checklists, explanations and questionnaires (available from the author) that can be used for internal, external and/or third-party audits of an organisation's Quality Management System.	Routledge ISBN 13: 978–1138025899

(*Continued*)

Title	Extracts from book reviews	ISBN
ISO 9001:2015 In Brief (Fourth Edition)	Now in its 4th edition, this book is particularly aimed at students, newcomers to Quality Management Systems and the busy executive with the overall intention of providing them with a user-friendly, very simplified, explanation of the history, the requirements and the benefits of the new standard. Using this book as background material will also enable organisations (large or small) to quickly set up an ISO 9001:2015-compliant Quality Management System for themselves – at minimal expense.	Routledge ISBN 13: 978– 1138025899
How to Convert from ISO 9001:2008 to ISO 9001:2015	The publication of ISO 9001:2015 in September 2015 signalled the start of a three-year transition period during which those organisations wishing to move to the new version of the standard need to make changes to their existing Quality Management Systems. *How to Convert from ISO 9001:2008 to ISO 9001:2015* provides step-by-step advice to help you through the transition and realise the benefits of ISO 9001:2015. It maps out a framework that guides you through the options and alternatives, ensuring that you have the knowledge and information you require to seamlessly make the necessary transition.	Herne European Consultancy Ltd ISBN-13: 978– 0992758509
MDD Compliance Using Quality Management Techniques	The Medical Device Directive (MDD) is difficult to understand and interpret, but this book covers the subject superlatively. In summary, the book is a good reference for understanding the medical device directive's requirements and would aid companies of all sizes in adding these requirements to an existing QMS.	Butterworth Heinemann ISBN-13: 978– 0750644419
Quality and Standards in Electronics	A manufacturer or supplier of electronic equipment or components needs to know the precise requirements for component certification and quality conformance to meet the demands of the customer. This book ensures that the professional is aware of all the UK, European and International necessities, knows the current status of these regulations and standards, and where to obtain them.	Newnes ISBN-13: 978– 0750625319
Environmental Requirements for Electromechanical and Electronic Equipment	This is the definitive reference containing all of the background guidance, typical ranges, details of recommended test specifications, case studies and regulations covering the environmental requirements on designers and manufacturers of electrical and electromechanical equipment worldwide.	Butterworth Heinemann ISBN-13: 978– 0750639026
CE Conformity Marking	CE marking can be regarded as a product's trade passport for Europe. It is a mandatory European marking for certain product groups to indicate conformity with the essential health and safety requirements set out in the European Directive. This book contains essential information for any manufacturer or distributor wishing to trade in the European Union. Practical and easy to understand.	Butterworth Heinemann ISBN-13: 978– 0750648134

Title	Extracts from book reviews	ISBN
Building Regulations in Brief (Ninth Edition)	This ninth edition of the most popular and trusted guide reflects all the latest amendments to the Building Regulations, planning permission and the Approved Documents in England and Wales. This includes coverage of the new Approved Document Q on security, and a second part to Approved Document M which divides the regulations for 'dwellings' and 'buildings other than dwellings'. A new chapter has been added to incorporate these changes and to make the book more user friendly.	ISBN-13: 978–1138285163
Building Regulations Pocket Book	This handy guide provides you with all the information you need to comply with the UK Building Regulations and Approved Documents. On site, in the van, in the office, wherever you are, this is the book you'll refer to time and time again to double-check the regulations on your current job.	ISBN-13: 978–0815368380
Wiring Regulations in Brief (Third Edition)	• Tired of trawling through the Wiring Regs? • Perplexed by Part P? • Confused by cables, conductors and circuits? Then look no further! This handy guide provides an on-the-job reference source for Electricians, Designers, Service Engineers, Inspectors, Builders, Students, DIY enthusiasts.	ISBN-13: 978–0415526876
Water Regulations in Brief	*Water Regulations in Brief* is a unique reference book, providing all the information needed to comply with the regulations, in an easy to use, full colour format. Crucially, unlike other titles on this subject, this book doesn't just cover the Water Regulations, it also clearly shows how they link in with the Building Regulations, Water Bylaws and the Wiring Regulations, providing the only available complete reference to the requirements for water fittings and water system.	ISBN: – 978–1856176286

INDEX

Note: Page numbers in *italic* indicate a figure. Page numbers in **bold** indicate a table.

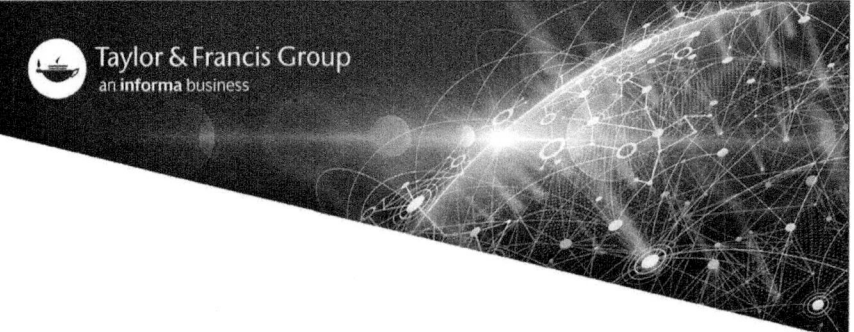